INDUSTRIAL POLICY IN BRITAIN

Also by David Coates

ECONOMIC AND INDUSTRIAL PERFORMANCE IN EUROPE (*editor*)
THE QUESTION OF UK DECLINE

Industrial Policy in Britain

Edited by

David Coates
*Professor of Government and
Co-Director of the International
Centre for Labour Studies
University of Manchester*

First published in Great Britain 1996 by
MACMILLAN PRESS LTD
Houndmills, Basingstoke, Hampshire RG21 6XS
and London
Companies and representatives
throughout the world

A catalogue record for this book is available
from the British Library.

ISBN 0–333–61528–X hardcover
ISBN 0–333–61529–8 paperback

First published in the United States of America 1996 by
ST. MARTIN'S PRESS, INC.,
Scholarly and Reference Division,
175 Fifth Avenue,
New York, N.Y. 10010

ISBN 0–312–15797–5

Library of Congress Cataloging-in-Publication Data
Industrial policy in Britain / edited by David Coates.
p.   cm.
Includes bibliographical references and index.
ISBN 0–312–15797–5 (cloth)
1. Industrial policy—Great Britain.   I. Coates, David.
HD3616.G73I53   1996
338.941—dc20   95–42142
                                                     CIP

10   9   8   7   6   5   4   3   2   1
05   04   03   02   01   00   99   98   97   96

Printed in Malaysia

Contents

List of Tables and Figures

Tables

Figures

Notes on the Contributors

Simon Bromley is Lecturer in Politics, University of Leeds, UK.

Tom Burden is Principal Lecturer, Leeds Business School, Leeds Metropolitan University, UK.

David Coates is Professor of Government at the University of Manchester, UK.

Ed Gouge is Lecturer in Politics, University of Leeds, UK.

Simon Lee is Lecturer in Politics, University of Hull, UK.

Chris Lord is Senior Lecturer in Politics, University of Leeds, UK.

Neill Marshall is Reader in Industrial Geography, Centre for Urban and Regional Development Studies, University of Newcastle, UK.

Paul Reynolds is Senior Lecturer in Contemporary Political Studies, Edge Hill College of Higher Education, Ormskirk, UK.

Kevin Theakston is Senior Lecturer in Politics, University of Leeds, UK.

Alan Tuckman is Senior Lecturer in Sociology, University of Humberside, UK.

List of Abbreviations

AACP	Anglo-American Council on Productivity
ACOST	Advisory Council on Science and Technology
AEI	Associated Electrical Industries
AGR	Advanced, Gas-cooled Reactor
BAe	British Aerospace
BC	British Coal
BGC	British Gas Corporation
BL	British Leyland
BNFL	British Nuclear Fuels
BNOC	British National Oil Corporation
BP	British Petroleum
BT	British Telecom
CAP	Common Agricultural Policy
CBI	Confederation of British Industry
CEGB	Central Electricity Generating Board
CLA	Country Landowners Association
CTC	Central Training Council
DoI	Department of Industry
DTI	Department of Trade and Industry
EAGGF	European Agricultural Guidance and Guarantee Fund
EC	European Community
EE	English Electric
EEF	Engineering Employers Federation
EFTA	European Free Trade Association
ERDF	European Regional Development Fund
ESI	Electricity Supply Industry
ET	Employment Training
ETSU	Energy Technology Support Unit
EU	European Union

FDI	Foreign Direct Investment
GATT	General Agreement on Tariffs and Trade
GDP	Gross Domestic Product
GEC	General Electric Company
GNP	Gross National Product
GPO	General Post Office
GTC	Government Training Centre
HMSO	Her Majesty's Stationery Office
IDC	Industrial Development Certificate
IDU	Industrial Development Unit
IRC	Industrial Reorganisation Corporation
ISDN	Integrated Services Digital Transmission
IT	Information Technology
ITB	Industrial Training Board
LEC	Local Enterprise Company
MAFF	Ministry of Agriculture, Fisheries and Food
MITI	Ministry for International Trade and Industry
MoD	Ministry of Defence
MSC	Manpower Services Commission
NAO	National Audit Office
NATO	North Atlantic Treaty Organisation
NCB	National Coal Board
NCVQ	National Council for Vocational Qualifications
NEB	National Enterprise Board
NEDC	National Economic Development Council
NEDO	National Economic Development Office
NFFO	Non-fossil Fuel Obligation
NFU	National Farmers Union
NSTAP	National Strategic Technology Acquisition Plan
NUM	National Union of Mineworkers
NVQ	National Vocational Qualification
OECD	Organisation for Economic Co-operation and Development
OFTEL	Office of Telecommunications
OPEC	Organisation of Petroleum Exporting Countries
PWR	Pressurised Water Reactor
R&D	Research and Development
RAF	Royal Air Force
RDG	Regional Development Grant
REC	Regional Electricity Company

RPI	Retail Price Index
RSA	Regional Selective Assistance
SGHWR	Steam Generating Heavy Water Reactor
SWP	Sector Working Parties
TEC	Training and Enterprise Council
TOPS	Training Opportunities Scheme
TPER	Total Primary Energy Requirement
UCS	Upper Clyde Shipbuilders
UKAEA	United Kingdom Atomic Energy Authority
UKIG	United Kingdom Industry Group
VANS	Value-added Network Services
VET	Vocational and Educational Training
WTO	World Trade Organisation
YOP	Youth Opportunities Programme
YT	Youth Training
YTS	Youth Training Scheme

Note: Throughout this book, the term 'European Community' (or EC) refers to anything before the ratification of the Maastricht Treaty in 1993; and 'European Union' (EU) to any subsequent or continuing process, even if begun prior to 1993.

I INTRODUCTION

1 Introduction

David Coates

The existence of this text, in the form in which it is presented here, is itself evidence of how the political agenda in contemporary Britain has begun to shift. The very term 'industrial policy' spent the 1980s out of fashion. It was not something that was widely referred to, except by those pursuing the sources of Britain's economic weakness. Commentators sympathetic to the philosophy and practice of Conservative governments after 1979 would look back to the twenty years before, see Conservative and Labour governments heavily and increasingly involved in the shaping of industrial activity, and use that involvement as a key to post-war economic under-performance. The ruling fiction of the 1980s was that the UK stopped having industrial policy, and had industrial recovery instead. The reality, of course, was simply that one kind of industrial policy was replaced by another, and that the new industrial policy could no more seal Britain from recession and de-industrialisation than had the one before. While the fiction held, the debate on industrial policy stalled; but at the end of the 1980s, as industrial output fell and unemployment rose, the debate began again.

This book hopes to make an academic contribution to the renewed debate. For, if the consideration of contemporary policy options is to be well informed, and if the claims made for particular policies are to be properly evaluated, whole bodies of new information will be required that are not at the moment readily to hand. To meet the requirements of informed discussion of what Chalmers Johnson has called the 'political agenda for the rest of this century – jobs, high technology, savings and investment, world competitiveness, orderly change of industrial structure' (C. Johnson, 1984, p. 4), the history of industrial policy in post-war Britain needs to be pulled back from the obscurity into which it has

3

settled, and freed from the mythology and caricature by which it is often beset. The philosophies underpinning the alternatives on offer need to be fully recognised, and the uniqueness claimed for them evaluated by some specification of how these things are done in more successful economies abroad. And the very terminology in play – economy, industry, intervention, the market – needs careful definition and delimitation, the better to clarify the tasks ahead and the real options in play.

We know of no one book which does all these tasks satisfactorily, though useful coverage of some aspects is provided by many texts, including Barberis and May, 1993; Clarke, 1993; Grant, 1982, 1990, 1991; Hart, 1986; Kirby, 1991; Morris and Stout, 1987; Shepherd, 1987. We have therefore set out here to fill what we take to be a major gap in the available literature. The purpose of this chapter is to lay the ground for our collective endeavour, by establishing some of the conceptual and comparative reference points on which the rest of the chapters will be built.

1.1   The case for industrial policy

The backcloth to the ebb and flow of industrial policy in post-war Britain has been the changing place of the British economy and state in the global economic and political order. As the first industrial nation, the UK as a whole (with its early industrial heartland firmly planted in a northern quadrant linking Liverpool and Newcastle to Glasgow and Belfast) enjoyed a brief Victorian period of world industrial monopoly, one accompanied by the consolidation of London as the world's leading financial centre and of sterling as the world's reserve currency. But, as every major history of the British economy makes clear, British-based manufacturing industry lost its position of world domination steadily from the 1890s. Late nineteenth and early twentieth-century British-based industry was initially lulled into a traditionalism of methods and markets by the memory of its mid-nineteenth century success; and was then denied systematic incentives to modernise by a banking system and set of state institutions which had themselves used that earlier success to construct different interests and concerns. Twentieth-century UK manufacturing went into decline under state policies which (as late as the 1950s) were still preoccupied with the defence of empire and sterling, and under a gap between industry and finance inherited from its nineteenth-century economic and social geography. Both before the First World War and more tentatively in the 1930s, political coalitions emerged to shift those priorities and to bridge that gap; but before 1945 neither Tariff Reform nor Bank of England-led industrial restructuring managed to transform the weakening base of British manufacturing industry (see Kirby, 1980; Newton and Porter, 1988; Pollard 1992; Coates, 1994). Victory in war, and the associated dislocation of war-time competitors, then gave British-based manufacturing industry its last brief period of Western European supremacy; and it was the rapid ebbing away of this brief and final interlude which brought the question of industrial policy on to the political agenda in the late 1950s as never before.

At the heart of the modern UK debate on industrial policy have been, and remain, attitudes to the relationships and roles of *states and markets*. For more than thirty years now, as politicians and academics have explored the appropriate relationship of the state to industry, they have moved back and forth along a broadly unchanging range of policy positions, which can essentially be expressed under the following five headings:

(i)   defending the market
(ii) creating/supplementing the market
(iii) managing the market
(iv) shaping the market
(v)   controlling/democratising the market.

In all but the first of these, the recognition of the possibility (and reality) of *market failure* has inspired policy to strengthen competition, to provide public goods, to handle external costs, to overcome inadequacies in capital provision, to restructure international competitive advantage, and/or to plan the economy's democratic control.

Very occasionally the main axis of debate (and the competing policies on offer) has been a very radical one, turning around number (i) and (v). Between the wars (around the issue of communism) and in the UK in the early 1980s (around the Labour Left's Alternative Economic Strategy), the debate on industrial policy raised questions about whether to have markets at all, and whether to leave those that remained under the control of private economic actors. But between those two periods, the policy debate was a much more moderate one, only oscillating between and within points (ii) and (iii): how to run

markets under private control in ways that could meet socially required
levels of employment and consumption. But that debate no longer holds
centre-stage either. Now the big issue around industrial policy really
turns on areas (i) and (iv): on the kinds of policy required to strengthen
the international competitiveness of locally-based, privately-owned
industrial concerns. Is it enough to leave industrial growth to market
forces, or do those market forces need to be reset by active state intervention? As we shall see in greater detail in the chapters to follow (and
especially in Chapter 10), the industrial policy debate in Britain since
1945 has moved between a broadly *social democratic* package –
(organised around points (ii) and (iii) – and a *neo-liberal* one – (organised around point (i); and is now being reset as a tussle between that
liberal position and a more interventionist one, a *third way*, encompass-
ing some elements of the arguments gathered here as point (iv).

What is at stake in these should become clearer if we examine the
arguments mobilisable under each of the five points in turn.

(i) Defending the market

At one extreme, liberal economists and policy-makers have advocated
(and continue to advocate) a very specific and highly restricted role for
the state in its dealings with industry. Dominant in the Conservative
Party after 1979, though in the 1970s very much a minority voice even
there, we find a position built around a faith in the capacity of markets
to act as optimal economic allocators, and in the ability of individuals
within those markets to pursue their own self-interests in ways that
maximise benefits for all. In the end, liberal arguments in favour of
private non-regulated processes of resource allocation always rest upon
a long-established set of general claims for the superiority of market
forces, that:

- markets necessarily act as a powerful incentive to producers to
  operate as efficiently as possible in order to survive;
- markets force firms perpetually to develop new products and
  production processes;
- markets co-ordinate, without conscious human intervention, the lit-
  erally millions of individual decisions made in a complex economy
  by a multiplicity of producers and consumers; and
- markets allow individuals greater freedom of choice as producers
  and consumers than they can experience in any system of managed

markets or centralised planning. (cited in Breitenbach *et al.*, 1990, p. 17)

These arguments are so generally accepted in British political culture these days that the onus of proof is always placed – in public discussions of industrial policy – on those who would argue for state action to mould or replace markets. Yet such neo-classical defences of market processes ought not to be thought of as intellectually neutral 'facts' of economic life. In reality they constitute a bundle of economic axioms which carry a powerful political message and preference: for economic decision-making to remain in the hands of the owners of private capital. They also carry a powerful specification of the proper role of the state: an insistence that the economic activity of the state should be restricted to the creation and guaranteeing of market conditions (and of the relationships of private property which underpin them in a capitalist market economy).

In such a view of the world, the task of government was (and is) to set the framework within which markets can function effectively. Governments ought thereafter to avoid any 'interference' (as liberal thought would see it) in the functioning of privately-based market processes within that framework, since these work best when left to themselves. On this set of understandings, industrial policy, if there is to be any, is conceived as 'policy to improve the general framework within which producer activities and consumer choices take place, and to facilitate an automatic process of industrial adjustment' (Jacquémin, 1984, p. 5). Indeed, as Jacquémin rightly points out, such an approach merely requires 'an infrastructure of quality, a professionally adapted labour force, accessibility to capital and credit, and a fiscal system which is not opposed to economic rationality' (ibid., p. 5). To get that, from a liberal perspective, a proper industrial policy is one geared to the *creation of sound money and open markets,* goals best achieved by reducing state activity and taxation, replacing public by private ownership, stripping away subsidies to capital and to labour, removing barriers to the rights of individuals to dispose of their property as they see fit, and allowing those individuals to make private contracts reflective of their relative standings in both labour and product markets.

At the heart of a liberal specification of the proper relationship of industry to government lies a profound unease with the state as an economic actor – both with the state as a *planner* of economic activity (that is, replacing market processes) and as a *regulator*. From this perspective, centralised systems of economic planning are seen as inherently flawed, because they are:

- unable to cope with the vast complexity of modern economic systems without eroding individual choice and seriously blunting industrial efficiency;
- bound to concentrate power in the hands of central state agencies and so jeopardise individual freedom;
- prone to bureaucratic stagnation and corruption, and to the emergence of new hierarchies of inequality based on bureaucratic position; and
- inevitably generative of a privately run black market as their crucial lubricant.

From this perspective too, even more modest attempts at state regulation of markets share many of the weaknesses and proclivities of full-blown central planning. Liberal defenders of unregulated market processes, that is, tend to the view that any form of active state involvement in what ought to be undisturbed private economic activities is bound eventually to be seriously counter-productive: with governments being prone to put short-term political considerations before long-term economic needs, incapable in any case of picking winners any better than markets can, bound to entrench inefficiencies by their dulling of the essential disciplinary role of the price mechanism – even prone (if successful) to eat away at what remains of 'individual liberties and pluralistic forms of government' (Curzon Price, 1984 in Bib, p. 130).

(ii) Creating/supplementing the market

At one notch removed from liberal orthodoxy stand economists and policy-makers who retain much of the faith in the power and superiority of market processes, but who supplement it with a recognition of the market's necessary limitations as an allocative device. From such a standpoint, industrial policy is not illegitimate. It has an important supplementary role to play, compensating for recognisable 'market failures'; but always in a context in which 'the precise reasons for the market imperfection or the market failure must...be identified, and a policy designed to solve the specific problem directly' (Jacquémin, 1984, p. 5).

Any systematic reading of the literature on industrial policy quickly makes clear that 'there is no uniquely valid way of analysing market failure'; but as James Shepherd argued in 1987, 'the following [sources/types of failure] have proved operationally useful':

- *information deficiencies* – particularly when technology is changing rapidly, participants in the market can lack the data base on which to make well-judged business decisions;
- *risk aversion by private economic actors* – an entirely rational attitude for individual companies to adopt when the cost of failure is high, but one that is not conducive to overall industrial dynamism;
- *externalities* – benefits/costs accruing elsewhere in the economy which open up a gap between what is financially viable for a company and what is beneficial at the level of the economy as a whole;
- *structure* – where there is insufficient competition, and barriers to entry, it may be in the public interest to help new competitors to break into the market.   (Shepherd, 1987, p. 59)

It is worth taking the last category first, for, at their most modest, market imperfections or failures may simply derive from the lack of competition itself. Indeed, much of civilian industrial policy in the UK in the 1950s was really *competition policy* (policy aimed at breaking up monopolies of producers or retailers – hence the creation of the Monopolies Commission and the banning of resale price maintenance); and industrial policy in the 1980s was similarly driven in part by a desire to break monopoly provision and control: of utilities by public corporations (hence privatisation) and of labour markets by strong trade unions (hence moves against the closed shop and secondary picketing). But the other 'market failure' which has long preoccupied British governments has been the failure of foreign markets, failures visible in the existence of artificially-closed export markets or heavily subsidised (and hence dumped) foreign-made imports. The biggest of all those markets – from which in the 1960s and 1970s British-based producers stood in danger of exclusion – was the European Community itself: which helps to explain why the key initiative on competition policy after 1960 came to be the pursuit of Common Market membership – with the explicit aim of gaining access to European consumers and of exposing British-based industry to European competition.

The whole issue of *public goods* has been another source of inspiration for certain kinds of industrial policy. For much of the post-war period, basic utilities were publicly-owned, because it was felt that their contribution to industrial output was too general to be left in private hands. Much basic research and its supporting infrastructure has been government-funded for similar reasons: that like many public goods it was 'non-appropriable – i.e. difficult or impossible to establish ownership rights which in turn make it difficult to recover sunk costs by charging for use, [and] non-depletable, i.e. when use by one person does not diminish the amount available to others' (Sharp and Pavitt, 1993, p. 5). Education and training programmes fit here too, since adequate levels of investment in human capital are notoriously difficult to generate through private market processes alone (problems of free-riding and uncertain futures getting in the way). Defence goods have been similarly treated, with the defence of the realm (and the orchestration of the military capacity to guarantee that) being seen as too general a concern simply to be left to the unplanned interplay of private economic actors, and too general a benefit to be sold as a commodity on the open market. Indeed, and because of the foreign policy aspirations and commitments of successive post-war British governments, the Ministry of Defence and its predecessor ministries consistently developed in the post-war period extensive policies for industry: policies focused on industries, firms and goods geared to military production and use, but policies with an enormous fallout (and significance) for the shape and performance of British-based industry as a whole.

(iii) Managing the market

This impulse to improve or supplement the performance of markets did not, however, exhaust the reasons for industrial policy. As often as not, post-war British governments were reluctant to leave things to the market not because of their abandonment of some principled commitment to the maintenance of pristine markets, but because of their dislike of the form which unregulated market outcomes were likely to take. Concern with employment levels, the balance of payments, the erosion of social services or even the distribution of wealth – all acted on occasion as spurs to the formation of particular sets of government-industry relations. As Martin Chick observed, 'in each case, concern for the political and social response to the outcomes of particular market operations has occasioned government intervention'. And if this has been a case of market failure, the failure was *political* as much as economic: 'the failure of markets to produce outcomes desired by politicians' (Chick, 1990, p. 2).

This is why industrial policy to contain 'market imperfections' has often also often been justified in the language of *externalities*. The argument has been that markets left to themselves often bring private sources of supply and demand into balance only at the price of public costs unacceptable to parties not directly involved in the actual private bargain made within the market. The biggest public cost of private market processes between the wars was mass unemployment; and the whole thrust of Keynesian economics thereafter served to legitimate state management of markets to prevent it. The characteristic policy instruments associated with Keynesian demand management for full employment did not constitute industrial policy as such. They were wider and more generally-focused than that; but more specific manifestations of this general market imperfection did inspire the development of policies directed towards particular industries and firms. As we shall see in more detail in Chapter 8, from the 1940s we find policies to soften the run-down of old industries, policies to even up regional inequalities in the distribution of employment and wealth, policies to set limits on the kind of labour practices companies could use in the pursuit of competitive advantage – even, lately, the beginnings of policy to add to private decision-making processes an obligation to cost environmental damage, a cost treated as entirely *external* to economic calculations in less regulated markets.

There is even a growing awareness in certain academic and political circles of the hidden *economic* costs of unregulated economic rundown – a recognition that, without state management, the first casualties of severe recession can be the *most* rather than the least efficient firms in an industry (those carrying the heaviest debts for new machinery, for example). In such circumstances, a wholly private set of economic calculations might leave a national economy with key parts of its industrial structure even more outmoded after recession than before it, as only companies with old equipment, long paid for, manage to survive: to the detriment not just of the firms that fold, but to the long-term competitiveness of the economy in total. Industrial policy can then be justified not simply as a device to create markets via competition policy. It can actually be legitimated as a way of managing market processes, as a means of producing distributions of resources different from those likely to emerge from the interplay of unregulated private actors.

(iv) Shaping the market

The last of the examples of 'externalities' cited above – that of the perverse ability of unregulated market forces to work against the efficient and to privilege the outmoded – is but one example of a more general tendency, observed by many advocates of active industrial policies, of private capital markets to act imperfectly as guarantors or suppliers of long-term, strategic, national economic interests. Critics of non-intervention have often pointed to the way in which the inherent *short termism* of private investment decisions, and the *high aversion to risk-taking* characteristic of many private financial institutions, often act as barriers to the adequate financing of small businesses or to the private sustenance of new industrial processes with long gestation periods and uncertain prospects. Nor can private investment sources easily sustain *infant industries* in the face of established competition; so the case is often also made for the provision of public funds to see new industries through to competitive viability (on this, see Wade, 1990).

Indeed the critique of market-led industrial recovery can go deeper. For, even when working well, markets tend to reflect and reinforce existing patterns of comparative advantage. They respond to, and reinforce, existing distributions of factor endowment, rather than, by some automatic mechanism, creating new ones. But it is new ones that economies in competitive difficulties actually need; so once it is recognised that the distribution of economic factors is not god-given and fixed in stone, a new role for industrial policy opens up – as a way consciously *to create international competitive advantage.*

This is very much the argument of policy-makers now active in and around the Clinton administration in the United States, that today in the USA the primary purpose of industrial policy 'must be to secure a dynamic competitive advantage in the global economy for American enterprise' (C. Johnson, 1984, p. 9). People like Laura D'Andrea Tyson and John Zysman have long argued that the competitive strength of particular industries (and thereby whole economies) is increasingly determined by policies adopted at corporate and state level to enhance the quality of local factor endowments; and that therefore it is vital for governments to consider (and to develop policies on) 'the role of economies of scale, learning-curve economies and technological innovation in shaping the competitive advantage of individual firms' (Tyson and Zysman, 1983, p. 32). The model and evidence underpinning this argument is often Japanese (or latterly more generally East Asian) in inspiration, predicated on the recognition that all advanced economies now compete 'in a world of developmental states' (Cohen and Zysman, 1987, p. 249): that because, in an increasingly integrated world economic system, 'competitiveness is more and more a matter of organised strategies in which governments lead, and less and less a product of natural endowments', industrial policy can become a vital mechanism through which permanently to 'alter the terms of international competition and irrevocably change the very structure of the market – [and] not simply distort an otherwise efficient market' (Thompson, 1989, p. 40).

Indeed the notion of 'efficiency' at play here is quite different from the static Pareto-optimality of most neo-classical models. It relies much more heavily on a Schumpeterian view of technical efficiency over time. Chalmers Johnson made this very clear in 1984 when he wrote:

> Industrial policy is the logical outgrowth of the changing concept of comparative advantage. The classical or static notion of comparative advantage referred to geographical differences and various national endowments among economies that were supposed to produce a global division of labour. The newer dynamic concept of comparative advantage replaces the classical criteria with such elements as human creative power, foresight, a highly educated work force, organisational talent, the ability to choose, and the ability to adapt. Moreover these attributes are not conceived of as natural endowments but as qualities achieved through public policies such as education, organised research, and investment in social overhead capital. (C. Johnson, 1984, p. 8)

On this argument, the task of industrial policy is not one of picking winners in a static market. It is one of creating them in dynamic markets – of taking the longer strategic view, and of deploying state and corporate resources to its attainment. The key task of economic policy is to lift the whole economy off a downward path of low productivity, low investment and low demand: to place it instead on an upward spiral of competitiveness, profitability and growth. Unregulated market forces will not do that. A strategically-planning and interventionist government can – by the quality of its *education and training* of industrial labour, and by its policies on *capital modernisation* (by its support of innovation and new technologies, and by its encouragement of their diffusion through industry as a whole). That at least is the claim made for industrial policy by those seeing it as the key priority of a developmental, modernising state.

(v) Controlling/democratising the market

Such a view of industrial policy then sits alongside an even more radical critique of market forces – one associated exclusively with intellectuals and parties of the left. Among socialists there has long been a general case against private market forms of economic allocation – a recognition that in capitalist economies:

● markets only work at the cost of the perennial insecurity of producers;
● markets allow the economically strong to drive out the economically weak, and so generate monopoly power (what Marx called the centralisation and concentration of capital) that robs workers and consumers of effective economic control:
● markets intensify social inequality;
● markets produce unavoidable cycles of expansion and contraction; and
● markets ultimately respond not to human need but to the distribution of purchasing power (which their propensity to create inequality continually pulls apart).

In the left-wing debate on the kinds of industrial policy needed in a weak economy of the UK kind, you then find varying degrees of recognition – shared with Tyson and Zysman – of the way in which market logics, left to themselves, tend to be 'cumulative rather than corrective' (Anderson, 1987, p. 72): that processes of uneven economic development created by the interplay of market forces at the level of the world economy cannot be unwound by those same market forces. To this sense of how market forces systematically favour the strong, the more left-wing advocates of industrial policy then add two other propositions: that no private economic institution is so structurally located as to be able or inspired to develop long-term strategic goals for the national economy as a whole (only the state is so located); and that the weight of transnational corporations in modern national economies is such that any national strategy will have to be politically imposed upon (or at least strenuously negotiated with) such private, global economic actors. All this comes together in a view of radical industrial policy as the key instrument through which democratic state institutions can insert

popular, national economic goals into a universe of private market
forces that would otherwise ride roughshod over them. It also comes
together as an argument for industrial policy geared to finding what
Dietrich called 'the missing market'. It comes together, that is, as an
argument that democratic public institutions should reorientate the
overall growth path emerging from the unco-ordinated private decisions of individual firms, by engaging in 'selective targeting and proactive intervention in strategically important activities', and by
developing 'a strategic consensus within which de-centralised (strategic) decision-making [can then be] located and focused' (Dietrich,
1992, p. 28).

This view of the necessary anarchy of market forces and the inequalities of market outcomes in economies dominated by privately-owned
firms can be given both a social democratic and a socialist inflection,
depending on how deep the contradiction between private, capitalist
interests and the public, social good is understood to be. In their moderate form, arguments of this kind lay behind both the attempts at indicative planning in Britain in the 1960s, and the corporatist initiatives
launched by the Labour Government between 1975 and 1979. Given a
more radical inflection, they underpinned the Labour left's call for
extensive public ownership and planning agreements with large, private
companies (the policy on which the Labour Party came to power in
1974); and were equally central to the Alternative Economic Strategy
on which the Labour left fought for party dominance in the early 1980s.
Their presence now is most evident in the arguments of economists like
Keith Cowling and Roger Sugden, tying industrial policy to the creation of strong, central, strategic planning agencies, new state-owned
investment banks and holding companies, enhanced powers for
regional planning bodies and the extensive democratisation of industry
and the state (Cowling and Sugden, 1990, *passim*).

In these more radical arguments – of both the Johnson/Tyson and
Cowling/Sugden type – the debate on market failures connects directly
to questions of development and underdevelopment, and to the forces
determining the positions of national economies in the international
division of labour. When these arguments prevail, governments intervene in industry to do more than create, supplement or manage
markets. They intervene to strengthen the position of their home industries in global markets, or at the very least to prevent the erosion of
local competitive strength. Yet the pursuit of economic growth and the
struggle against economic decline invariably brings into the policy

frame a vast range of possible political initiatives, very few of which focus directly on industry as such: a range that stretches from the reform of labour laws, through questions of education and culture, out to patterns of income distribution, housing, welfare benefits and the like. Industrial policy is then situated on a much wider canvas: and because it is, a full understanding of its character and role in the post-war UK requires that we shift now from exploring why we might need industrial policy to a delineation of what industrial policy actually entails. We need to move, that is, from a discussion of justifications to one of definitions.

1.2   The boundaries of industrial policy

Arguments of these kinds generate industrial policies of widely varying types and intensity. So if we are to be clear on which kinds of industrial policy have actually been in play in post-war Britain, we need to be able to recognise precise variations of policy amid the broad run of state–economy relationships of which they are only a part. To do that, we need some definitional precision on both terms in the label: 'industry', and 'policy'.

(i) Industry

To take 'industry' first, it is not immediately obvious how, if at all, the term is meant to be distinguishable from a specification of 'the economy' in total. If 'industry' is the place *where people work* (are 'industrious'), then in principle all spheres of labour which contribute to the reproduction of the society ought to fall within its remit. Work in the home, work in offices and factories, work in mines and fields – all should be understood as part of Britain's industrial system. But so wide a notion of industry robs the term of its cutting edge, and does not sit well with the popular and more restricted notion of industry as the place *where things are made* (or *dug up*, since mining seems always to be seen as an industry as well). In popular discussion, 'industry' and 'manufacturing' tend to be synonymous; with 'industry' often carrying an image of paid manual work under factory conditions, to set alongside other work at the edges of the industrial core: unpaid, domestic work in the home on the one edge, and routine, white collar work in the service sector on the other.

Yet that equation – of industry with manufacturing – is itself not without its problems. If industry is the place where things are made, rather than where services are provided, then many people working in industry perform an internal service function not dissimilar in kind to their white collar equivalents elsewhere. If industry is where manual work is done, then to restrict it to manufacturing is to exclude similar work processes in the provision of basic utilities, in transport and in construction. And if manufacture is the key – if industry is where things are made (and as commodities, are then sold), then so too is the output of the agrarian sector, of the extractive industries, and of many service companies as well. Indeed, of late, in terms both of international trade and of employment, agriculture, fuel and banking have been among the more successful of Britain's productive sectors, at the very time when the number of people working in more conventionally understood manufacturing industries has been steadily in decline, and when manufacturing's traditionally positive contribution to Britain's trading surplus has given way to a growing dependence on the import of foreign manufactured goods.

Nor can we with any ease treat industry as the private sector and non-industry as the public. These days the public–private boundary is too fluid for that (with public ownership rising in the 1970s, and privatisation developing apace in the years since); and, in any, case, certain publicly-owned institutions do produce tradable goods, do employ manual workers, and do even on occasion trade abroad. The weight of what we shall term 'industry' is in fact now located in the private sector, so *industrial policy as we will understand it will be in the main policy linking public institutions to private companies.* But it will not be exclusively so. In the past to a greater extent, and in the present to a lesser, the state has directly owned and managed part of Britain's industrial base; and because it did and does, any study of industrial policy in the post-war period has also to include a discussion of policy initiatives taken within the nationalised sector itself.

In fact the literature on, and popular discussion of, any modern economy's internal structure abounds with overlapping and potentially conflicting classificatory categories. There is the public and the private, the tradable and the non-tradable, manufacturing and services, primary, secondary and tertiary sectors, old and new industries, heavy and light, high-tech and low-tech, and so on. The literature also abounds with lists – of industrial sectors picked out to constitute the 'core' of the country's manufacturing base. The CBI, for example, recently offered these twelve for that purpose: aerospace and other transport equipment; electronics and electrical engineering; chemicals; metals; paper, printing and publishing; minerals and mineral products; metal products; motor vehicles and components; food, drink and tobacco; clothing and footwear; and textiles (CBI, 1991, p. 66). We also face an official *Standard Industrial Classification of Industrial Activities* which in its 1980 version grouped activities into ten basic categories/orders, and in its latest (Central Statistical Office, 1992) version has replaced that ten with seventeen:

A: Agriculture, hunting and forestry
B: Fishing
C: Mining and Quarrying
D: Manufacturing
E: Electricity, gas and water supply
F: Construction
G: Wholesale and retail trade, etc.
H: Hotels and restaurants
I: Transport, storage and communication
J: Financial Intermediation
K: Real estate, renting and business activities
L: Public admin and defence: compulsory social security
N: Education
O: Health and Social Work
P: Other community, social & personal service activities
Q: Extra-territorial organisations & bodies

   Classification systems of these kinds are only as valuable as the purposes to which they are put; and so if we clarify our purposes here, the classification systems we shall need should come into view. The contemporary debate on industrial policy has been sparked by a more general concern with standards of life, possibilities of employment, and achievement of trading surpluses in the increasingly competitive world of the 1990s. The availability of employment will depend on the size of the entire economy (on expansion in any or all seventeen of the SIC's new categories); and the standards of life those jobs can sustain will critically turn on the productivity of the labour processes dominant in each, and on the ability of local producers to finance the purchase (through exports) of the products of labour processes situated abroad. In that constellation of complex economic and social relationships, *it is the productivity and competitiveness of the tradable section of the economy which is ultimately critical* and the bulk of what is traded across international boundaries comes not from the welfare sector, internal transport, utilities, construction and retailing but from extractive and manufacturing industries, and from the output of the agrarian sector and of large financial intermediaries.

So if we are to focus on 'industry' in the context of surveying policies to enhance international competitiveness, we need to focus on those sectors producing commodities which participate directly in international trade, and allow the rest of the economy to creep in only at the margin. *We need to concentrate, that is, on the core, exporting, industries.* Historically, that core lay in manufacturing itself. Manufacturing industry – broadly defined to take in textiles, transport equipment, machinery, iron and steel, chemicals, minerals fuels and lubricants – provided 83.9 per cent of all UK exports by value as late as 1973; but that percentage fell rapidly, to 65.9 per cent a decade later (Foreman-Peck, 1991, p. 150). The slack left by weakening manufacturing performance was increasingly taken up by *extractive* industries – oil and gas rather than coal: 'between 1979 and 1985 the fuel balance of trade improved by some 3 per cent of GDP' (Wells, 1989, p. 50). Agriculture too has made an important contribution to the recent easing of balance of payments constraints on UK economic performance, with food imports falling from 19.5 per cent to 6.4 per cent of the total import bill between 1973 and 1983; and financial services continued to do the same. In fact, the balance of earnings (exports minus imports) in the service sector actually settled 'throughout the 1980s...at a percentage of GDP...considerably below the levels attained in the mid 1970s' (Wells, 1989, p. 44), as overseas spending on shipping, civil aviation and especially tourism ate away at the margins created by the City, and by earnings from consultancies, engineering and royalties. But none the less oil and financial services definitely, and agriculture to a lesser degree, helped to cushion the diminishing overseas earnings generated by UK-based manufacturing industry in the second half of our period, and so must fall within our core definition of industry itself. Of course, their contribution to the UK's balance of trade cannot be adequately charted without some allowance for the contribution of activity elsewhere in the economy to which they are linked: to construction and internal transport, to basic utilities, to more domestically-focused services and to welfare provision. But for clarity of exposition we shall need to prioritise the core, and deal predominantly with policy towards the industries we find there.

(ii) Policy

So, if these sectors are the focus of our concern, with which type of *policy* affecting them do we need to be primarily concerned here? The answer has to be that we need to be concerned with only some of the vast range of government policies which have repercussions on industrial performance. If we do not restrict our concerns in this way, we shall be in no position to isolate industrial policy from the rest. Nor shall we be able either to characterise that policy over time or to locate its place in the government's overall scheme of things. Indeed, only by differentiating industrial policy from more general economic policy shall we be able to decide if the two are in harmony or in tension; and only by isolating individual strands of industrial policy itself shall we be able to locate points of internal tension among the whole set of state initiatives to industry. Since those tensions invariably exist, we need to go into the study of industrial policy with a very detailed specification of what that policy is, and where its boundaries lie.

Yet that definitional task is easier to proclaim than to deliver. As David Audretsch has correctly observed, 'an actual definition of industrial policy may be as difficult to formulate as it is prevalent in practice...you know it when you see it, but you can't define it' (Audretsch, 1989, p. 10). Indeed, as Andre Blais reported to the Canadian Royal Commission on Economic Union and Development, in much of the literature recently produced in this area, 'the need for an exact definition of the term has not been strongly felt', and where a definition has been proposed, it was 'generally disposed of in a paragraph, with the author not taking care either to justify the definition or to indicate some of the problems it may contain' (Blais, 1986, p. 3).

The result is a literature riddled with a set of conflicting definitions, with the centre of gravity of each as much conditioned by positions in the arguments laid out in Section 1.1 above, as by any precise sense of where industry ends and policy begins. For, as Malcolm Sawyer has observed, 'each approach has to some degree built within it a definition of industrial policy: in other words the definition of what constitutes industrial policy is paradigm-specific' (Sawyer, 1992, pp. 4–5). That is why analysts of a neo-classical persuasion tend to give the definition of policy a narrower focus, whereas those keen to see industrial policy creating market advantage give it a wider one. As we approach a working definition of industrial policy, we shall need therefore to relate the width and content of our definition to a sense of where it fits into the wider paradigmatic arguments about the strengths and weaknesses of unregulated market processes. We shall also need to go beyond the definitional sloppiness of much of the literature in this field, armed with the recognition that in much of it the term is often 'left as a rather vague and general [one], or something that encompasses a very broad range of adjustment mechanisms' (Thompson, 1989, p. 58).

In that literature, some analysts have chosen to define industrial policy as anything that bears on the question of industrial competitiveness. Chalmers Johnson, for example, chose to define industrial policy as 'a summary term for the activities of governments that are intended to develop/retrench various industries in a national economy in order to maintain global competitiveness' (C. Johnson, 1984, p. 7). Writing to a sceptical American audience, he chose to define industrial policy very generally indeed, as

first of all an attitude, and only then a matter of technique. It involves the specific recognition that all government measures – taxes, licenses, prohibitions, regulations – have a significant impact on the well-being or ill-health of whole sectors, industries, and enterprises in a market economy.   (ibid., p. 7)

And he explicitly placed it as 'the third side of the economic triangle, to the government's monetary and fiscal policies' – realising that all three of them affected industry, but wanting to keep industrial policy as the label for all 'the government's explicit attempts to co-ordinate its own multifarious activities and expenditures and to reform them using as a basic criterion the achievement of dynamic competitive advantage' (ibid., p. 11).

The problem with defining industrial policy so broadly, however, is that it runs the risk of subsuming within the definition the whole complex of state activity touching the economy: policy on levels of demand, growth, employment, welfare, even environmental issues and incomes control. – By being so ambitious in its coverage, it actually serves to hide and obscure the nature of industrial policy as such, making it an axiom of policy-making rather than a choice. Wildavsky, for example, using this wide definition, was quite able to conclude that: 'there is no such thing as not having an industrial policy. Action and inaction alike affect the condition of industry' (in Audretsch, 1989, p. 11). We can see what he means, but the observation hardly helps us to specify with any precision the business that we are about.

So industrial policy is hard to locate if it is not properly designated. It is also hard to locate because in practice it never stands alone. As Grahame Thompson has persuasively argued, one of the main problems with the study of industrial policy is the way in which – in recent US and UK experience – policy to industry has been called upon to do too many things and to meet too many objectives. Industrial policy is – in his words – 'over-determined by other policy areas'.

> Thus industrial policy can be called upon at times to solve employment problems, problems of regional imbalance, defence policy issues, social welfare issues, and housing policy among others. In addition, tax and fiscal policy can substitute for industrial policy, as can domestic and/or international competitiveness and trade policy.... What tends to happen with industrial policy therefore is that it gets fused together with this range of other policy areas and/or it gets substituted by other policy areas, or a combination of the two of these. This makes unravelling what is the specific domain of industrial policy rather difficult, but quite necessary.   (Thompson, 1989, p. 59)

But why is it necessary? The Thompson answer is that the proper understanding of industrial policy requires that it be analytically distinguished from the other areas with which in practice it is combined (or, as he would put it, articulated) – so that strategic issues associated with industrial policy can be discussed in isolation, and so that the scale and nature of its articulation with other policy areas can be recognised and assessed. To those ends, Thompson (and many other scholars of industrial policy) then drop a level of generality. They differentiate broad policies affecting the economy as a whole from those more directly focused on specific sectors, industries or firms: and restrict the term 'industrial policy' to this second category of policy initiatives alone. Industrial policy then narrows down to 'any policy implemented by government which is directed towards a particular industry with the objective of improving that industry's competitive position' (Clarke, 1993, pp. 141–2), and becomes characterised as 'long run supply-side initiatives aimed at restructuring/promoting the activities of particular firms and sectors' (Dietrich, 1992, p. 17).

As this last citation makes clear, this definitional narrowing invariably also involves a differentiation of policies working on the demand side of the economy from those directed to supply-side issues, and of 'macro-economic management' from 'microeconomic intervention'

(Hall, 1986a, p. 269): with 'industrial policy' again understood as referring only to the second of each of these. In other words, they do what Wyn Grant does, and restrict the definition of industrial policy to

> a set of measures used by governments to influence the investment decisions of individual enterprises – public and private – so as to promote such objectives as lower unemployment, a healthier balance of payments, and a more generally efficient industrial economy. (Grant, 1982, p. 7)

This seems to be a wise and necessary move to make, so long as we do not then discount or ignore the effects on individual industrial sectors of those broader economic and social policy initiatives and concerns. That is why we shall follow here the definition of industrial policy suggested by Daniel Okimoto, that industrial policy:

> involves the government's use of its authority and resources to ... address the needs of specific sectors and industries (and, if necessary, those of individual companies) with the aim of raising the productivity of factor inputs. By contrast, public policies dealing with the economy as a whole, not just its micro-industrial parts, falls into the domain of macroeconomics. [And like him we will need to recognise that] between the two poles – industrial policy and macroeconomics – are grey areas that can be grouped at either bend of the continuum, depending on the uses to which they are put. Fiscal budgets, for example, have an impact on the whole economy, but individual items in the budget – like public procurements or research and development subsidies – can be used to promote specific industries and hence ought to be included in the category of industrial policy.   (Okimoto, 1989, pp. 8–9)

In fact, to meet that recognition, we need to establish the existence of what we might call both *direct* and *indirect* industrial policy. *Direct industrial policy* is policy geared specifically and explicitly to enhancing the market performance of particular industrial sectors or that of their component industries or firms. *Indirect industrial policy* is the effects on those sectors which flow from the often unanticipated impacts of more general economic and social policy concerns. These other areas of policy then shade into indirect industrial policy in so far as they help to promote (or indeed hinder) the efficiency and competitiveness of particular sectors, industries and firms. This distinction parallels closely others common in the literature on industrial policy: between 'discriminatory' and 'non-discriminatory' measures, or between what D. T. Jones in 1981 called 'vertical' and 'horizontal' industrial policy (Jones, 1981, p. 154). At the core of industrial policy are initiatives directed to particular firms or industries; but behind them, and often informing them and providing their rationale, are broader (more horizontal, less discriminatory) sets of policies applying across industry as a whole. Training, general policy on R&D funding, and policies on ownership, management and democracy, all fit here. In other words, some general policies are more obviously to be understood as indirect industrial policy than are others – and it is into that penumbra that we would certainly want to place lots of labour market policy, and policy on social infrastructure.

If we go forward equipped with this distinction between direct and indirect industrial policy, at least two things follow for the analysis we shall build and the histories we shall narrate.

One is that the proper study of industrial policy will have a set of core concerns, and an associated awareness of the need to map interactions, overlaps and boundary problems with other areas of government policy. The imagery it needs is well captured in a recent attempt at such a mapping (Figure 1.1).

The other is that – within Thompson's central box – are to be found a distinct and recognisable core set of policies and practices. These will be united – and therefore specifiable – around a linked chain of concerns, procedures, areas and instruments. At the core of the *concerns* of industrial policy invariably lies the desire both immediately to enhance the efficiency, productivity and competitiveness of home-based industrial producers, and also to see the consolidation through time of an industrial structure strong enough (in terms of productivity and competitiveness) to underpin other long-term social and political goals. In the pursuit of those concerns, industrial policy invariably emerges from a distinct set of government institutions, whose *practices and procedures* are always marked by what Peter Hall called the three component elements of any industrial policy: 'the volume of funds [channelled] to industry; the set of criteria that govern the choice of sectors, firms and projects to be supported; and the degree of government pressure that is brought to bear on the re-organisation and reallocation of resources within industry' (Hall, 1986a, p. 272). And in the pursuit of industrial concerns through recognisable policy channels

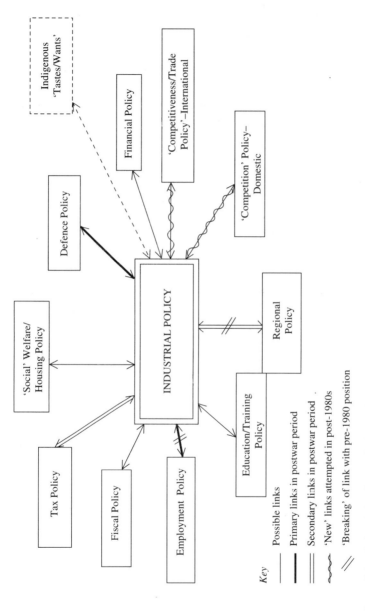

Figure 1.1 *Industrial policy and other policy areas*
(SOURCE: Thompson, 1989, p. 60)

and procedures, governments invariably prioritise certain *areas* of action (any or all of competition policy at home, foreign trade policy, and direct regulation and industrial targeting) which they work on through the use of a number of policy *instruments* (any or all of procurement policy, administrative and legal regulations, the disbursement of public funds, and the direct or indirect supply of infrastructure and factors of production).

It is these areas and instruments that take us to the core of industrial policy. Across Europe as a whole in the last twenty years, and not just in Britain, governments have pursued their industrial concerns by developing policies on some or all of the following:

- *creation and exploitation of markets* – both in relation to foreign trade (through attitudes to protection by themselves and by others, and through export promotion) and through internal policies on monopolies, mergers and support for infant industries;
- *industrial ownership, management and democracy* – policies on the scale of the public sector, on the rights of workers and managers, and on the degree of public regulation of decision-making procedures in private industry;
- *investment in plant and equipment* – its scale and origin, the terms of its provision, its geographical distribution, and its distribution between industries;
- *industrial structure* – encouraging local investment by multinational concerns, and seeking ways of stimulating and strengthening small and medium-sized enterprises;
- *new industries* – identifying future growth areas and providing support for them: especially in industries such as information technology, micro-electronics, biotechnology, robotics and energy;
- *older industries* – to facilitate their restructuring or demise;
- *new technology* – on the encouragement of R&D, the dissemination of technical knowledge and the launch of new products;
- *labour supply* – education, training and retraining: both in relation to specific industries and skills, and through general reforms of educational syllabuses for specifically industrial purposes.

It is with the pattern of government activity in Britain since the Second World War under these headings that the chapters which follow will be most centrally concerned.

1.3 Typologies of state action

Peter Hall, in the quotation cited above, referred to the different degrees of government pressure characteristically associated with a style of relationship between industry and the state. His reference is doubly important here, both to draw attention to an important element of industrial policy for which we must look, and also as a reminder of the existence of a broader dimension of industrial policy that has also to be kept in view. That broader dimension is the place occupied by industrial policy as a whole in the institutional arrangements and governing philosophies of different state systems. Industrial policy is not shaped just by the exigencies of particular industrial problems. It is also shaped by the persistence of more deeply entrenched and longer established habits of mind and ways of acting in the political system and industrial structures of which it is a part. Around the edge of the study of industrial policy therefore, we shall need to look for and identify these broader, more general characteristics of state–industry interaction.

The literature on industrial policy in post-war capitalist economies suggests the existence of at least three types of such state traditions and ways of linking government to industry – the *liberal*, the *developmental*, and the *negotiated/consensual* – and contrasts each with the centrally planned *command* economies characteristic of the Soviet bloc prior to 1989. In a liberal state-industry relationship, industrial policy has only a limited and non-directional role. The way in which a liberal state and its industries interact is overwhelmingly through market processes, with the state maintaining a broadly 'hands-off' approach when faced with industrial difficulties: intervening reluctantly, reactively (rather than proactively), and only in cases of visible market failure or political crisis – and then primarily simply to guarantee the creation of open market conditions again. Direct industrial policy in such a situation is limited, reactive and non-directional.

In a developmental state–industry relationship, industrial policy is exactly the reverse: it is directional, it is proactive, and it is extensive – and it is all these things because state institutions and traditions exist to bind governments and industry together, with both sides accepting the role of the state as the long-term strategic planner of industrial structure and performance. Between the two models, liberal and developmental, we can also imagine a third – one in which there is a high degree of negotiated interaction between state and industry (and often between both and labour as the third partner), with the state providing industrial support, and demanding high levels of labour protection and social provision, in an attempt to harness both sides of industry to a project of permanent industrial modernisation and change.

Such a typology of state regimes, then, overlays the arguments we met earlier for different kinds and scale of industrial policy, and is associated with the prioritisation of different sets of more discrete industrial policies. The relationship between the three layers (state regime, state involvement in industry, and discrete policy initiatives) can be captured – in preliminary and schematic form – as shown in Figure 1.2.

Of course, each of these models is, at best, only an ideal type – such that to label any particular set of state–industry relationships as liberal, developmental or consensual would be to accentuate only part of their overall profile. States invariably combine elements of one or two of these models: either by policy changes over time (now more liberal, now less), or by creating policies for one sector of industry which fit one model, and for other sectors which fit another (liberal to civilian industry, developmental to military goods producers, and so on). Certainly in the British case (and as Chapter 2 will make clear in more detail) we shall see liberal attitudes to state–civil industry relations in the 1950s and again in the 1980s being challenged briefly in the intervening decades by attempts at a more consensual corporatist mode of

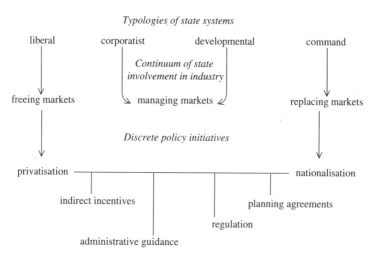

Typologies of state systems

Figure 1.2   *State systems and industrial policy*

industrial planning. We shall also see elements of a developmental relationship persisting between the Ministry of Defence and the military-industrial sector even during the heyday of liberal civilian economics.

But with such caveats, it is still possible to say that the British state – over the post-war years as a whole – has been in general more liberal than developmental in its relationship to industry and in its attitude to the role, scale and character of industrial policy; and that only at certain times has it attempted to replace that liberalism with a more consensual and negotiated relationship with both capital and labour. One task of the chapters to come, therefore, will be, where appropriate, to chart the rise and fall not just of individual industrial policies, but of the shifting centre of gravity of industrial policy as a whole on this liberal–consensual–developmental continuum. Indeed it is the fusion of the detailed policy analysis and the broader understanding of state traditions which can best capture what has happened in Britain since the Second World War, and best clarify the nature of the choices facing governments and electorates in this key area of policy-change in the 1990s and beyond.

II SECTORS OF POLICY

2 Manufacturing

Simon Lee

2.1 Introduction

The performance of manufacturing industry is an especially important question for industrial policy in Britain for three reasons. First, manufacturing contributes, and has contributed during the post-war period, by far the largest share of exports. In 1992, manufactures accounted for 62.6 per cent of total British exports compared to only 23.4 per cent in the case of services. Secondly, since only about 20 per cent of service output can be exported, manufacturing, because of its greater tradability, is vital to Britain's capacity to pay for her imports of food, raw materials and foreign manufactures. For every one per cent decline in Britain's exports of manufactures, its exports of services have to increase by 2.5 per cent merely to compensate for such a loss. Thirdly, a significant and increasing proportion of the service sector is dependent on manufacturing. Indeed, as we shall discuss in more detail in Chapter 3, the distinction between manufacturing and services is becoming harder to identify (House of Commons, 1994, pp. 21–2). Therefore, domestic manufacturing is vital to Britain's trade performance, the prosperity of her population, and the competitiveness of the non-manufacturing sectors of her economy.

Though the share of GDP in constant prices accounted for by manufacturing has declined in all the major industrial countries, Britain is unique amongst them in experiencing almost stagnant manufacturing output in the 1970s and 1980s. In 1992, British manufacturing output was less than one per cent above its 1973 peak, whereas in the same period output in France had risen by 27 per cent, in Germany by 25 per cent, in Italy by 85 per cent, and in Japan by 119 per cent (House of

Commons, 1994, pp. 20–2). From 1963, when the value of the Britain's trade in manufactures was 275 per cent greater than that of her manufactured imports, to 1983 the UK sustained an annual balance of payments surplus on her trade in manufactures of between £1.5 bn and £6.0 bn (House of Lords, 1985, p. 7). But from 1984 to the present day, through periods of both economic boom and recession, Britain has sustained a substantial deficit on her trade in manufactures. Indeed, the recession of 1990–3 was the first in Britain during which manufactured imports have risen.

The most damaging consequence of the relative decline of manufacturing in Britain is that the size of the tradable sector of the national economy is now too small for Britain to be able to pay its way in the world. Having accounted for 32 per cent of Britain's GDP in 1972, and 28 per cent in 1980, manufacturing contracted so rapidly in the following decade that by 1992 it was responsible for generating only 20 per cent of GDP (Davis *et al.*, 1992, p. 46). Singh has contended that an 'efficient' manufacturing sector is 'one which (currently and potentially) not only satisfies the demands of consumers at home, but is also able to sell enough of its products abroad to pay for the nation's import requirements', provided that those objectives are achieved at 'socially acceptable levels of output, employment and the exchange rate' (Singh, 1977, p. 118). By any of Singh's criteria, Britain now possesses, and is likely to possess for the foreseeable future, an 'inefficient' manufacturing sector. In the case of employment in manufacturing, for example, the total fell nationally by more than 1 m between 1968 and 1976 and then, as even one of the most ardent Thatcherites has acknowledged, by a further 2 m or 14 per cent of the total employed in manufacturing during the recession of 1979–81 (Lawson, 1992, p. 55). These disturbing industrial trends have not passed unnoticed. In 1985, a House of Lords Select Committee report on *Overseas Trade* asserted that a poor performance in manufacturing undoubtedly contained 'the seeds of a major political and economic crisis in the foreseeable future' (1985, p. 56). In 1991, the House of Lords' Select Committee on Science and Technology warned that Britain's manufacturing base was in decline, that its home markets were increasingly penetrated by imports, and that its share of world markets in manufactures was too small. The Committee concluded that 'The implications for our future prosperity are grave' (House of Lords, 1991, p. 29).

There are many contending explanations for Britain's relative economic and industrial decline: strong trade unions, inadequate financial institutions and inappropriate state policies being among them (Coates, 1994). This chapter lacks the space to explore the way that the absence of a network of state-owned or private sector development banks (capable of supplying long-term and affordable finance to manufacturing industry) has acted as a major constraint on UK post-war industrial development. But it will be organised to demonstrate another important cause of UK post-war economic under-performance: namely the relative priorities given to civil and defence manufacturing in post-war industrial policy, and the way in which a disproportionate share of national industrial and technological resources have been devoted to the manufacturing of weapons. It will argue that whereas state assistance to defence manufacturers has been regarded by successive British governments as a wholly legitimate and necessary form of intervention in manufacturing industry, civil industrial policy has been characterised by a series of sporadic and often ineffectual interventions of a far less sustained kind. It will also argue that the industrial policies of the Thatcher and Major Governments should be understood both as a reaction to, and a critique of, these failed interventions in civilian manufacturing industry. The industries covered in this chapter are privately-owned manufacturing ones. Policy towards service industries, energy and agriculture will be dealt with in the chapters that follow.

2.2 Policy towards manufacturing 1945–1964

The immediate post-war years are important for any analysis of Britain's post-war relative economic decline, not least because many influential commentators have contended that this period witnessed the failure of the Attlee Government to develop the sort of technocratic industrial policy instrumental in the post-war recovery of the French, West German and Japanese economies. Correlli Barnett, for example, has attributed this key failure to the primacy given to the expansion of the welfare state (Barnett, 1986, p. 11); and Peter Hennessy, more appropriately, has described the reorganisation of Whitehall after 1945 as 'the missed opportunity' for industrial modernisation (Hennessy, 1989, p. 125). Warfare rather than welfare was in fact the key eroder of post-war industrial competitiveness. The Attlee Government never managed to turn its commitment to nationalisation into a proactive industrial policy for civil manufacturing; and it failed to do so, in part at least, because it was simultaneously determined to maintain Britain's status as a Great Power. This determination entailed, among other things, the procurement of large amounts of expensive military equipment from domestic manufacturers. This had a particularly adverse effect on the performance of civilian manufacturers.

(i) Civil industrial policy

Addison has documented how Labour's wartime plans for extending the peacetime role of civil industrial policy were limited to only a few industries where state ownership was felt to be vital (1975, p. 262); and Cairncross has noted how few people actually stopped to consider how the expanded role for state intervention under nationalisation should be organised (1985, p. 300). Labour's 1945 manifesto recognised that, in conditions of scarcity, controls would be required on investment, the allocation of resources for production, and the promotion of exports; but the manifesto was silent on how those controls would be combined and on what form planning would take. As a result, the British working parties that were created compared unfavourably with, say, their French equivalents: so that France after 1945 had an effective civil industrial policy while Britain possessed 'at best, only a collection of unrelated expedients' (*The Economist*, 14 December 1946, cited in PEP, 1960, p. 222).

On the civilian front, the major policy shift which occurred after 1945 was the transfer from private to public ownership of a number of basic utilities. Industries and firms already in the public sector (the Port of London authority, the Central Electricity Generating Board [CEGB], the BBC, the London Passenger Transport Board, and the British Overseas Airways Corporation [BOAC]) were joined by the Bank of England, coal mining, the supply of gas and electricity, the railways system and a section of road transport, civil aviation, telecommunications and iron and steel. Though the Attlee Government's nationalisation programme was often treated subsequently as a key element of social reform, its public ownership initiatives (as we shall see in more detail in Chapter 4) were largely driven by considerations of economic modernisation; and certainly no attempt was made to alter modes of management within the newly nationalised concerns, nor were more than limited funds provided for new investment there.

In fact, public ownership was also seen as a mechanism for circumventing problems of private monopoly power; and competitive pressures in British industry after 1945 were also strengthened by the creation in 1948 of the Monopolies and Restrictive Practices Commission (MRPC), to which the Board of Trade could refer cases in which more than one-third of the supply, processing or export of certain goods came from one source. Competition policy was then extended by the Conservatives in the 1950s, by the splitting of the MRPC into the Monopolies Commission and the Restrictive Practices Court in 1956, and by the beginnings of moves against resale price maintenance in 1958. Indeed, as we had cause to mention in Chapter 1, although the Conservative governments of the 1950s did not reverse Labour's public ownership initiatives (except in relation to iron and steel), they did relocate the priorities of their industrial policy – attaching far more centrality to the encouragement of competition within the private sector than had been the case under Attlee.

The immediate post-war problem of competitiveness for British manufacturers lay less with questions of ownership or external monitoring, however, than with relatively sluggish industrial productivity. Three of the most important initiatives in civil industrial policy under the Attlee Government were the creation of the Anglo-American Council on Productivity (AACP), the establishment of sector working parties, and the setting up of four development councils. The AACP produced no fewer than sixty-six reports about a diversity of manufacturing industries in which a number of obstacles to greater industrial efficiency were identified, not least, the shortcomings of British management. To overcome these weaknesses in civil industry, seventeen working parties were appointed to analyse the problems of specific industries, principally those concerned with the manufacture of consumer products. Their reports resulted in eight ministers being empowered to create a development council in a specific industry or for a group of related industries. Ministers were also given the power to assign as many as twenty functions to the development councils, including provisions for scientific and technical research, product design, certification and standardisation, recruitment and training, and advice to the minister about the industry (Henderson, 1952, pp. 454–7). However, the development councils were given few compulsory powers and did not become proactive instruments of intervention capable of radical industrial reorganisation. Their role was limited, largely reactive and advisory; and in the event only four of them had even been established before Labour left office.

Interventions in civil manufacturing in the 1950s were largely confined to the steel, cotton textile and aircraft industries. In the case of the steel industry, statutory control over the distribution of iron and steel was reintroduced in February 1952 and remained in place for six further years. However, the most important state intervention concerned the location of a fourth steel mill in Britain. Rather than constructing a large, modern integrated plant at Newport, the optimal industrial location, the Government bowed to the pressure from strong regional and departmental rivalry and split the investment between two smaller and less efficient plants, one at Newport and one at Ravenscraig in Scotland (Henderson, 1952, pp. 348–9). Meanwhile, the cotton industry's demands for protection from duty-free imports from Commonwealth manufacturers went largely unheeded, and in 1959 the Cotton Industry Act enabled compensation to be provided to cotton manufacturers scrapping redundant machinery and mills. The reorganisation schemes initiated for the cotton industry in July 1959 elicited a far larger response from manufacturers than had been anticipated. If the cotton industry was in any sense representative of the condition of civil manufacturing in Britain at the end of the decade, there must have been a much wider but latent need and demand for similar modernisation programmes in other industrial sectors.

The civil aircraft industry, on the other hand, appeared to be in a sufficiently healthy condition in 1951 for the Churchill Government to restrict its support largely to the retention of a 'buy British' policy. However, this policy of state disengagement and reliance on private sector initiatives was abandoned in 1954 after the withdrawal of the certificate of airworthiness from the Comet, the world's first jet airliner. The failure of the Comet threatened the survival of De Haviland as a major British aircraft manufacturer. The Treasury was content for De Haviland to close, but the Ministry of Supply was not. It subsequently ordered 18 aircraft from De Haviland for the RAF and offered an eventual £10 m in loans and procurement contracts to the company (Hayward, 1983, pp. 19–20). Indeed, between 1950 and 1964, state payments to aircraft manufacturers covered 70 per cent of the industry's total output.

It had become apparent by the mid-1950s that most British firms in the aircraft industry lacked the financial resources to be able to finance privately the escalating costs of R&D, especially at a time of declining procurement of military aircraft (Hayward, 1983, p. 28). The responsibility for rationalisation of aircraft manufacturing was not entrusted to the private sector but was undertaken in 1959 by the newly created Ministry of Aviation, which made it clear to manufacturers that future state funding of civil projects would be conditional upon the rapid and comprehensive implementation of a process of concentration within the industry. It was subsequently disclosed that the Ministry had a very precise blueprint for the future structure of the industry, in which there would be a reduction from seventeen to five principal manufacturers. The British Aircraft Corporation and the Hawker Siddeley Group were to be responsible for airframe development, Rolls-Royce and Bristol Siddeley were to handle aero-engine manufacture, and Westland helicopter manufacture. Within two months of the first public reports of Sandys' ultimatum to the aircraft industry, this rationalisation had taken place. The fact that such a detailed programme of industrial reorganisation was confined to an industry vital to Britain's military interest is indicative of the priorities of the post-war British state, and the particular factors that have moved it to undertake proactive intervention in manufacturing.

(ii) Military industrial policy

If the institutional structures of civil industrial policy in post-war Britain constituted 'a collection of unrelated expedients', those of military industrial policy were far more coherent. Drawing on the lessons of wartime, two White Papers on defence in 1946 proposed a central organisation of defence (which emerged as the MoD in 1947). To oversee military industrial policy, the Joint War Production Committee was created, which worked for the Ministerial Production Committee. To oversee military research, a Committee on Defence Research Policy was established. To each committee was appointed a permanent chairman who, with the Chief Staff Officer and Permanent Secretary at the Ministry of Defence, constituted the four principal ministerial advisers. It is testament to the continuity in the institutional structures shaping weapons production that, forty years later, as Broadbent has noted, these four same pillars can be identified in the form of the Chief of Defence Procurement, the Chief Scientific Adviser, the Chief of the Defence Staff, and the Permanent Under-Secretary of State (1988, p. 17). As we shall see in more detail in Chapter 7, such continuity is conspicuous by its absence from post-war civil industrial policy-making structures.

Critical to the subsequent health of British manufacturing industry was the growth of spending on military equipment after the onset of the Cold War. As late as 1947 that growth did not look inevitable: the defence White Paper that year stated that it was 'both inevitable and right that rehabilitation of the civil economy should increasingly absorb the country's efforts and resources, to the diminution of activities in the defence field' (Chalmers, 1985, p. 34). But the British response to the onset of the Cold War ensured that this set of priorities in industrial policy was soon reversed. Despite the sterling crisis of August 1949, the Attlee Government began to devote more resources to defence, spending £200 m on equipment in 1949/50 out of a total defence budget of £760 m, or 7 per cent of national income (Carver, 1992, p. 15). The communist invasion of South Korea in 1950 then drew from the Attlee Government in 1951 a £4.7 bn, three-year programme which effectively doubled Britain's defence spending within two years (Chalmers, 1985, p. 50). Given that unemployment at this time was only 1.5 per cent and manufacturing industry was operating at near to full capacity, the Government's insistence that weapons must be procured from domestic manufacturers meant that the expansion in military manufacturing could only be realised by diverting resources from civilian manufacturers' investment and exports (Chalmers, 1985, p. 51; see Burnham, 1993, p. 5 for an alternative view). In fact, Korean rearmament generated an increase in inflation from 3 per cent in 1950 to 12 per cent in 1951, while the balance of payments surplus of £300 m in 1950 was converted into a £400 m deficit in 1951. With the switch of national resources from civilian to defence manufacturing, the total volume of exports of manufactures stopped growing in 1951, declined by almost 9 per cent in 1952 and did not recover to its 1950–1 level until 1955 (Cairncross, 1985, p. 231).

Even before the Conservatives' General Election victory of October 1951, the consequences for manufacturing industry of Britain's refusal to abandon her pretensions to Great Power status were apparent. The Attlee Government had been forced to attempt to control defence spending by spreading rearmament programmes over a longer period than the original three years (Dockrill, 1988, p. 44). Having in opposition attacked the Attlee Government for its tardiness in rearming Britain, Winston Churchill as Prime Minister now conceded that its plans for weapons procurement were 'utterly beyond our economic capacity to bear' (Chalmers, 1985, p. 54). A reappraisal of defence policy was therefore undertaken, as a consequence of which a greater salience was given to the development of the hydrogen bomb, and the production of a V-bomber to deliver it was accelerated. It was thought that the manufacture of such high-technology weapons would be more effective both in strategic and cost terms than the maintenance of large, conscript armed forces. However, escalating defence costs were not contained by this strategic reappraisal. In 1954, defence spending accounted for nearly 10 per cent of the national budget (Dockrill, 1988, p. 51). Furthermore, the failure of the 1956 Suez invasion demonstrated not only the paucity of Britain's pretensions to Great Power status, but also that relatively high levels of defence expenditure would not automatically deliver victory on the battlefield. A further major review of defence policy was therefore undertaken by the Macmillan Government, with both the Prime Minister and his new Minister of Defence, Duncan Sandys, known advocates of defence economies. The April 1957 Defence White Paper claimed to be 'the biggest change in military policy ever made in normal times', but after an initial fall in 1957–8 defence spending levelled off before starting to rise again from 1960–1 onwards (Chalmers, 1985, p. 68). The burden of Britain's overseas commitments on its industrial performance would therefore remain a constant impediment throughout the 1950s.

Government policy towards the procurement of military aircraft was shaped by the cancellation of a series of projects, the emphasis in military strategy placed upon the V-bombers, and Duncan Sandys' belief in 1957 that the future lay with missiles rather than manned aircraft. Most of the frontline fighter aircraft serving with the RAF in the 1950s were the product of the 1940s. Only the Hawker Hunter and the Lightning saw service in any numbers, and several other supersonic fighter programmes were cancelled. The Churchill Government's reappraisal of defence policy had committed Britain to a domestically manufactured, strategic nuclear bomber force – the V-bomber force of Victor, Vulcan and Valiant bombers which were projected to cost an additional £600 m over 15 years (Chalmers, 1985, p. 57). However, towards the end of the decade, concern was expressed that these bombers might be vulnerable to improved Soviet anti-aircraft defences. To surmount this potential threat to Britain's deterrent, Duncan Sandys authorised the production of the Blue Streak long-range ballistic missile which, it was envisaged, would eventually replace manned aircraft altogether. In addition, the operational life of the V-bombers would be extended by arming them with the Blue Steel, a stand-off, airborne missile (Dockrill, 1988, p. 69). Despite this new emphasis on missile manufacturing, development work did begin in 1959 on one major new aircraft project, the TSR2.

So, overall, between 1945 and 1960 the military concerns of successive British governments justified heavy public funding for R&D in a number of critical industries: in nuclear power, aerospace, shipbuilding and electronics in particular. 'In the 1950s more than half of total national R&D spending was devoted to defence' (Edgerton, 1993a, p. 10); and defence R&D as a percentage of total defence expenditure (at 14.7 per cent in 1958) was way higher even than in the USA (10.10 per cent) and certainly than in France or Germany. The aircraft industry was the main beneficiary of this state largess. Three-quarters of its output remained military as late as the mid-1960s; and in the mid-1950s 'government spending on R&D in the aircraft industry was only just under what private industry and nationalised industries spent on their own R&D' in total (ibid.). Government civilian R&D expenditure in 1960/61 was £44 m. R&D expenditure by defence departments that year was £242 m (Grove, 1967, p. 268).

2.3   Policy towards manufacturing in the 1960s

The 1960s was a decade in which there came to the fore the question of whether manufacturers in Britain, in both the civil and defence sectors, possessed sufficient resources to be able to develop products that would enable them to remain competitive in world markets. There was a marked trend towards increasing industrial concentration (motor vehicles and electronics) and international collaboration (civil and military aerospace) in important sectors of manufacturing. This was a process (accelerated by the state's interventions) which was to have important repercussions for governments in the 1970s.

(i) Civil industrial policy

Competition policy was extended through the decade by the banning of resale price maintenance in 1964, the public overseeing of mergers as well as monopolies from 1965, the toughening of legislation on restrictive trade practices in 1968, and the attempt to enter the European Community from 1961. Throughout the decade, the state supplied funding to a number of civil aerospace projects, but two were of particular importance: the RB-211 jet engine project at Rolls-Royce (which was subsequently to confront the Heath Government with a major dilemma over its industrial policy) and the Anglo-French Concorde project to develop a supersonic jet airliner. Work on the concept of a supersonic transport aircraft began in Britain in the early

1950s, with a technical feasibility committee being established in November 1956. From the outset it was accepted by the Government that the development of such an aircraft would be beyond the means of the private sector, but the eventual decision to proceed with the project on a collaborative basis with the French was only in part motivated by questions of industrial logic (the opportunity to share development costs and to strengthen European technological collaboration as a bulwark against industrial competition from the USA). Political considerations were also a major factor. Indeed, the signing of the collaborative agreement in 1962 coincided with Macmillan's attempts to gain EEC membership. Apparently at no stage was the Cabinet presented with a detailed analysis of the project's benefits to either the aircraft industry or the national economy, being told simply that the British aircraft industry would not survive a decision not to proceed (Hayward, 1983, p. 56). The Concorde project was to prove one of the most costly errors of post-war industrial policy in Britain. The development costs alone, which had been projected at the signing of the treaty at between £150 m and £170 m by 1970 escalated to £275 m by the time the Wilson Government assumed power and had reached £825 m by the time that it left office in 1970 (Reed, 1973, p. 91). This was the dividend on an aircraft of which fewer than twenty were sold, and then only to the national airlines of France and Britain.

While international industrial collaboration was identified as a means to secure the future production of aircraft, industrial concentration through mergers was regarded as a source of competitive advantage in the electronics and motor vehicles' industries. Particularly significant here was the decision of the Labour Government to create the Industrial Reorganisation Corporation, the IRC (for details, see Chapter 7, p. 167). Behind the IRC's creation lay the belief that too few British firms possessed the necessary scale to be able to finance the R&D necessary to remain competitive in world markets, and that although market forces had been promoting a degree of concentration, this was not proceeding at a pace which was felt to match the needs of the national economy. The IRC was therefore given the capacity to draw up to £150 m to accelerate the concentration of manufacturing industry and to 'establish or develop, or promote or assist the establishment or development of any industrial enterprise' (Young and Lowe, 1974, p. 40). The IRC eventually became involved in more than fifty mergers or takeovers, although the number of IRC-inspired mergers was to prove less significant than their long-term impact upon the development of major manufacturing industries. In the electronics industry, for example, the IRC provided finance to English Electric (EE) and Elliott Automation to facilitate their merger. The IRC then played a major role in the takeover of Associated Electrical Industries (AEI) by the General Electric Company (GEC), and subsequently supported GEC's takeover of EE.

In the case of the motor vehicle industry, the Wilson Government inherited a very difficult situation from the previous Conservative administration, which had chosen to encourage car manufacturers to locate new plants away from existing manufacturing capacity and markets in regions of higher unemployment, such as Merseyside, or Linwood in Scotland. Such investments did nothing, however, to promote corporate profitability; and in the instance of Rootes, a small British car manufacturer, led to a deal that saw Chrysler, one of the so-called 'Big Three' US vehicle manufacturers, purchase what was close to a controlling voting equity in the UK company (Wilks, 1984, p. 89). In opposition, Wilson had criticised the Conservatives for too easily surrendering control of the British car industry, but when he sought an alternative 'British' solution he was unable to persuade the chairmen of either of the two major British car manufacturers to enter negotiations with Rootes. Eventually, the Wilson Government allowed Chrysler to take over Rootes, but only after the IRC had acquired a 15 per cent stake in the new venture and after a series of undertakings had been secured from Chrysler, including a confirmation of expansion at Linwood, and a requirement to 'export more than average' (Wilks, 1984, p. 93). Nor was Rootes the only manufacturer in which the IRC was to acquire an equity stake: it acquired stakes in a number of other manufacturers, and loaned money on eleven separate occasions to individual firms not facing mergers but wishing to make capital investment in new or existing manufacturing plants. On three other occasions, the IRC used its full range of powers to intervene decisively in takeover battles, buying shares in businesses to enable the company it had chosen to support to acquire another manufacturer. Firms not facing merger were also assisted, provided that they undertook industrial modernisation as a precondition of assistance (Young and Lowe, 1974, pp. 66–8).

(ii) Military industrial policy

The principal influence on defence manufacturers in this period came not from industrial concentration but from the threat posed by project cancellation and contraction in procurement budgets. Thirteen years of Conservative government had seen the cancellation of twenty-six major aircraft projects at a cost of £300 m, while the remaining projects tended to be both over-budget and behind schedule (Carver, 1992, p. 72). The 1965 Defence White Paper cancelled not only the fifth Polaris submarine, but also the replacements for both the Hunter and a medium transport aircraft. In April 1965, the Labour Government cancelled the TSR2, where R&D and production costs were estimated to have risen to £750 m, or £5 m per aircraft – twenty-five times as much as the Canberra bomber it was intended in part to replace (Reed, 1973, p. 57). The P-1154 supersonic version of the Harrier jump-jet and the HS-681 tactical transport aircraft projects were also cancelled only two years into their design stage. But further potential savings from the cancellation of domestic defence procurement programmes and the purchase of equipment from overseas suppliers were then diluted by the decision to fit Rolls-Royce engines and British avionics to the US Phantom jet on order for the RAF, which increased the cost of the aircraft by 40 per cent (Carver, 1992, p. 72). One important project that was given the go-ahead in 1967 was the production of the Tornado multi-role combat aircraft, a collaborative venture between German, Italian and British manufacturers. Britain's share of the project's costs was projected at £4 bn, with the aircraft becoming operational in the 1970s (Dockrill, 1988, pp. 91–3). It was believed that collaboration would bring about substantial savings in development costs and enable British manufacturers to compete against their US rivals in world markets. Military industrial collaboration with France also extended to the Jaguar fighter-bomber, and subsequently to the Lynx, Puma and Gazelle helicopters (Taylor and Hayward, 1989, p. 100). At the same time, the process of industrial concentration in civil manufacturing was paralleled in the military sector in 1966 with the takeover of the aero-engine manufacturer Bristol Siddeley by Rolls-Royce.

Overall, the 1960s witnessed a new government concern with shifting the public funding of R&D from military research to civilian; and 'indeed for the first time in its history the British state spent more on civil R&D than on military R&D' (Edgerton, 1993a, p. 11). In 1965 the Government spent £1720 m on defence R&D (at 1985 prices) and £1543 m on civilian R&D. By 1970 those figures had reversed in size: to £1325 m for defence R&D and to £1790 m for civil R&D (Edgerton, 1996). However, it should be said that by 1970 public spending on military-related R&D was rising again; and even prior to that, neither state-induced industrial restructuring nor a resetting of state innovation policy could stem continuing relative industrial decline. Between 1964 and 1970, the UK's share of world exports of manufactures fell by an annual average of 4.5 per cent (Walker, 1987, p. 203).

2.4   Policy towards manufacturing, 1970–79

The 1970s saw the faltering performance of manufacturing industry in Britain reflected in a series of rescues of ailing manufacturers by both Labour and Conservative Governments. The Conservatives spent their years of opposition between 1964 and 1970 developing a programme for government which emphasised administrative reform of central government, limited disengagement of the state from industry, British membership of the EEC, and removal of the disruptive influence of trades unions on the management of British industry, as the keys to an improved industrial performance. Harold Wilson sought to burden Edward Heath with the label of 'Selsdon Man', raising the spectre of a return to nineteenth-century *laissez-faire* policies. In truth, as Holmes has suggested, if 'Selsdon Man' ever existed, he was a 'technological, managerial man looking to a European commitment to aid the regeneration of competition in industry and personal initiative in the wealth creating process rather than the wealth distributing process' (1982, p. 11). Heath's policies for reviving the competitiveness of manufacturing did not challenge the principle of the mixed economy, but they were to be implemented through 'a new style of government' based on a 'fresh' (in effect, technocratic) approach to decision-making that would be 'deliberate and thorough', and use the 'best advice' and 'up-to-date techniques' (Conservative Party, 1970, p. 13).

By contrast, the Labour Party in opposition in the early 1970s drifted to the Left in its industrial policies. In *Labour's Programme 1973*, the Party revealed the three principal instruments of its intended future policies towards manufacturing. These were, first, the establishment of a state holding company, the National Enterprise Board (NEB), with extensive powers to purchase profitable private sector companies and to intervene to assist lame duck industries; secondly, planning agreements, which would be established with leading manufacturers to provide a systematic and coherent basis to state intervention in manufacturing; and, thirdly, a new Industry Act which would provide the state with the full panoply of powers that were required for economic and political objectives to be met. For the Wilson and Callaghan Governments between 1974 and 1979, as for the Heath Government of 1970–4, the industrial policies developed on the opposition benches were undermined by the necessity of managing a series of economic crises in which the trades unions were once again identified as an important contributory factor to industrial decline. The state's interventions in manufacturing were largely reduced to reactive rescues of lame ducks rather than proactive interventions to nurture industrial winners.

(i) Civil industrial policy

Despite the initial promise not to intervene to save lame ducks, the industrial policy of the Heath Government was soon to become preoccupied with the rescues of Rolls-Royce and Upper Clyde Shipbuilders (UCS). Rolls-Royce's problems in January 1971 largely arose from the mismanagement of launch aid to the aerospace industry during the 1960s. The company had initially estimated the cost of development of its RB-211 jet engine at £60.25 m, with the state agreeing to finance 70 per cent of the development costs. However, the civil service lacked the industrial expertise to monitor effectively the progress of this most ambitious technological project, and this, coupled with ineffective cost control, left the Heath Government with a project whose costs had escalated to £169 m and which was six to nine months behind schedule (Hayward, 1983, p. 107). Initially, the Government refused to give an open-ended commitment to Rolls-Royce and would provide only 70 per cent of the £60 m that the company had to find to finance the project's overrun costs. However, in January 1971, it became clear that Rolls-Royce would require £110 m of state assistance rather than the £60 m it had been provided with in November 1970. Since Rolls-Royce faced cancellation costs of £300 m for the RB-211, the Government decided to rescue the company by means of a selective nationalisation of those company assets relating to defence and collaborative ventures (Hayward, 1983, pp. 109–20).

By rescuing Rolls-Royce, the Government saved the nation's fourteenth-largest employer and a company at the forefront of technology, albeit at an estimated cost to the taxpayer of £170 m. The logic behind the rescue of UCS was not so immediately apparent – it had been in trouble and had received £20 m in grants and loans before the election of the Heath Government. The company approached the DTI in 1970 because of its liquidity problems and was eventually granted further state assistance in February 1971. However, when John Davies indicated barely one month later that no further assistance would be forthcoming, and it appeared that the workforce would have to be cut from the existing 8500 to an eventual 2500, a fourteen-month work-in began at the shipyards. The work-in was terminated only after the future of the yards had been secured with a large injection of state finance and a written parliamentary reply from Davies that the state would continue to support UCS for a further five years or until it was back on its feet, whichever came sooner (Young and Lowe, 1974, p. 160).

Although the rescues of Rolls-Royce and UCS were an important indication of the Heath Government's proclivity for managerialist solutions to the problems of manufacturing industry, it was the enactment of the 1972 Industry Act which constituted the clearest expression of this. Section 7 of the Act provided for discretionary assistance for projects that created or safeguarded employment in the assisted areas or regions, and Section 8 provided for aid to be allocated to individual companies or projects, in the form of grants, guarantees, loans or equity (Grant, 1982, p. 50). Active use was made of these powers. It was later calculated that state industrial assistance to the private sector had totalled £1.18 bn (at 1979 prices) in 1972–3, and £1.24 bn the following year (Grant, 1982, p. 53).

The Wilson and Callaghan Governments' attempts to remedy Britain's relative industrial decline focused on the three elements of their industrial policy. The first was the NEB, which accounted for almost one-third of the state's total spending on general aid to industry from 1975–6 to 1978–9 (£608 m out of £2.06 bn at 1978 prices). Having initially been given a statutory borrowing limit of £1 bn, by 31 March 1979 the NEB had received £777 m, of which £569 m had been spent on an ailing British Leyland (BL). This is illustrative of the way in which the NEB, which had been intended as a means by which the state might acquire a developmental role in nurturing innovation in some of the nascent manufacturing companies at the forefront of technology, had become a hospital for sick companies (Sawyer, 1991, pp. 160–2). Some 95 per cent of the NEB's resources were devoted to the rescue of major manufacturers, most notably British Leyland, Rolls-Royce, Alfred Herbert and Cambridge Instruments.

The second element of Labour's industrial policy was its proposals for establishing planning agreements between the state and leading manufacturers. These proposals were outlined in the White Paper, *The Regeneration of British Industry*, and enacted in the 1975 Industry Act.

In practice, only one planning agreement was signed with a manufacturer in the private sector (the other agreement was with the National Coal Board), and that not until March 1977. This agreement was with Chrysler (UK), the British subsidiary of a major US car manufacturer, whose production had been disrupted by poor industrial relations and whose 1976 programme of redundancies had caused much bitterness among its workforce. For Chrysler (UK)'s management, the planning agreement appeared to offer a means by which attitudes within the company could be changed through a more open, supportive and participatory style of management. For the trades unions, the agreement gave them access to corporate information which they would otherwise have been denied, but this did not dispel their suspicion sufficiently to persuade them to add their signatures to those of the Government and the company on the agreement itself. Nor were the unions prepared to abandon the principle of collective bargaining or to enter binding agreements on working practices. Plans were drawn up for a second agreement, despite reservations among both workers and management, but they were eventually abandoned when Chrysler (UK) was the subject of a proposed takeover by Peugeot Citroën.

The third element of the Labour Government's policies for civil manufacturing was its industrial strategy, which was set out in its November 1975 White Paper, *An Approach to Industrial Strategy*. This very title, as Sawyer has suggested, betrayed the very tentative nature of Labour's approach, which did not itself constitute a strategy but rather the provision of a flexible framework within which strategic decisions could be taken (1991, p. 166). The White Paper sought to identify both the causes of and remedies for the poor performance of manufacturing. Among the causes identified were excessive public spending, interference with nationalised industries, declining industrial profitability, low and inefficient investment, inadequate training policies, sharp and frequent changes in government policy, and problems with the provision of finance to industry, especially for medium-term and longer-term investment. These problems were to be remedied by providing better co-ordination and more effective use of industrial policy instruments, drawing in particular on advice of the tripartite SWPs, which covered more than thirty industries and about 40 per cent of manufacturing output.

From 1974 to 1979, no fewer than fifteen sectoral schemes were in operation to assist individual manufacturing industries. Initially, general assistance to manufacturers took the form of the Accelerated

Projects Scheme, which provided £72 m of state assistance to 111 projects between April 1975 and June 1976 at a cost of £568 m. This
scheme was succeeded by the Selective Investment Scheme, which
sought to encourage companies, especially in engineering, to proceed
with projects that otherwise might not have been undertaken. This
scheme provided a further £106.5 m of assistance, in the form of grants
averaging 10.5 per cent of project costs to eleven projects (Grant, 1982,
p. 51). However, the major problem with these and the subsequent
Microprocessor Application Project and Microelectronics Industry
Support Programme, which were intended to promote awareness of and
investment in the products of the microelectronics industry, was that of
'additionality'. It was very difficult to establish whether state assistance
was being provided to a project which was genuinely additional, or
whether it was in effect reducing the risk of a venture that would have
gone ahead regardless. Furthermore, the introduction of new support
schemes could not disguise the fact that overall state spending on
industrial and regional support had fallen around 25 per cent below the
planned level in 1978–9, in large part because of a lack of demand for
assistance from firms reluctant to initiate new projects (Grant, 1982,
p. 52). So unsuccessful was Labour's record of intervention in manufacturing that in February 1979, Sir Douglas Wass, the Permanent
Secretary at the Treasury, was able to compose a memorandum in
which he noted that no less than seven of the Government's schemes to
subsidise jobs in manufacturing were not only unlikely to break even
but were also expected to run up losses more rapidly than the rate of
economic growth.

In addition to its many assistance schemes, the Callaghan
Government's most notable interventions in manufacturing were its
nationalisations of the aerospace and shipbuilding industries. Although,
Labour's October 1974 General Election manifesto had promised the
nationalisation of these industries, it was not until April 1977 that
British Aerospace (BAe) was created from Hawker Siddeley, the
British Aircraft Corporation and Scottish Aviation. Eric Varley, the
Secretary of State for Industry, asserted that nationalisation was a
recognition that the state was the aerospace industry's major sponsor
and customer and that such dependence meant that the industry could
not be regarded as a 'genuine example of private enterprise' (Hayward,
1983, p. 194). Nationalisation would capitalise on this dependence on
state assistance not only to improve the general control and accountability of state investment in aerospace projects, but also to give man-

agement greater freedom to complete the long overdue rationalisation
of the airframe manufacturing sector. The nationalisation proposals
were met with great hostility from the Opposition, which regarded
Labour's claims about greater control and more detailed management
of state investment as no more than pious hopes and a licence for costly
interference in the day-to-day management of companies. The nationalisation of the shipbuilding industry in July 1977 through the creation of
British Shipbuilders was less controversial than that of aerospace, and
was motivated more by the need to manage the industry's long-
standing decline than by any hope that state ownership could serve as
a platform for expansion and modernisation. Indeed, as Sawyer has
suggested, the fact that British Shipbuilders was eventually privatised
through a sale of its constituent parts rather than as a whole is demon-
strative of the fact that state ownership and control did not integrate the
activities of the formerly independent shipbuilding companies (1991,
p. 165).

Finally we should note – in relation to civil industrial policy through
the 1970s – the continuation of a set of initiatives designed to
strengthen competitive pressures on British-based firms: overwhelmingly by the decision to join the European Community in 1973, but also
by measures to encourage fair trading (1973), ban restrictive trade practices (1973–6) and give consumers enhanced rights (1973–7).
Collectively these initiatives created a new Office of Fair Trading and a
renamed Monopolies and Mergers Commission.

(ii) Military industrial policy

Throughout the 1970s, governments were also faced with the additional
burden of a continuous struggle to contain Britain's rising defence
costs. Despite the 1964–70 Wilson Governments' attempts to control
and reduce the costs of Britain's military programmes, defence spending in 1972–3 was as high in real terms as it had been in 1964–5
(Chalmers, 1985, p. 89). Heath took office believing that Wilson had
cut back the defence budget too far, but that under the management of a
Conservative Government the economy could sustain defence spending
at 5.75 per cent of GNP rather than the 5 per cent that Wilson had
intended for the period 1968–73 (Dockrill, 1988, p. 104). Not only that,
but Heath's administrative reforms within Whitehall would ensure that
the defence budget was more efficiently spent. However, despite major
reorganisations of the structures managing weapons procurement, the

fact that new equipment programmes continued to be funded throughout the decade, while existing major procurement programmes (most notably the Tornado multi-role combat aircraft programme) were simultaneously escalating in cost, ensured that defence continued to consume a higher proportion of GNP than in any other major industrial nation. Indeed, in the light of a perceived increased threat from the Soviet Union, and with the cushion of North Sea Oil, the Callaghan Government agreed in May 1977 to implement NATO's target of a 3 per cent annual increase in real terms in Britain's defence spending, with the proviso that economic circumstances might affect what could be achieved (Chalmers, 1985, p. 99). The industrial dividends of the Cold War for British defence manufacturers were therefore not yet exhausted.

Despite the recurrent economic crises experienced during the 1970s, spending on military equipment remained buoyant. One impetus behind new procurement programmes was the creation by the European members of NATO of a European Defence Improvement Programme. Britain's contribution included the announcement in the February 1972 Defence White Paper of an accelerated procurement programme of Type-42 destroyers and Type-21 frigates for the navy, and extra Buccaneer and Nimrod aircraft for the RAF. In April 1973 authorisation was also given for the construction of three through-deck cruisers. Having originally been a 12 579 ton ship with only a helicopter-carrying capacity, the design of the through-deck cruiser was soon transformed into a 19 000 ton aircraft carrier with the capacity to carry the Harrier vertical take-off and landing aircraft. So, just months after an attempt to cut costs, in May 1975 the Wilson Government ordered Sea Harriers for these ships – raising the total cost of the carrier programme to £2.36 bn over twenty years (Chalmers, 1985, p. 102).

Between 1974–5 and 1978–9, spending on defence equipment increased by 29.5 per cent in real terms, whereas spending on personnel in the same period declined by 8 per cent (Chalmers, 1985, p. 98). Denis Healey, as Chancellor of the Exchequer, had proposed an annual cut in defence spending of £500 m in 1975 because he thought that the defence industry was too large and that scarce skilled labour should be released to civil manufacturing ready for an upturn in economic growth. To achieve this cut would have meant the cancellation of three major defence equipment programmes – the Tornado fighter, the through-deck cruiser and the Chevaline project. The Cabinet refused to agree to these cancellations but, as Chalmers has suggested, the justification for cancellation of these projects was no different from that which had led the first Wilson Government in 1965 to cancel the TSR2 and the CVA-01 aircraft carrier programme (Chalmers, 1985, p. 101). Admittedly, the Defence Review of December 1974, which aimed to reduce defence spending from 5.5 per cent of GNP in 1975 to 4.4 per cent by 1985, had seen the navy lose one-seventh of its surface fleet (Dockrill, 1988, p. 103). Despite these cuts, new procurement projects continued to be funded; for example, the decision in September 1978 to order a new Main Battle Tank for the British Army at a cost of £1 m each, three times the cost of its predecessor, the Chieftain (Dockrill, 1988, p. 109). At the same time, throughout the 1970s, £1 bn was being secretly spent on the Chevaline project, the modernisation of the warheads on Britain's Polaris missiles. In consequence, defence manufacturing remained both a prominent source of employment and a major drain on the Exchequer and performance of the civil economy at the end of the 1970s. In 1979–80, it was estimated that around 400 000 jobs in manufacturing were sustained by the military procurement programme, while a further 140 000 jobs were derived from export contracts for British military equipment (D. Smith, 1980, p. 113).

2.5 Policy towards manufacturing since 1979

As with so many other areas of public policy, the election of the first Thatcher Government in April 1979 marked a watershed in the development of industrial policy in Britain. For the first time in the post-war period, a government was elected that did not believe in state intervention as the solution to manufacturing decline. On the contrary, during their years in opposition from 1975 to 1979, Mrs Thatcher and Sir Keith Joseph led an ideological assault on the notion that the state should be the prime agency of social and industrial change. They argued that state intervention was a principal cause of deindustrialisation, because manufacturers had become accustomed to acting as entrepreneurs in the realm of politics, concentrating their efforts on lobbying ministers for subsidies as successive governments engaged in the ultimately futile exercise of attempting to pick industrial winners (Burton, 1979). It should not be thought, however, that governments after 1979 lacked an industrial policy. They did not. Through their policies of privatisation and deregulation, their promotion of inward investment in Britain by foreign manufacturers as the most effective means of improving Britain's trade performance in manufactures, and their continued support for defence manufacturers, both the Thatcher and Major Governments pursued a very clear and consistent set of industrial policies.

(i) Civil industrial policy

One of the most intractable industrial policy problems confronting the first Thatcher Government in 1979 was the future of manufacturers based in the public sector: most notably British Steel and BL, the sole remaining British-owned volume car manufacturer. The possibility of a wholesale liquidation or break-up of BL (as a signal to manufacturing industry that it would have to survive in future without state subsidies) was thought to be neither politically nor economically feasible, 150 000 people were employed by the company (many of them in marginal seats in the Midlands) and the closure of the company would cost the balance of trade in manufactures an estimated £2.2 bn and the Government up to £1 bn. Since the economic costs of closure to the Government were almost identical to the £990 m cost of funding BL's corporate plan, but the political costs were infinitely higher in a period of recession and growing social unrest, Thatcher concluded that 'the political realities had to be faced' (Thatcher, 1993, p.121); and BL was duly rescued. So too was British Steel, whose debts were even higher than those of BL. In 1981 the Government wrote off £3.5 bn of British Steel's capital and allowed the company to borrow an additional £1.5 bn without parliamentary approval. The Department of Industry also guaranteed loans of £200 m to ICL, the troubled state-owned computer manufacturer.

The competitive advantage given to many state-owned manufacturers by the large cash injections and/or government contracts that they benefited from in the early 1980s has been overlooked too readily by those advocates of the benefits of privatisation who have sought to argue that it is the act of transfer itself (from the inescapably inefficient public sector to the inherently more efficient private sector) which has been the most important factor in these companies' performance since privatisation. However, when the early and heavy costs to the taxpayer that were incurred on the road to privatisation are set aside, the 1980s may legitimately be seen as the decade in which Conservative governments dismantled the entire structure of direct state subsidies to civil manufacturers that had accumulated during the 1960s and 1970s. The list of privatised manufacturers, which includes BAe, Amersham International, Cable & Wireless, British Telecom, ICL, INMOS, Jaguar, Rolls-Royce, Ferranti, British Shipbuilders, the Royal Ordnance Factories, British Steel and the Rover Group bears testament to the extent both of previous state intervention in manufacturing and the degree of disengagement achieved by the Thatcher Governments.

The 1980s was the decade in which competition policy regained centre-stage in the government's approach to industrial regeneration. As early as 1980 a Competition Act was passed, allowing the Director of Fair Trading to investigate (and to refer to the Monopolies and Mergers Commission) any suspected anti-competitive practices, regardless of whether questions of monopoly or merger were involved, or whether the company or companies concerned were in the private or the public sector. The privatisation measures taken to end public monopolies were accompanied by the creation of consumer watchdog bodies with statutory powers, and by the encouragement of competition within and around the newly privatised concerns. The government signed up for the European Single Market, and reset its Department of Industry as a 'department of enterprise' in 1988. The Major Government followed this with a much-vaunted deregulation initiative, moving as many rules and restrictions as possible off the corporate sector, and particularly off small-businesses, whose creation and sustenance it (and its Thatcher predecessors) tried systematically to encourage.

If privatisation and deregulation were the first plank of industrial policy after 1979, the second was the promotion of Britain as a location for foreign direct investment (FDI) by multinationals wishing to benefit from the creation of the Single European Market. During the 1980s, Britain attracted more than 40 per cent of total US and Japanese investment in Europe. In 1990, foreign-owned companies accounted for 22 per cent of manufactured output, 27 per cent of capital investment and 16 per cent of manufacturing employment in Britain (CBI, 1992, p. 12). Indeed, in 1990, FDI into the UK accounted for 3.8 per cent of GDP, which was more than twice the EC average of 1.7 per cent (Davis *et al.*, 1992, p. 62). Given their hostility towards state intervention in manufacturing, inward investment offered the Thatcher governments a primarily market-led solution to the problem of how to re-enter lost export markets and improve the UK's trade performance. By exposing domestic manufacturers to greater competition from foreign companies operating in Britain with more efficient management techniques and working practices, they hoped that inward investment would also act as a catalyst to the more rapid growth of productivity, output and investment across the whole of UK manufacturing. Furthermore, the very presence of so much foreign investment would serve as one of the clearest vindications of the Government's own investment of a large amount of political capital and taxpayers' money in the reform of both the trades unions and personal and corporate taxation so as to deliver a disciplined work-force and incentives for higher productivity and profitability.

Privatisation, deregulation and the attraction of FDI have remained key elements of the civil industrial policy of the Major Governments since 1990. Those governments have steadfastly refused to provide state assistance to struggling manufacturers: notably the commercial vehicle manufacturer, Leyland Daf, and the shipbuilders, Swan Hunter. Moreover, the importance of inward investment to the performance of British manufacturing has also remained a central theme of policy: with the car industry again the flagship for the benefits of this kind of capital movement. But, in one respect at least, the replacement of Margaret Thatcher by John Major did effect a change of policy emphasis, of importance to us here – a reaffirmation of the importance of manufac-turing industry to overall economic competitiveness. Following his narrow General Election victory in April 1992, John Major sought in a series of interviews and speeches to emphasise the importance that he personally attached to the performance of UK manufacturing. In March 1993, he proclaimed not only that he 'passionately believed' in the necessity of widening and expanding the industrial base, but also that during the 1980s he had in fact held to a minority view against the Thatcherite orthodoxy that service industries would be enough to sustain national prosperity (*Independent*, 4 March 1993). Just over a week later, Major asserted that his ambition was to help industry to fight its battles. However, in setting out his own six-point strategy for assisting industry, he was quick to qualify his emphasis on manufactur-ing, in case anyone should be given the mistaken impression that his government was moving towards support for the type of proactive national industrial strategy advocated by some trade associations (EEF, 1992). Not only did Major acknowledge the importance of recovery in every sector of the economy, with no special priority or significance being attached to any recovery in manufacturing, but he also identified the importance of the services sector of the UK economy in general and the City of London in particular as a huge generator of export earn-ings. Furthermore, any increase in the DTI's budget or salience within Whitehall was ruled out by Major's affirmation of his refusal to return 'to a failed past of subsidies and state control' and his desire 'to get government off business's back' (*Daily Telegraph*, 12 March 1993).

The litmus test for the Major Government's policies towards manufacturing came with Michael Heseltine's appointment as Secretary of State for Trade and Industry in a Cabinet reshuffle following the 1992 General Election. Following his resignation from the Cabinet in 1986 over the Westland helicopter crisis (Linklater and Leigh, 1986), Heseltine had published two volumes of non-Thatcherite Conservatism in which he had identified a leading role for the state in a national industrial strategy (Heseltine, 1987; 1989). Heseltine's analysis was simple. The UK's relative industrial decline could be stemmed if the Government possessed the appropriate political will – his! If ever he became installed at the DTI, he would 'dispel the false belief which has misled too many in my party, that there is a heresy called "intervention" to which unsound Conservative administrations eschew' (Heseltine, 1987, p. 82). As for manufacturing, Heseltine had pointed to the 'initial brusque reaction' of the Government (of which he was then a part) to the Aldington Report. The decline of manufacturing should not be accepted as inevitable, not least because it remained the key wealth creator for the present. It would therefore be 'complacent to assume that manufacturing can be allowed to decline further without undermining economic recovery' (Heseltine, 1987, p. 90). However, after his appointment at the DTI, careful steps were taken by his Thatcherite cabinet colleagues to deny Heseltine the opportunity to fulfil either his previous promises to pursue a proactive state policy towards manufacturing or his subsequent pledge at the 1992 Conservative Party conference to intervene 'before breakfast, before lunch, before tea, and before dinner'; and the prospects for intervention waned still further with Heseltine's initially less than impressive stewardship of the pit closures programme, his department's passive stance towards the collapse of the Leyland DAF commercial vehicle manufacturing business and the BMW takeover of Rover, and the reports of rows with cabinet colleagues over his proposal for an English Development Agency.

(ii) Military industrial policy

During the 1980s, the Thatcher Governments also sought to instil greater efficiency and value for money in the procurement budget by introducing increased competition for defence contracts, moving financial risk from the customer to the supplier, and maintaining closer control of costs at each stage of production. In this way, it was hoped that an end might be brought to overpricing, 'cost-plus' contracting and escalating project costs. To this end, in 1981 the Government announced organisational changes within the MoD designed to give greater ministerial control over the procurement process at an earlier stage than in the past; and in 1984 Peter Levene, an industrialist, was appointed as Chief of Defence Procurement with a remit to make the Procurement Executive 'more commercially minded' and to promote competition for contracts (Taylor and Hayward, 1989, p. 79). To facilitate the transfer of technology from the defence to the civil sector, the then Secretary of State for Defence (Michael Heseltine) also created Defence Technology Enterprises (DTE) in 1984 to identify commercially applicable innovations that could be transferred from military R&D programmes to civil industry.

Heseltine's reforms could not deflect the controversy surrounding either the rescue of the Westland helicopter company, which led to the resignations both of Heseltine at the MoD and Leon Brittan at the DTI, or the decision to purchase the US0 AWACS airborne early warning system after hundreds of millions of pounds of taxpayers' money had been poured unsuccessfully into a British Nimrod-based system. The 1987 Defence White Paper announced that the MoD would participate in the Government's 'Next Steps' civil service reforms to delegate executive functions of government to agencies by examining the feasibility of uniting the main defence research establishments into one agency (Carver, 1992, pp. 150, 153). The Defence Research Agency was duly established, albeit not until April 1991. In the interim, in 1989, the Cabinet's Advisory Council on Science and Technology (ACOST) had proposed that the Agency should exploit the expertise at its disposal by developing a much wider role in industrial policy as a national centre of excellence in technology. However, the Cabinet soon put a stop to any possibility of a revival of proactive intervention by the backdoor by rejecting ACOST's proposal.

Their commitment to defence as the first charge on Britain's national resources must be seen as the third major element in Conservative industrial policy since 1979; and a further source of continuity between the Thatcher and Major Governments. The privatisation of some of Britain's largest defence manufacturers during the 1980s, through the sale of BAe, Rolls-Royce, Shorts, British Shipbuilders' warship yards, the Royal Ordnance Factories, Ferranti, and the management of the

Royal Dockyards, neither weakened the dependence of these companies upon domestic procurement contracts, nor diminished the status of the MoD as the most important provider of direct state assistance in Whitehall. On the contrary, all the signs indicate a continuation of this heavy state bias towards defence manufacturers in the first half of the 1990s, in spite of the projected 16 per cent decline in real terms of UK defence spending between 1990–1 and 1996–7. The White Paper, *Realising our Potential: A Strategy for Science, Engineering and Technology*, revealed that the Government intended a further reduction in its spending on R&D which would leave it one-fifth lower in real terms in 1995–6 than in 1987–8 (HMSO, 1993, p. 39). Defence-related R&D spending alone was expected to fall by about one-third. Yet, despite these cuts, defence spending by the MoD's Procurement Executive has remained a far more important influence on UK manufacturing than the much smaller budget of the DTI. For example, the 1993 Defence Estimates projected that the MoD's procurement budget for 1993–4 would total £9915 bn, providing £636 m for research, £2134 bn for development, and £7145 bn for production. British-based industry had won contracts for 75 per cent of the value of the equipment procured during the previous five years, while in 1991 alone, the MoD had placed 37 000 new contracts with 6400 contractors, thereby taking its total of active contracts in 1992 to 127 000 placed with over 10 000 contractors. In 1993, the defence sector still accounted for about 9 per cent of manufacturing GDP and employed about 400 000 people, bringing new export orders worth about £6 bn, second only to the USA and approximately 20 per cent of the world market for armaments.

The fear has been that Britain's 'peace dividend' will take the form of a decline in manufacturing output, profitability, and competitiveness unless measures are taken to stimulate the civil sectors of manufacturing. But those measures will have to come from the DTI, not the MoD; and there the situation is very different. Aerospace, for example, remains one of the few manufacturing sectors employing advanced technologies in which Britain remains a major global player. Indeed, in 1991, Britain captured an 11.7 per cent share of world markets for aerospace products, against an 8.7 per cent share of world markets for manufactures in general. BAe has been in the vanguard of those companies supporting the DTI's own Aviation Committee's National Strategic Technology Acquisition Plan (NSTAP) which had called for a £1 bn state investment over ten years. This recommendation, which has been endorsed by a report from the House of Commons Trade and Industry

Committee (House of Commons, 1993), would demand an almost fivefold increase in the existing level of state support for R&D in the aerospace industry. Ironically, on the very eve of the announcement by the German government of their own version of NSTAP, the Secretary of State for Trade and Industry, Michael Heseltine, was informing the Trade and Industry Committee that the Government would not sanction further state support for civil aerospace. In fact, under existing expenditure plans, state support for aerospace R&D is projected to decline from £26 m to £22 m per annum over the next five years. The then Industry Minister, Tim Sainsbury, suggested to British aerospace companies that rather than look to the British government for additional assistance, they should look overseas for industrial partnerships in order to defray the costs of R&D.

2.6   Conclusion

In 1994, Britain achieved its lowest current account deficit since the last surplus in 1985. However, the deficit of £168 m with the rest of the world, which had stood at £11.8 bn in 1993, was not the product of an improved performance by UK manufacturing. Although the trade deficit on visible goods declined to £10.7 bn in 1994 (composed of a £3.9 bn deficit with the EU and a £6.8 bn deficit with the rest of the world) from £13.4 bn in 1993, the principal cause of the improvement was Britain's record surplus on its invisible trade, which reached £10.4 bn in 1994 – not least due to the continuing flood of direct investment overseas by UK companies, which grew by £19 bn in 1994, following a £17 bn increase in 1993. Despite this poor trade performance, the domestic privatisation programme of the 1980s and 1990s, allied to the emphasis internationally on the deregulation of markets, has meant that the British government has been able to become semi-detached from questions of industrial policy and interventions in civil manufacturing. This, in spite of the fact that the privatisation process itself has entailed major intervention and has had extremely detrimental impacts upon certain sectors of UK industry, notably the manufacturing of buses, trains and mining equipment.

At the same time, the continuing provision of massive state assistance to defence manufacturers in Britain has ensured that, despite the end of the Cold War, the Major Governments have continued to face sensitive decisions about weapons procurement and embarrassing parliamentary and public inquiries about the sales of arms to suspect regimes. The political weight of defence procurement has also served to reinforce a culture that has emphasised the importance of political entrepreneurship in Westminster and Whitehall to win defence contracts from the public sector, rather than industrial entrepreneurship in the much larger but more competitive markets of the private sector. (No fewer than 373 'insiders' from the civil service and armed forces have moved during 1993 and 1994 to jobs in private industry to join rival defence contractors [*Guardian*, 25 January 1995].) Given that the House of Commons' Public Accounts Committee has found not only that about 80 per cent of major defence equipment projects are running behind schedule by an average of 32 months but also that there are 'large cost over-runs' on a significant number of projects (*Financial Times*, 15 December 1994), the longer-term dividend to the competitiveness of British manufacturing of present policy priorities is at least highly questionable. When to such economic costs are added the questions – of national identity, foreign policy and Britain's place in the world – that arise from decisions about arms procurement, the political dividend of continuing to devote such a large proportion of state assistance to defence manufacturers also looks suspect. The major social and economic crisis in national affairs in the foreseeable future predicted by the Aldington Committee in 1985 may have moved much closer one decade on.

3 Services

Neill Marshall

3.1 Introduction

The last two decades have witnessed a growing prominence of service activities in the British economy. Between 1971 and 1991 employment in the British service sector increased by almost 4 million jobs, and by 1991 services accounted for 71 per cent of total employment. A similar though slightly less pronounced trend is to be found in the data on output. In 1991 service industries accounted for 66 per cent of national output, measured in current prices, and had increased from 57 per cent in 1981 (Table 3.1).

This growth of the service sector is part of a long-term trend. The proportion of total employment in service industries has increased throughout most of the twentieth century (Table 3.2). However, the shift towards services has been particularly sharp in the 1980s, because it has coincided with a marked contraction in manufacturing employment and, at times, output. The growth and increasing economic significance of services has produced a lively policy debate. If the 1980s really was a decade of 'service-led' expansion, a large manufacturing sector might no longer be so important for wealth and employment creation. However, many commentators, including academics and industrial lobbyists, argue that despite the growth of services, manufacturing remains fundamental to the creation of wealth and trade. For them the growing prominence of services in Britain reflects the poor performance of the manufacturing sector.

Participants in this debate often pay insufficient attention to the differing characteristics of individual services, and the differing roles they play in the economy. The services sector includes a whole variety of

Table 3.1 *Employment and output change, by sector in Britain, 1971–91*

Sector	Employment (000s)			
	1971	*1991*	*Change 1971–91*	*% Change 1971–91*
Manufacturing	7 890	4 720	–3 170	–40.2
Services	11 388	15 370	+3 982	+35.0
Other	2 370	1 642	–728	30.7
Total	21 648	21 732	+84	+0.4

Output, by sector in Britain, 1981–91 (%, current prices)

	1981	*1991*
Agriculture, etc.	2.1	1.7
Energy	10.3	5.4
Manufacturing	24.1	19.9
Construction	5.7	6.4
Distribution	12.1	13.9
Transport and communication	7.1	6.6
Finance	11.0	16.8
Ownership of dwellings	6.1	6.7
Public administration	7.2	6.6
Education and health	9.1	9.5
Other services	5.3	6.5
Total services	57.8	66.6
All industries	100.0	100.0

SOURCE: Employment Gazette Historical Statistics; Employees in Employment; Central Statistical Office Blue Book.

industries which are only loosely related. Public as well as private services are included in the sector. The former include both central and local government, and the health and education services; and the latter financial services (such as insurance and banking), a variety of retailing, transport, communications and distribution activities, as well as a plethora of specialist business services (such as market research, management consultancy, accountancy and computer services). The idea of a service sector, then, is a 'chaotic conception', which has evolved through custom and practice. In the nineteenth century, economists'

Table 3.2   *Percentage change in service employment in Britain, 1861–1991*

Service sector employment in Britain, 1861–1991 (%)

1861	28
1871	31
1881	33
1891	35
1901	35
1911	36
1921	41
1931	49
1951	46
1961	49
1971	53
1981	62
1991	71

Employment change in British service industries, 1981–91 (%)

Fastest-growing service industries

Computer services	188.0
Business services not elsewhere specified (nes)	122.3
Auxiliary services to banking	121.3
Commission agents	89.4
Professional and technical services nes	75.3
House and estate agents	60.2
Legal services	58.5
Auxiliary services to insurance	58.1
Other services	57.6
Accountancy, auditing, etc.	57.1
Other financial institutions	54.3
Restaurants, snack bars, cafés	53.9
Social welfare, etc.	51.0
Renting of moveables	49.7
Cleaning services	46.8

Slowest-growing/declining service industries

Sea transport	−49.2
Retail distribution, confectionery, tobacco	−25.8
Railways	−24.7
Defence	−21.1
R&D	−21.0

Table 3.2 *continued*

Central Offices	−16.7
Wholesale distribution, agriculture, textiles, fuels, ores, etc.	−15.7
Public refuse and sanitation	−13.0
Telecommunications	−9.9
Wholesale distribution, food, drink, tobacco	−7.3
Distribution of motor vehicle parts and petrol	−2.5
Dispensing and other chemists	−0.6
Local government (nes)	−0.1
Other inland transport	1.5
National government and social security	1.8

SOURCE: Department of Employment Historical Statistics; Employees in Employment.

attention focused on manufacturing industries and the primary sector as the heart of the economy, and other activities were allocated to a residual or service sector. Though academic views have changed since, statistical systems still 'emphasise older or even declining economic activities' (OECD, 1986, p. 20). The notion of a 'residual' or service sector has thus persisted, and has become increasingly unsatisfactory as service activities have grown.

The diverse character of service industries makes it very difficult to talk about industrial policy towards services as a whole. Nevertheless, it is fair to say that during most of the twentieth century services have tended to be neglected in industrial policy. There has persisted a negative view of services which goes back at least to Adam Smith and Marx, who in their different ways believed services to be non-productive (that is, contributing nothing to wealth creation). The service sector has been variously regarded as a less efficient one (which because of its labour intensity acts as a drag on labour productivity growth in the economy) or as a sector which is both closely linked to and dependent upon manufacturing industries, the economic base of the economy. These views underpinned one of the few policies ever designed explicitly with service employment in view, the Selective Employment Tax of 1965. This was levied specifically on service employees, and sought to reduce the drift in employment in the economy from manufacturing to services by making service employees more expensive.

As the economic significance of services has increased, their profile in industrial policy has grown. As we saw earlier, after 1979 successive

Conservative governments introduced a new accumulation strategy or model of economic growth, making a sharp break with the post-war aims of full employment, demand stabilisation, extensive state intervention in industry and markets, and an expansive welfare system. In its place a neo-liberal vision of the economy was developed, in which control of inflation, sound public finances, the promotion of competition, efficiency and labour market flexibility were substituted as legitimate economic goals. Free markets, individual entrepreneurship and self-reliance replaced state intervention and subsidy as the motive forces of economic growth. The growth of service industries was then used to support this shift in policy and the reduction of subsidies towards manufacturing, on the grounds that services could substitute for any contraction of the manufacturing sector. Equipped with such a set of understandings and concerns, government ministers in the mid 1980s came to the view that deindustrialisation did not matter, since the service industries were to become the focus of an 'enterprise strategy' (DTI, 1988, p. 41), designed to create an economy characterised by market competition and a culture of individual enterprise.

This chapter takes three industries, conventionally regarded as service industries, and outlines government policy in relation to each. It describes government intervention to promote a more competitive and, therefore, more innovative and dynamic *financial sector*: perhaps the most far-reaching, and best-known, example of government attempts to create a more open economy. Privatisation has also been used by successive Conservative governments since 1979 to introduce or significantly enhance competition in public services, and the *telecommunications industry*, which is an important source of service innovation and growth, is taken as an example of this. Privatisation and the opening of markets has normally been associated with the establishment of new regulatory bodies charged with policing the operations of firms in accordance with market principles, and ensuring the quality of customer service. In contrast to financial services, where self-regulation of the industry has predominated, in telecommunications government has established a watch-dog with responsibility for enforcing competition. However, not all government activities could be so readily privatised, especially core services of the state such as defence, social security and taxation. Nevertheless, the determination of Conservative governments since 1979 to control public expenditure has led to a systematic reorganisation of what *public services* remain. This chapter shows the way government has sought to improve public sector performance by enforcing strict manpower and expenditure controls, and by introducing where possible quasi-market forms of competition into the public sector.

3.2   Financial services

As Table 3.1 shows, the financial sector was at the leading edge of service industry growth during the 1980s. Growth in financial services also encouraged the expansion of a plethora of related accounting, legal and specialist business services. The conspicuous consumption of staff, on seemingly ever-increasing salaries, 'golden hellos' and 'golden handshakes', also produced growth in a range of consumer services. However, the importance of the financial sector cannot be measured simply in terms of employment. In the introduction to 'Global Finance and Urban Living' Budd and Whimster (1992, p. 1) describe the financial sector as a vanguard sector, and a symbol of the economic changes taking place in Britain during the 1980s. The financial sector was intimately involved in the Government's plans to create, as one strand of its enterprise culture, a 'people's capitalism' which included wider ownership of shares and homes and greater personal financial self-reliance, through the establishment of new small businesses, and the expansion of personal pensions, life insurance and savings plans. The growth of financial services also went along with the creation, at the Government's behest, of a more internationally open and nationally dominant financial sector, based primarily in London, which it was hoped would continue to be competitive with New York and Tokyo as a world financial capital.

The evolution of any financial sector is shaped by the nature of its regulatory framework: that is, by the rules that govern trading, established by government and implemented by financial institutions (Rybczynski, 1988, p. 6). In the post-war period in the UK, this framework was constructed around a number of regulatory pillars: the central banking authority and supervisory control provided by the Bank of England, exchange controls, credit rationing, and the delimitation of the activities of key institutions. Through these regulatory arrangements, a set of relatively self-contained financial markets was established – these were characterised by 'restrictive practices, anti-competitive mechanisms, and self-imposed constraints... condoned, if not positively encouraged by regulatory authorities' endorsed by government (Llewellyn, 1990, pp. 16–17). The system was designed to control and segment the financial sector; to 'balkanise' it, so that speculation and turbulence in one part would have a limited impact on the rest of the sector, and ultimately the rest of the economy. On to this highly structured national system was superimposed the supranational institutional fabric of the Bretton Woods Accord, which fixed exchange rates to the dollar, and international institutions (like the International Monetary Fund and World Bank) which provided stability and promoted growth and investment in the world economy.

During the last two decades or so, changes in financial markets, and the greater use of computer technology in trading, have helped establish an integrated global financial market in equities trading and in corporate and international banking. This internationalisation has made it' difficult for governments to control financial markets, and put pressure on them to liberalise or regulate the markets more lightly to attract increasingly mobile international funds. In this regard, the election of the Conservative Government in 1979 marked a significant turning point, when these general pressures to reduce regulation in financial markets broadened into a government-inspired reorganisation of the regulatory framework in the financial sector. It is important to realise, though, that these changes happened specifically 'because state power was used to override ... business interests' (Moran, 1991, pp. 12–13).

The decision to make a 'bonfire' of market controls, and to develop prudential safeguards for the personal investor (see Table 3.3 for the main changes) reflected the new government's view that a less restrictive market for financial services would encourage growth because it would be more innovative, offer greater customer choice, and be more attractive to international investors. Writing in 1989, Nigel Lawson saw the benefits of regulatory changes as follows.

Throughout the economy the operation of normal market forces was constrained in 1979 by a battery of direct controls ... These were all swept away ... The most striking example ... is in the financial sector. The historic decision to abolish all exchange controls in 1979 opened up a new range of investment opportunities ... The abolition of the corset and other controls on the behaviour of the banks and building societies has generally increased the flexibility of financial markets ... Housing finance... has now been transformed into a highly competitive and innovative market place. (Lawson, 1989, pp. 28–9)

Table 3.3   *The main changes in British financial regulation since 1979*

1979	Ending of guidelines limiting mortgage lending by building societies
1979	Ending of exchange controls
1980	Ending of the corset (Supplementary Special Deposit Scheme) introduced to curb bank lending
1981	Abolition of reserve asset requirement requiring banks to lodge at least 12.5 per cent of their deposits in a specified range of liquid assets
1982	Ending of hire purchase restrictions
1983	Collapse of the building societies cartel
1983	Building societies given access to wholesale money markets
1986	Big Bang opening up trading in the City of London
1986	Building Societies Act
1986	Financial Services Act
1987	Schedule 8 clarifies Building Societies Act
1986	Withdrawal of mortgage lending guidelines
1989	The abolition of Control of Borrowing Order
1991	Composite Tax on building society deposits abolished. Deposits charged at basic rate of tax.
1994	Announced that new powers to be granted to building societies as part of review of 1986 Act. Societies can increase their activities on wholesale money markets, own life insurance companies and expand their non-property lending.

There were three key elements to government reforms after 1979. First, domestic financial operators were increasingly exposed to the rigours of international competition. This is seen most clearly in the 'Big Bang' where, once the rules on membership of the Stock Exchange were relaxed, the introduction of foreign firms into the market initiated a widespread restructuring. Secondly, the regulatory changes dissolved 'the demarcation lines between those operating in ... three areas, deposit banking, long term savings and capital markets' (Rybczynski, 1984, p. 24). Institutions then used their greater freedom of operations to diversify into new areas, thus integrating financial markets; and new financial 'products' associated with this diversification were introduced (such as endowment mortgages, interest bearing current accounts, more targeted insurance policies or lending by building societies outside the property sector). The third aim of government policy was to establish a new regulatory regime protecting investors from financial malpractice. The tradition of industry self-regulation was respected by the 1986 Financial Services Act, which created the Security and Investments Board, sitting on top of a series of self-regulating organisations (SROs) responsible for specific financial sectors.

Yet, despite all its changes, there are increasing signs that even the present Conservative Government is still dissatisfied with the operation of capital markets, not least because the recasting of regulation designed to ensure customer protection has proved problematic. The complex structure of consumer protection in the financial sector fits somewhat uneasily within other components of the regulatory framework, and has received considerable criticism for being overly bureaucratic. In addition, it has not managed to stamp out malpractice, as witnessed by the Maxwell, Barlow Clowes, Polly Peck and BCCI scandals. After mounting criticism, two of the SROs (FIMBRA and LAUTRO, which oversee, respectively, independent financial advisers and the life insurance industry) have been replaced by the Personal Investment Authority, with stricter membership requirements for firms. However, many contemporary financial commentators regard this as a stopgap-solution, and are calling instead for industry self-regulation to be discarded in favour of a formal system of legally enforceable government system of regulation. The largest building societies also believe their activities to be unduly curtailed. This lies behind the decision of the Halifax–Leeds to become a public limited company, and the merger of the Cheltenham and Gloucester building society with Lloyds Bank. Industrial policy, in relation to financial services at least, must therefore still be understood to be in a process of flux and change.

3.3   Telecommunications

There are political, technological and economic dimensions to government telecommunications policy. The government has responded to significant changes in the industry by privatising the telecommunications network, hitherto run as a public sector monopoly, and by liberalising the market for telecommunications services. Privatisation is part of a series of government policies aimed at improving the performance of public services, and making them more responsive to commercial demands. The next section discusses public services more fully. This section outlines the complex questions concerning regulation which arise following privatisation, including maintaining competition and ensuring a level playing field for key players in the sector. Furthermore, a system of regulation primarily based around market principles finds it difficult to handle broader national concerns and interests. Thus far, in a liberalised telecommunications industry, it has proved difficult to ensure the development of a national high-grade telecommunications network. This, in turn, threatens the universal availability of telecommunications services, a significant benefit of monopoly provision, and as a consequence national capacity for innovation and service development may yet be damaged.

During the last twenty years, technical developments have altered the traditional telephone network so that a 'superhighway' of advanced telecommunications and data transfer is a real possibility. The capacity of the telecommunications network to carry digital computer information has been increased by the introduction of optical fibres as a replacement for copper cable, by the computerisation of telephone exchanges, and by the expansion of satellite broadcasting. It is now much easier for industry to integrate increasingly pervasive computer equipment. Advanced telecommunications also facilitate innovation in specialist computer processing, consultancy, advertising, market research, accountancy, media and publishing services, all of which rely on electronic flows of information and data processing. Technical improvements are also bringing closer the possibility of a variety of new home-based services (such as home banking, shopping and entertainment).

Until 1979 the telecommunications industry remained a public sector monopoly. The industry was nationalised in 1911 because private sector companies had been reluctant to invest on a scale necessary to produce a national system. In 1969 telecommunications was made the responsibility of the General Post Office (GPO), a public corporation, which had more autonomy than a government department. The GPO determined what equipment could be connected to telecommunications networks, what telecommunications lines could be used for, and what prices should be charged for services. Monopoly provision facilitated the cross-subsidisation of routes, most notably the local telecommunications network, which was supported by long-distance trunk and international business, which was more profitable. This allowed the telecommunications carrier to maintain a genuinely national service. Of course, new investment in networks and services did not take place everywhere at the same time, but there was a commitment to universality of service.

The rationale for placing telecommunications in the public sector included, 'national security considerations, the "natural monopoly" of the telephone network, the public service character of the telephone service and the need to maintain the technical integrity of the network' (Morgan and Sayer, 1988, p. 9). Perceived economies of scale in telecommunications, the importance of equity of access for all sub-scribers, and possible market failures also supported a public sector monopoly. However, as technical changes integrated the lightly regu-lated world of computers with tightly regulated telecommunications, the GPO was slow to introduce new services and equipment, and telecommunications charges were expensive, especially relative to those prevalent in the USA. There was also political interference in the telecommunications service, as lobbying by the equipment supply industry, unions and rural pressure groups influenced the development of the network and services, and held the industry to a development path other than one suggested by purely commercial criteria. All this stimulated pressure for change, especially from large companies that recognised communications and information technologies were vital to their commercial interests, but which felt constrained in what they could do by the facilities and capacity supplied by the telecommunica-tions carrier. The prominence of the financial sector in the national economy, which was particularly reliant on telecommunications for its success, also encouraged change. From the government's point of view, the large-scale investment needed to improve the telecommunications infrastructure was believed to be beyond the capacity of the public purse. In any case, in a fast moving and complex industry, the private sector was deemed more likely than government to make the right commercial decisions.

The Conservative Government therefore decided to liberalise telecommunications. There were three elements to their new policy: telecommunications was separated from the Post Office; the supply of terminal equipment and services was opened to competition; and the telecommunications network was privatised. The 1981 British Telecommunications Act created a new state-owned company, British Telecom (BT). Shares in BT were sold to the public in three tranches, the third and final tranche being completed in 1993. The 1981 Act also broke BT's monopoly on terminal equipment, which remained only for the first telephone set.

Following privatisation, BT was retained intact, unlike the electricity and water industry, where public sector companies have been split into regional units. It was deemed necessary to retain a 'national champion' in an important, increasingly global, industry requiring massive investment. A new regulatory framework was therefore established to avoid anti-competitive behaviour from BT, and to simulate market forces. The DTI was provided with important regulatory controls, including the power to grant licences for competitive networks to BT. Almost immediately, and with active government co-operation, Mercury Communications was established as an alternative telecommunications carrier to BT.

The DTI also holds responsibility for the regulation of cable television, satellite licences and the resale of BT capacity. During the 1980s and early 1990s the DTI has granted a number of cable television licences, mainly to American and Canadian telephone companies, and it is intended that they should ultimately provide alternative local telephone services to BT. In the meantime, BT has been prevented from using its network to provide competitive television services. A liberal attitude has also been taken by the DTI to the development of private business telecommunications networks, which provide services such as store and retrieval systems, mailboxes, data bases and management information packages. Eventually third-party use of these value-added network services (VANS) was permitted. Large companies such as British Rail and Racal have developed virtual network services on lines leased from BT, and British Rail is expected ultimately to offer telecommunications services which will compete directly with BT.

The Office of Telecommunications (OFTEL), an autonomous agency financed by the DTI, was given responsibility for supervising compliance with existing telecommunication licences and ensuring the quality of service provided to the customer. OFTEL also supervises the operation of a price formula for BT services, whereby BT must maintain the price of a basket of services at the Retail Price Index minus x per cent. However, unlike its counterparts in the USA and Canada, OFTEL can only make recommendations: it has no statutory authority. Nevertheless, OFTEL has adopted a more aggressive approach to regulation than many expected: for example, following its advice, BT's participation in new mobile telephone services was restricted.

The Government has staked considerable creditability on the increasing effectiveness of Mercury as a network competitor for BT, and in consequence Mercury was initially given an exclusive licence to compete with BT until 1990. In the 1990 duopoly review this licence was extended for international infrastructure and telephone services.

Mercury was also given advantages over BT; it need not offer a universal national service, and its prices were unregulated. The connection of Mercury's network to that of BT's was also settled on terms which the industry believed to favour Mercury.

In 1991 the DTI presented its views on the future development of the telecommunications industry in *Competition and Choice: Telecommunications Policy for the 1990s*. The White Paper signalled a shift from managed competition to more open markets. Cable, satellite and cellular telephone companies were given greater flexibility and connectivity to offer telecommunications services. The price cap on BT was also tightened and currently stands at RPI minus 7.5 per cent. Within this price control formula BT is further limited in the price of individual services. No other operators are controlled in this way. Nevertheless, there remains considerable concern about the dominant market position of BT. This is expressed in the debate about the terms of interconnection between BT and its competitors, and the portability of subscribers' telephone numbers. BT's competitors claim that forcing subscribers to change telephone numbers when changing operators acts as a constraint on competition.

There is also a recognition that, without BT's investment, a national high-grade optical fibre network (Integrated Services Digital Transmission – ISDN) will be slow to develop. BT wants to be able to broadcast television and entertainment services over its network, which would both open up new markets and justify investment in optical fibres for the local loop between the home and the nearest telephone exchange (which currently remains copper cable). This would then make economic a whole range of additional services (such as video on demand, remote medical advice, and home shopping). As things stand, however, BT is excluded from broadcasting, at least until 1998, and the government is currently relying on cable TV operators franchised to develop a local entertainment and telephone network in competition with BT. Cable operators are worried about the ability of BT to circumvent current legislation, and damage their long-term prospects. The upshot is that a national optical fibre telecommunications network is still some way off.

Since 1991, Britain has been adapting a regulatory regime established to deal with a duopoly to suit a system of multiple provision. In the autumn of 1994 it was decided to conduct a fundamental review aimed at devising a regime more suitable for encouraging the growth of competition. So far the effects of privatisation and liberalisation seem to be following the US pattern – the USA having a longer history of liberalised telecommunications. In both countries, telecommunications 'are evolving into a complex patchwork of private networks, local area networks, overlays, microwave towers and satellite transponders, [and] cable television nets' (Muligan, 1991, p. 226) – all built in response to demonstrable demand. Since these components of the telecommunications system are unevenly distributed, the government's competitive framework for telecommunications visibly works better in some places than in others. Whereas large businesses and consumers in large cities increasingly have access to alternative telecommunications networks and services, smaller cities, peripheral regions and rural areas with less demand for such services are more likely to face monopoly BT provision and a basic telephone network. As Noam suggested, 'British telecommunications policies have created an entity [BT] similar to the pre-divestiture AT&T in the United States – a private, dominant and regulated carrier with limited competition'; and because they have, it remains unlikely 'that the transformation of British telecommunications [has yet] reached a stable equilibrium' (Noam, 1992, p. 132).

Nevertheless, despite failing to provide a satisfactory regulatory regime, Britain has demonstrated that liberalisation of telecommunications can produce a wider range of services at a lower cost. As a result it has influenced much thinking in other western European countries, and has started a trend towards liberalisation, with the support of the European Commission. An important lesson which has been learned from the British experience is that the regulatory regime introduced with competition needs to be thought through carefully, otherwise companies take advantage of regulatory issues rather than compete in terms of services and price.

3.4 Public services

Many public services do not lend themselves easily to privatisation. Some services are a 'pure public good'. They cannot be provided by individuals, and are not normally supplied by the private sector; and yet they are, like law and order or defence, vital to the country. Other 'social' services (health, education, social welfare) are regarded as essential, but cannot be afforded by significant sections of the population. Ideally people should have equal access to these services, and this may be more readily ensured by state provision. The administrative and regulatory role of the state also requires services such as tax collection and international relations.

Such public services were supported by direct taxation and national insurance during the 1950s and 1960s, and their efficiency was generally not subject to systematic scrutiny. Since the 1970s, however, concern over rises in public spending have coincided with economic slow-down and produced pressures for greater efficiency in public services. Increases in unemployment, brought about by the slow-down of economic growth in the 1980s and 1990s, have placed strains on the welfare state, by increasing demands for services while reducing the tax base for raising finance. The increasing openness of national economies has exposed the limitations of public expenditure as a means of stimulating the national economy. Public services are now more likely than they were immediately after the Second World War to be viewed as a cost of production in globally competitive markets, rather than as a means of maintaining domestic consumption.

The slow-down in economic growth in the advanced economies since the 1970s, has coincided with, and in part helped to produce, a structural gap between public service spending requirements, expressed in a growing demand for labour-intensive public services, and the willingness or ability of government to pay for them by raising taxation. Changes in government attitudes are particularly important. Since 1979, the Conservative governments' economic ideology has made changes in the scale and character of the public sector particularly central to their entire economic project. Their avowed intention to curb trade union power, reduce the public sector borrowing requirement, and control public expenditure, all led to a desire to change the way the public services operated (Tyson, 1987, p. 57). Most Conservative politicians also had little faith in the need for big government, supplying standard services to a mass population, and argued instead for a more customised, selective and entrepreneurial approach in public services. They also complained that many services had been 'captured' by producer interests, and needed to develop a stronger emphasis on customer service. The commitment in government circles to market forms of provision also meant that the public sector was regarded there as less effective, or even 'parasitic' – and as such, a major constraint on the operation of the private sector.

There have been four strands to the Government's approach to the public sector since 1979. First, the size of the public service has been reduced to control public expenditure. Secondly the scope for private sector involvement in service provision has been increased by contracting out public services to the private sector, or by the privatisation of public services. Thirdly, the Government has sought to improve the managerial capacity of middle-ranking and senior government officials, and at the same time to reduce the power of the public sector unions. Along with these changes, financial constraints have been placed on the public sector to reduce the costs of its operations, and encourage the development of more efficient practices. Fourthly, the Government has sought to 'de-privilege' public sector employees.

Initially some parts of the public sector were opened to the disciplines of market competition via sales to the private sector. An example of this process was included in the previous section on telecommunications. But the bulk of central and local government could not be dealt with so easily. So, in the face of an inability to reduce dramatically the functions of the state, the main thrust of government policy became to improve 'value for money': by encouraging staff to carry out their existing functions more efficiently, by using fewer resources and reducing costs. Of course, these objectives were not new, but the weight placed on them certainly was.

Tight central control was imposed on the public service. In the local authority sphere, the proportion of local expenditure provided by central government was increased, and capping mechanisms were used to limit the amount authorities could levy from local taxpayers. This produced a series of bitter disputes, particularly with Labour-controlled authorities, which resisted cuts in public services. So local authority responsibility was increasingly circumvented via the introduction of new agencies directly under central government control. The Government also sought to remove one tier of local administration: metropolitan authorities were abolished in the mid 1980s, and a single tier of local authorities was introduced in Scotland in 1995. The Local Government Commission has been directed to produce single unitary authorities in England, thus doing away with the county tier of local government in all but a few rural areas.

In the civil service, departmental manpower targets were used to reduce the number of civil servants. Departments were also given a cash limit and this was extended to budgetary controls. These activities were supplemented by an efficiency unit, initially under Lord Rayner, directly responsible to the Prime Minister, which promoted investigations of individual departments' activities. The financial management of the civil service was also reformed. The Financial Management Initiative, launched in 1982, was designed to improve the allocation, management and control of resources throughout central government. The theory was that management was primarily about financial control. Information on costs, therefore, was broken down to the lowest administrative level possible: managers at lower levels could then be given responsibility for controlling them.

By the late 1980s, it began to look as though the Government's drive to change the public sector was running out of steam in the face of employee resistance, the deterioration of public services, and the limitations of a policy which concentrated largely on getting more out of the same resources. However, a new policy direction has been established since 1990. There are two key elements in this new policy: the creation of subsidiary organisations such as agencies or trusts within the public services, and the introduction of market competition to ensure that their managers face pressures similar to those facing private industries. As the 1991 White Paper *Competing for Quality* (Cmnd. 1730) announced:

> Greater competition ... has gone hand in hand with fundamental management reform of the public sector. This means moving away from the traditional pyramid structure of public sector management. The defects of the old approach have been widely recognised: excessively long lines of management with blurred responsibility and accountability: lack of incentives to initiative and innovation: a culture that was more often concerned with procedures than performance ... Public services will increasingly move to a culture where relationships are contractual rather than bureaucratic.   (quoted in Harrison, 1993a, p. 4)

Using the market as a discipline to improve the efficiency of public services was first introduced into local authorities in the early 1980s. If local authorities wished to carry out building work, or highways construction and maintenance using directly employed labour, they were required to win the right to do so by competitive tendering with the private sector. In the late 1980s and early 1990s competitive tendering was significantly extended into refuse collection, street and building cleaning, and parks and leisure management. In addition, the introduction of local management of schools meant that schools could purchase their own services from the local authority or elsewhere.

Similar changes can be identified in the National Health Service (NHS) from 1983, when the circular *Competitive Tendering in the Provision of Domestic, Catering and Laundry Services* established the practice of compulsory contracting out to the private sector. Health

Authorities responsible for the delivery of services in their area were required to submit plans for the contracting out of ancillary services, including cleaning, catering and laundry services; and competition from private contractors was used both to exert a downward pressure on the costs of in-house provision, and to create an alternative source of supply. The procedure was widened in 1988 to include portering and security, and in 1992 to include the purchase of information technology, consultancy and maintenance of buildings.

Management reorganisation has gone alongside this trend towards contracting out. In the NHS, the 1990 National Health Service and Community Care Act was widely seen as 'a watershed in the development of publicly provided health care' (Harrison, 1993b, p. 89). At the beginning of the 1980s the Health Service was organised into four tiers of management: the Department of Health and Social Security at the centre, and below this, regional, area and district levels. In the early 1980s, the hierarchy was simplified by removing the area level. Then, in 1991, a more market-like environment was created by dividing each District Health Authority into two entities: a providing arm (the hospitals, community health and ambulance services) and a purchasing arm. The purchasing arm had the task of assessing the health needs of the population, and drawing up purchasing plans to meet them. These requirements were met by placing contracts with their own provider units, as well as those of other districts. Many general practitioners have been given control over their own budgets, and act, together with the purchasing arm of the Health Authorities, on behalf of the individual in the marketplace. Providers, usually the hospitals, have been established as 'Trusts', and have been delegated powers and greater freedom to manage and handle their own assets and staff. The 1990 reforms linked the finance available to the level of activity in individual provider units, more or less as in an ordinary market. Provider units were (and are) recompensed at whatever prices they set for their services. That means they have been reset as genuinely trading bodies.

Management reforms have also included the introduction of agencies into the civil service. The Ibbs report argued:

> The central Civil Service should consist of a relatively small core engaged in the function of servicing Ministers and managing departments ... Responding to these departments will be a range of agencies employing their own staff ... and concentrating on the delivery of their particular service.   (Cabinet Office, 1988, p. 15)

Based on the Ibbs report, by February 1994, 94 agencies employing approximately 60 per cent of the civil service had been established, and another 21 per cent of civil service employees were under consideration for agency status. Though staff remain civil servants, each agency is a separate unit of management under a chief executive who has the day-to-day responsibility for delivering services. In each case, a framework document now sets out the way the agency should operate. This establishes the financial regime under which it should work, and performance targets. With greater delegation of responsibility to the local level, it is intended that agencies should be better placed to be more responsive to the needs of those who use their services. However, the move to agencies represents a further tightening of the financial screw on the civil service, because strict financial discipline is being imposed.

The expansion of agencies has encouraged the development of a quasi-market or contract culture within the civil service. This suggests to some that the private sector can take over traditional civil service responsibilities. As Graham Mather, the former Head of the Institute of Economic Affairs puts it, 'The Rubicon has now been crossed and anything that can be put into an agency can also be tested in the market' (Mather, 1992, p. 2). This philosophy lies behind the market testing of 130 000 civil service jobs by making civil servants compete against the private sector to carry out their particular functions. Together with the passing of the Civil Service Act in 1993 (which alters the definition of a civil servant) the way is now being cleared for the privatisation of even 'core' parts of the public sector.

The White Paper on the Government's future plans for the civil service (*The Civil Service, Continuity and Change*, 1994, HMSO) envisages the development of a less hierarchical, more flexible civil service, with fewer layers of management and an end to central wage bargaining. It proposes greater delegation to Whitehall departments, giving them freedom to decide on the numbers of staff they need, develop plans for their agencies, press ahead with their own market-testing programme, and set many of their own rates of pay. It also suggests further moves away from tenure towards fixed contracts, moves which will be introduced against the background of continuous cuts in civil service manpower. Between 1994 and 1998, it is envisaged that civil service manpower will fall to below 500 000.

It is difficult to be conclusive about future directions in the civil service. Some observers see, 'a clear trend towards breaking up the unified civil service' (Corby, 1991, p. 39). Or, in a more critical tone, 'the dismemberment of government ... is being achieved through a combination of stealth and public indifference' (Phillips, 1992, p. 21). Certainly the *Next Steps* document was explicit that 'to strengthen operational effectiveness, in agencies there must be freedom to recruit, pay, grade and structure in the most effective way'. There has also been a modest shift away from uniform conditions of employment. Greater flexibility is being introduced to attract and financially reward staff, and management have the opportunity to adapt salaries to local labour market conditions. Effectively this means that agencies will have the freedom to pay more to attract staff in the South-East and London, because this is where they have the greatest difficulties with recruitment: the differences between public and private sector wages are smaller in other regions.

More generally, if such agency or 'trust' structures are more fully adopted, contracting out extended, and agencies 'hived off' to the private sector, it is possible to envisage the emergence of a 'minimalist' or 'enabling' state (Ridley, 1988). Under such conditions, public sector employment would shrink, and the delivery of services would be largely left to the private sector, with the public sector merely being responsible for setting the terms of contracts and monitoring compliance. However, so far, the changes that have been made are some way from this. They have not been as dramatic as the rhetoric of government or its critics suggest. Changes take time to implement, and there is resistance from public sector employees to big change. A strong 'public service' ethos runs against strict market-based forms of operation. There is an inherent conflict in the new model of public sector organisation, between the delegation of responsibility to new agencies and the Treasury's desire to enforce strict financial control. The new structure, with the separation of politicians and their advisers from the delivery of services, also raises questions about the accountability of staff in the new agencies to both parliamentary scrutiny and the local electorate. The policy regime surrounding the civil service therefore, like the policy regimes established elsewhere in the service sector after 1979, is still in a process of development and flux.

3.5 Conclusion

The growing economic significance of service industries in the British economy has raised their profile in government policies. The diversity of service industries and their differing roles in the economy means that the details of policy differ considerably. Nevertheless, there are a number of common threads running through the three industries reviewed here. Since 1979, the government has opened up service industries to greater competition. In the financial sector this has been achieved by reducing regulations which restricted the operation of financial institutions, and removing informal agreements which limited competition. Public sector organisations have been privatised and this has been supported by regulations to limit anti-competitive behaviour from the large, dominant, private sector firms which have been created. Quasi-market arrangements have also been introduced into the remaining parts of the public sector.

The three industries examined also highlight the growing significance of international influences on national government policies. This is clearest in the telecommunications and financial sectors, where regulatory changes have been used as a competitive weapon to attract footloose international investment and to provide domestic industry with a competitive advantage. The relatively free regulatory environment in the USA acted as a spur to the British Government to engage in a 'bonfire' of market controls in the financial sector and 'hive off' BT, and this has in turn spurred similar moves elsewhere in Europe. Even in the public sector, policy is framed in the context of the need to reduce the scale of public sector provision, so that business costs are not increased by excessive taxation, which may in turn undermine the competitive position of locally-based industry in international markets.

It is also clear that in relation to the service industries considered here, far from standing back from intervention and letting market forces operate, governments since 1979 have become increasingly involved: either directly (as the manager of their own staff) or indirectly (as a regulator, taking responsibility for establishing the rules which govern business behaviour). For all their rhetoric about rolling back the state and letting market forces act freely, the Conservative Governments since 1979 have not fully deregulated either the finance or the telecommunications industry. What policy changes they have introduced – for these two industries at least – have really only made adjustments to the regulatory framework within which each industry is still obliged to operate; and the persistence of such regulation still leaves unanswered a number of questions. This chapter will close by posing four.

First, to what extent should regulation take into account the *national interest*? Such issues are particularly difficult where clashes of commercial interest are involved. This can be most readily observed in the debate about the development of ISDN in telecommunications, which is seen as a critical basis for innovation in a range of telecommunications and computer-based services. Until comparatively recently ISDN was seen as the ideal technical solution to delivering an advanced telecommunications infrastructure across the whole country, and was seen as a natural extension of the monopoly provision provided by the public telecommunications operator. Today the debate about ISDN is more complex, because in a more competitive telecommunications market, ISDN is a vital component of BT's competitive strategy, enabling it to exploit economies of scale and scope in network and service provision, and to gain an edge over its competitors. To other competitors, such as large companies with their own networks (for instance, Mercury and cable TV companies) BT's development of ISDN is seen as overly restrictive, preventing them from undertaking their own network developments. They therefore argue for a more open and diverse approach to the development of an advanced telecommunications network, which allows them to compete successfully with BT. At present, there is a danger that such conflicts of commercial interest will prevent the development of a national 'information highway' of high-quality cable, which will act as the catalyst for a range of new services.

Secondly, the sectors studied here highlight the manner in which unregulated commercial pressures encourage the spatial fragmentation of the British economy, and so raise questions of the *regional interest*. It is widely recognised that government reforms of the financial sector, which encouraged growth close to London, played a key role in the widening of regional disparities in the economy during the 1980s. The rationalisation of the public sector has also had an uneven spatial impact, because half of all white collar civil servants are located in only twenty-one local labour markets. Investment in telecommunications infrastructure inevitably has spatial consequences. The move away from universal service provision and the concentration of new services in selected locations of high demand is inevitably favouring specific locations over others. This raises questions (which will be considered in more detail in Chapter 8) about whether spatial concerns should be given a higher priority in government policy, either incorporated in the remit of regulators, or via urban and regional policy.

Thirdly, there is the question of what is the most appropriate regulatory structure for each industry, and what should be the balance struck between industrial autonomy and what we might term the *democratic interest*? Should regulation be left in the hands of the industry itself, as has been tried in the financial sector? This minimises government interference, but is open to abuse because regulations tend to be voluntary rather than enforceable. In addition, where regulators are given considerable freedom of operation, this may limit government discretion in industrial policy. The government could, of course, be more directly involved as a regulator either in an advisory capacity or by laying down legally enforceable rules. However, greater government control might discourage international investment.

Fourthly, there is the question of the relationship between market regulation and the *public interest*. During the rest of the 1990s, as large parts of the public sector – including parts of the core of the welfare state – operate under commercial and quasi-commercial conditions, there is likely to be an intensified debate as to whether such modes of operation are compatible with the social welfare goals and equity of service provision typical of public services. Traditional supporters of the welfare state argue that public servants are motivated by a public service ethos, and that their individual integrity and loyalty will lead to effective performance in providing services to clients. If they are right, activities which are classified as public services need not be solely judged by measures of commercial efficiency, but rather against criteria of effectiveness (judged, that is, by the quality of the service provided and by its impact on recipients). On the other hand, the present Conservative Government and its supporters see public sector bureaucracies as inherently inefficient. Public officials are seen as individuals pursuing their own ends. Where services are supplied free at the point of consumption, there are few limits to demand because costs are unknown to consumers; and when there are public monopolies there is no competition to encourage efficiency. This debate too seems set to continue.

4 Energy

Simon Bromley

4.1 Introduction

Before the Second World War, British energy requirements were very largely met by domestically produced coal. Indeed, as late as 1947 coal still accounted for some 90 per cent of Britain's total primary energy requirement (TPER). The modern coal industry had its origins in the industrial revolution, reaching a peak production in the period immediately before the First World War. In 1913 there were around 3000 mines, producing 300 million tonnes a year and employing 1 million workers. As a consequence of the inter-war recession, together with the loss of export markets to US coal producers, production contracted. In addition, the fragmented ownership structure of the industry and the conflict-ridden labour relations within it inhibited new investment and technical improvements. The depredations of the Second World War further damaged the industry. The nationalisation of the industry in 1947 was thus as much a means to the rationalisation of a chronically backward sector, as an assertion of a new pattern of state ownership. At the time of the formation of the National Coal Board (NCB), there were 958 mines, producing 200 million tonnes a year with 700 000 workers. Pre-war levels of production were achieved by 1952 and then the industry remained more or less stable at this level until 1957, when a large-scale contraction began.

If the first and originally dominant pillar of the British energy sector was the nationalised coal industry, then the other legs were the electricity supply industry (ESI), taken into state control in 1948, and the gas industry, nationalised in 1949. For England and Wales, the Electricity Act (1947) and subsequent reorganisations in 1955 and 1957 established the basic structure of regional distribution companies and a centralised, monopolistic generating and transmission body, the Central Electricity Generating Board (CEGB). (In Scotland a slightly different duopolistic structure was put in place.) Similar legislation in 1948 also reorganised the fragmented gas industry into a number of regional boards and a unified Gas Council, and this arrangement was later reshaped into the British Gas Corporation (BGC) in 1973. The CEGB had a near monopoly over the generation and transmission of electricity (though later the United Kingdom Atomic Energy Authority (UKAEA) and British Nuclear Fuels (BNFL) also played a limited role), and the BGC came to have a near total monopoly over the production of manufactured (town) gas, the purchase of North Sea (natural) gas and general gas distribution.

Much of the subsequent history of British energy policy can be told as the story of the decline of coal (albeit within a framework of limited protection), both in terms of its falling share of expanding energy requirements and in terms of an absolute decline in the levels of output and employment in the industry. The contraction of coal's industrial market was largely the result of a shift to cheaper oil imports, largely sourced from the Middle East. In 1950 the price of oil imports was roughly twice that of coal, whereas by 1970 oil was perhaps 25 per cent cheaper. Later, coal's gas and domestic markets were hit by the discovery of natural gas: in the early 1960s, more than 90 per cent of British gas was produced from coal, by the end of the decade more than 80 per cent was manufactured from oil, and by the late 1970s both coal and oil had been replaced by natural gas. Lastly, coal's share of the electric power generation market was challenged not only by oil, but also by the state-supported civil nuclear power programme. Thus, between 1957 and 1971 around 400 of the 700 pits were closed, with the loss of 400 000 jobs. Falling demand and productivity improvements accounted equally for the employment loss. As a result, coal's share of TPER fell steadily from 90 per cent in 1947 to 50 per cent by 1969, and to 33 per cent by 1974.

The other economies of Western Europe were also dominated by coal in the immediate post-war years, though not to quite the same extent as Britain. For the shift towards an oil-based, car-owning economy, pioneered by the USA during the inter-war years, did not occur in Western Europe (and Japan) until the long boom of the 1950s and 1960s. Thus, in 1950, the share of coal in the TPER of the countries that were later to form the European Community (EC) was some

75 per cent. Thereafter, there was a general and rapid shift away from coal. Oil and gas captured most of the industrial, railroad, commercial and residential fuel markets and thereby overtook coal as energy sources in much of the Western world. Coal was increasingly confined to electric power generation and coking coal was used for the production of iron and steel – the former market expanded roughly in line with national output until the 1970s and continued to expand until the recessions of the early 1980s, while the latter was stagnant for much of the period and then declined rapidly in North America and Western Europe. The net result was that the share of coal in TPER for the EC states fell to 20 per cent in 1971. On the other hand, the share of oil in TPER rose from 10 per cent in 1950 to 60 per cent in 1971, and most of this oil was imported from the Middle East and North Africa.

In many respects, then, the changes in the British energy balance were similar to those of Western Europe as a whole. However, the pattern of change in Britain was marked by a number of particular features. In the first place, the original degree of coal's dominance in Britain was unique. Second, the threat posed to coal by the general trends noted above was further enhanced by the discovery of large reserves of natural gas and oil in the North Sea in the 1960s and 1970s. A third distinguishing aspect was the strong position of British Petroleum (BP) and Royal-Dutch/Shell in the international oil industry. Finally, there was the civil nuclear power programme. Originally an off-shoot of the military programme, from the late 1950s through to the 1970s the use of nuclear power to generate electricity received considerable support from all governments.

It is important to recognise that policy, just as much as prices, drove these developments within the European and the British energy sectors. Indeed, in many cases, it was often policy which determined prices. Throughout the post-war period all governments in capitalist countries have intervened directly and extensively in both their domestic energy 'markets' and those of others. Most obviously, the cheap oil that fuelled the post-war boom was underwritten by the political and military role of the leading Western states, above all the USA, in the Middle East. Until the late 1970s, there was no free market for crude oil. Moreover, the large, vertically-integrated oil companies (the majors) effected a degree of cross-subsidisation of fuel oil (which competed against coal) by petrol (which had no direct competitors) in their European markets. This attempt to displace coal was further underpinned by the fiscal regimes adopted by many European governments, which kept taxes high on petrol and low on fuel oil. At the same time, shortages of public investment retarded the modernisation of the coal sector. Finally, in all cases the development of civil nuclear power has received large (if often hidden) public subsidies.

Against this background, British energy policy until 1974 was basically one of nationalisation followed by a pragmatic regulation, with little variation according to political party. Indeed, until the 1960s, energy policy received little sustained attention. Britain ended the Second World War as a one-fuel economy and with a severely depleted coal industry. The NCB was geared towards physical production targets, but lacked the investment capital to modernise and move away from low-productivity, high-cost pits. During the period of the gradual shift towards a two-fuel economy (coal and oil), there were two official reports concerned with the energy implications of post-war reconstruction – the Simon Report (1946) and the Ridley Report (1952). Reflecting the need to conserve foreign exchange, to rebuild production and to construct new housing, the Simon Report was principally concerned with the issues of domestic heating and the efficiency of fuel use. The Ridley Report argued that there was little room for increased oil imports because of the strategic risks of import-dependence (the Iranian nationalist leader, Mussadeq, had persuaded the Majlis to nationalise the Anglo-Iranian Oil Company (BP) in the Spring of 1951) and because of the foreign-exchange costs of dollar-denominated imports. (In fact, oil imports rose at three times the rate estimated in the Report over the next decade.)

Both the Simon Report and the Ridley Report argued against a strategic plan for the energy sector as a whole, recommending instead competition between fuels to encourage efficiency in what were in many cases otherwise effective monopolies. Inter-industry competition, set within a general framework of public ownership and the general requirement to break even, was reckoned to be the best route to an efficient use of fuel. Such competition between alternative fuels only became a reality in the late 1950s, when the technology to use oil for electricity generation became available. It was speeded up by the displacement of coal with slum clearances, the 1956 Clean Air Act and the switch by British Rail from coal to diesel and electric traction. Further competition for coal's markets came with the public and private sector exploitation of North Sea gas in the 1960s and early 1970s, and with the private sector development of North Sea oil coming on-stream in the late 1970s.

4.2 The emergence of a bipartisan energy policy

Thus the first fuel to challenge coal's dominance of the energy sector was oil, and this was imported mainly from the Middle East. As a result of this import-dependence, and especially because of its adverse implications for Britain's precarious balance of payments position, the potential importance of petroleum (oil and gas) discoveries in the North Sea was obvious. If economic growth was constrained by the weak balance of payments (and this was certainly the official perception in the late 1950s and 1960s), then the discovery and exploitation of domestic petroleum supplies could be critical. Paradoxically, the adverse balance of payments implications of oil imports were exacerbated by the fact that the UK was host to BP and Shell, since governments considered that the latter's international interests depended on a high oil price. Accordingly, by 1965 the average import price of oil into Britain was some 25 per cent above the West European average, and now that oil was contributing one-quarter of TPER this represented a considerable deficit item on the balance of payments.

The international petroleum industry first became interested in the North Sea after the discovery in 1959 of a large natural gas field (Groningen) at Slochteren in Holland. To begin with, the British Government refused permission to companies seeking to develop the North Sea. This was for two reasons. First, the Convention on the Continental Shelf adopted by the First United Nations Conference on the Law of the Sea (1958) had not been ratified by the British and the other North Sea littoral states. Second, the Government lacked any legislative powers to control economic activities on the continental shelf. Nevertheless, by 1963 many companies had made their interest clear through conducting preliminary seismic surveys. In April 1964 the Continental Shelf Act was passed, and this 'had two principal effects: firstly, it amended British law to allow the implementation of the Continental Shelf Convention and secondly, it extended the licensing provisions of the Petroleum (Production) Act 1934 to the area beyond territorial waters' (Cameron, 1983, p. 73).

In order to work out the details of policy for the North Sea, the Conservative Government established two committees drawn from the oil industry to advise on the legal and licensing aspects of North Sea development. An inter-departmental committee was also established to formulate policy, composed from the Treasury, the Ministry of Fuel and Power and the Cabinet. Strongly reflecting Treasury concerns and

the general economic climate, the inter-departmental committee argued
that the overriding need was for a contribution to the balance of payments and that this implied a strategy of rapid exploration and exploitation. The first round of allocating licences for exploration and
exploitation was rushed through before the 1964 General Election, and
a second round was completed by the Labour Government in 1965. The
Gas Council was designated as the sole purchaser (monopsonist) of any
gas produced.

With the return of a Labour Government in 1964, and in the context
of the heightened importance attached to indicative planning, the task
of the White Paper *Fuel Policy* (Cmnd. 2798, 1965) was to elaborate
the principles on which a co-ordinated national fuel policy could be
based and to outline the policy instruments open to the Government.
The prime concern was with the coal industry: rising oil imports and
technological change in the gas and electricity sectors were producing a
continuing fall in the demand for coal. The basic assumption continued
to be that coal would remain central to Britain's energy supply, but that
the gas industry would be given a powerful stimulus if North Sea
development proved to be successful. The bottom-line, however, was
that the fuel sector should make its full contribution to strengthening
the economy in general and to the balance of payments in particular.
(Notwithstanding the importance attached to the balance of payments,
Fuel Policy argued that oil imports could not be restricted without damaging the economy.)

A second White Paper, *Fuel Policy* (Cmnd. 3438, 1967), was neces-
sitated by the discovery of natural gas in the North Sea and the altered
position of nuclear power. In 1965 an ambitious second generation programme of expansion for nuclear power was launched, based on the
advanced, gas-cooled reactor (AGR). The discovery of North Sea gas,
in combination with the new AGR programme, implied that the central
concern of Government energy policy would be how to run down the
coal industry. In the light of these changes, coal output was projected to
decline still further. At the same time, the Government published a
White Paper on *Economic and Financial Objectives of Nationalised
Industries* (Cmnd. 3437, 1967) which emphasised the need both for
strict new financial criteria and for an arms-length relationship between
sponsoring ministries and industries. Like its predecessor, *Fuel Policy*
(1967) was concerned with the costs and problems of running down the
coal industry, but it also looked at questions of the security of supply,
fuel efficiency and the balance of payments. Two new departures were

the open recognition of the need for the Government to co-ordinate industry plans, given the magnitude of the investments concerned and their long lead times, and the use of future demand projections to assist in policy planning. *Fuel Policy* (1967) was to provide the basic policy framework for energy planning until 1973. It represented the first co-ordinated attempt to formulate a national energy policy and, despite some major forecasting errors (notably on oil price movements and in relation to the expansion of nuclear power), it was not without some success.

In addition to these general policy statements for the fuel sector as a whole, the Labour Government undertook a detailed review of North Sea policy. This was carried out by an inter-departmental committee composed of officials from the Department for Economic Affairs, the Cabinet Office, the Treasury and the industrial ministries. Two questions had to be settled: first, the degree of public sector participation in this newly expanding domain; and second, the division of the economic gains from gas exploration between the private producing companies and the Government.

On the question of public sector participation, when in opposition the Labour Party had called for the formation of a National Hydrocarbons Council. Its thinking on this issue was influenced by the argument of Peter Odell that outright nationalisation was not only difficult, especially given the requirement for rapid development, and potentially prejudicial to Britain's overseas interests, but also unnecessary. Instead, Odell argued that state co-operation with and direction of the large oil companies was a better alternative. In 1967 Labour's NEC followed the report of the party's study group on the North Sea in recommending the setting up of a National Hydrocarbons Corporation. This body was to be vested with control of all licensed blocks in the North Sea, to acquire the existing public sector assets in this sector (that is, those belonging to the Gas Council and the National Coal Board), and to participate in on- and off-shore operations.

Although the policy was endorsed by the Labour Party conference and compulsory state participation was to be instituted by the Norwegian Government in its second licensing round (1969–71) for Norway's sector of the North Sea, no such policy was carried through by the Labour Government. Both ministers and officials concerned with the formulation of policy believed that such proposals would be extremely difficult to implement against the opposition of the major petroleum companies, and that any disputes would only serve to slow down the speed of development within the North Sea sector. In addition, ministers felt that an attempt by the British Government to impose control on the US petroleum companies would have adverse implications for the operations of BP and Royal-Dutch/Shell in the USA and Canada.

The question of the division of economic benefits was simpler and the Government's stance was tougher. The petroleum companies wanted a price for North Sea gas based on that of competitive energy forms, whereas the Gas Council (in its position as the legal monopsonist) offered a cost-plus formula, thereby denying any excess profits to the companies. The Government's economic adviser, Thomas Balogh, strongly supported the latter proposal, and in essence this became Government policy. By these means, any 'rents', or above average profits, generated in North Sea gas production were to be appropriated by the taxpayer and the consumer, not by the private companies. Despite this, the third licensing round (1969/70) was successful, and between 1970 and 1975 the volume of exploration in the North Sea rose dramatically. These developments in the gas sector laid the basis both for a rapid and large-scale switch from manufactured to natural gas and for a significant expansion of the share of gas in the energy market.

The first real sign of the potential of the North Sea in relation to *oil* arrived with the announcement of the discovery of the Forties field by BP in October 1970 and of the Brent field by Shell–Esso in July 1971. It was clear from these and other finds that the UK could become self-sufficient in oil by the end of the 1970s, and remain in surplus at least for the 1980s. Under the new Conservative Government, every conceivable interest was now pushing for a rapid exploration and development of the North Sea: the DTI wanted to discover more about the North Sea's reserves; the Treasury wanted as big an impact on the balance of payments as soon as was possible; and the Barber boom was in part premised on the expected payments surpluses of the future. The fourth licensing round (1971/2) was the largest thus far, and it marked both the transition from a focus on gas to oil and from the phase of exploration to that of development and production.

The overall context in which British North Sea policy was formulated, therefore, dictated a strategy based on as rapid an exploration and development as possible, in order to make an early and significant impact on the generally weak balance of payments position of the economy as a whole. The logic of energy policy was thus subordinated to that of macroeconomic policy. This connection between policy for the North Sea and the more general management of the macroeconomy was further tightened with the large-scale increases in oil prices in 1973/4. Future oil earnings became increasingly central to the Government's management of both the foreign exchange markets and its own finances. What Carson (1981) has aptly termed 'the political economy of speed' came to dominate policy formulation.

Against this background, and notwithstanding its earlier failure to inject a significant degree of public sector control into the North Sea, the Labour Party Manifesto for the February 1974 election argued that the status of North Sea petroleum as a publicly-owned resource should be guaranteed and that its production and distribution should be placed under full government control with majority public participation. But in addition to the Government's desire for a rapid development of the North Sea, its freedom of manoeuvre was further limited by the developments that had already taken place between 1964 and 1972. For, as Cameron (1983) has detailed, oil areas tend to have a life-cycle where the best finds are made early on, and thus the companies' hands are strengthened in relation to the licensing authority; the initial North Sea discoveries coincided with buoyant demand for oil and rising prices, and this attracted the major international companies into the sector; by 1972 the state had played its strongest cards, having determined the timing, the size and the conditions of the licences; and by 1975 US companies controlled some 60 per cent of the acreage in the British sector of the North Sea. Thus despite the creation of the British National Oil Corporation (BNOC) and Britoil to participate in North Sea activity, the Labour Government's attempts to renegotiate licences and to extend state control over the sector proved unsuccessful.

Finally, throughout this period, there was the important subsidiary story of the development of civilian nuclear power. Originally the off-shoot of the military programme, the civilian effort was launched in the mid-1950s and was based on the Magnox reactor design. A second and much bigger round got underway in 1964, based on the AGR, but substantial technical difficulties and cost overruns threatened to derail the whole case for nuclear power by the early 1970s. In response, the Conservative Government rationalised the nuclear construction industry in 1973, forming the National Nuclear Corporation as the sole constructor. Fortunately for the industry, the combination of the oil price increases and problems in the coal industry in 1973/4, together with active lobbying by the commercial interests behind the US-designed Pressurised Water Reactor (PWR), kept the nuclear case alive within the CEGB and the state.

4.3   Energy policy to 1979

As the above review of post-war energy policy has tried to indicate, it has been characterised by a number of related features. In the first place, the policy can be seen as one of managing the transition from a one-fuel (coal) economy to a more balanced mix of energy sources. Second, the dominant actors in the supply of energy have been nationalised public sector corporations. A third feature, however, has been the failure to extend this public sector control beyond the immediate post-war nationalisations of coal, electricity and gas: the existence of a technologically advanced and well-capitalised international petroleum industry meant that the development of the North Sea was largely carried out under private sector auspices. Moreover, despite this dominance of the public sector, a fourth characteristic has been the absence of an overall strategic plan for energy supply and demand. This has been in part a result of the final distinguishing feature, the formulation of energy policy through inter-departmental committees, usually characterised by Treasury dominance, and thus the subordination of energy policy to general macroeconomic considerations.

Turning to the policy-making process itself, this regularly involved three kinds of actors: first, the nationalised supply industries; second, the relevant Government ministries and committees; and third, the major private sector companies which operate in the energy industries. Since the first post-war Labour Government, the major fuel industries have been under public sector control. The vast bulk of the coal industry was nationalised and came under the control of the NCB in 1947. The domestic gas industry came under the control of the BGC, which had a vertically integrated monopoly from the production of gas through to final distribution. Electricity supply was very largely the monopoly of the CEGB in England and Wales and a duopoly existed in Scotland. This public sector dominance was, of course, somewhat undermined by the private-sector led development of North Sea gas and oil.

As to the relevant government ministries (discussed in more detail in Chapter 7), responsibility for energy has been subect to considerable institutional migration. Traditionally, energy came under the purview of the Board of Trade, but during the Second World War the Ministry of Fuel, Light and Power was established (1942). In 1945 this became the Ministry of Fuel and Power (and the Ministry of Power after 1957). The Ministry of Power was then absorbed into the Ministry of

Technology in 1969, which itself was incorporated into the DTI in 1970. Then in 1974 the Department of Energy was created in response to industrial unrest in the coal industry and the huge increases in the price of crude oil in 1973. The relation between the various ministries, the nationalised energy industries, and the private sector construction and engineering companies may be described as a mixture of clientelism and corporatism. Industry managers and civil servants largely determined the course of policy, with only limited participation by workers' representatives and almost a complete absence of consumer representation. Major issues of policy direction were often settled by more or less *ad hoc* inter-departmental committees representing the nationalised industries, the ministry and usually the Treasury and the Cabinet Office. The evidence from Richard Crossman's *Diaries* and Harold Wilson's account of *The Labour Government 1964–1970*, for example, is that at no time was energy policy seriously considered at full Cabinet level. The direct attention energy policy did receive came from the civil service, to the extent that the 1965 and 1967 White Papers were, according to Crossman, written totally by officials, and no Minister had taken any active part in their drafting.

Finally, a number of private sector concerns have been involved in the policy-making process. Essentially, these have been of two kinds: first, there are a small number of large construction and engineering companies that have been involved in the building of power plant for the electricity supply industry; and second, there are the major international petroleum companies which have been centrally involved in developing the gas and oil resources of the North Sea. Particularly in the latter case, the relation of these companies to the relevant ministry has often been clientelist. For example, traditionally the Ministry of Fuel and Power relied on refining companies for investment and security of supply, while the Treasury 'looked to Shell and BP for help in keeping their funds in sterling and co-operating on currency flows' (Hamilton, 1978, p. 18). In return, successive governments gave the industry diplomatic and price support. These relations were further extended as governments came to rely increasingly on the major international petroleum companies for the development of the North Sea. Similar consideration have applied to the nuclear lobby.

Overall, then, the framework for public policy formation, especially under Labour's maximalist approach, was broadly corporatist in relation to the public sector and clientelist in regard to the private sector. For coal, electricity generation and gas, public sector dominance was secured through the incorporation of producer groups within the process of both policy-making and implementation. This created a series of 'insider' groups with privileged access to decision-makers in the state, such as the CEGB, the NCB, British Gas and the UKAEA. Similarly, private sector 'insider' groups were created by the clientelist relations established with the major oil companies and the construction and engineering companies which built power stations. A number of implications for the general character of post-war energy policy followed from these arrangements. In the first place, given the incorporation of producer groups within the policy process, policy was largely supply-driven, determined by producer interests in the public sector and subject to clientelist usurpation by private sector demands. One important consequence of this was that the concerns of consumers were neither determined nor able to make their voice heard. Another was the creation of 'outsider' groups which had little weight in the policy-making process, such as the lobbies for energy efficiency and for renewable sources of energy.

The absence of an overall plan for the energy sector and its subordination to broader questions of macroeconomic policy resulted in a second set of problems to do with the efficiency of energy supply. For the Morrisonian model of public ownership left at least two issues unresolved: first, the exact nature of the arms-length relationship between the industry and the ministry; and second, the procedures for monitoring performance in relation to non-market, social obligations. The nationalised industries were rarely able to pursue clear managerial objectives without ministerial interference. Equally, there were no clear procedures for ascertaining either the extent of cross-subsidisation or the efficiency with which non-market obligations were being met. It was simply assumed that inter-industry competition, coupled with financial control of the nationalised industries, would deliver an efficient service to the final consumer.

A final implication of this overall framework was the limited degree of party political input, whether through the Cabinet or through Parliament. There were, of course, White Papers, Bills, Select Committee Reports and Parliamentary debates, but because of the nature of policy formulation energy policy rarely became a subject of sustained party debate or attention. At least until 1979, ambitious plans formulated while in opposition – such as the Labour Party proposals noted above – came to little or nothing when in government.

Let us now try and take stock of the evolution of British energy policy in this period of broadly social democratic and corporatist attempts at regulation. Social democratic attempts to plan energy production – as in the proposals for a National Hydrocarbons Corporation in the mid-1960s, or in the White Papers associated with the National Plan, *Fuel Policy* (1965) and *Fuel Policy* (1967) – failed to get off the ground. It is certainly true that some forecasting was adopted, and energy policy was more closely integrated with concerns about the balance of payments. But overall, Labour followed the interventionist but unco-ordinated policies set by the Conservatives, while taking a slightly tougher stance on the distributive question of how to tax monopoly profits by using the Gas Council's monopsonist position. The failure to consolidate a more planned approach to the formulation of energy policy meant that control over key decisions pertaining to the rate of exploitation of North Sea reserves increasingly passed to a private sector that was dominated by the major international oil companies.

In 1973/4 came the first of the so-called 'oil shocks', with the price of oil rising roughly eightfold between 1973 and 1979. Competitive changes in the international oil industry, adverse developments in the strategic position of the USA and a greater degree of market control by the Organisation of Petroleum Exporting Countries (OPEC) had demonstrated the macroeconomic and energy dilemmas associated with high levels of import dependence for oil. The common response among the governments of the advanced capitalist states was to attempt to reduce their reliance on oil imports. In particular, they sought to increase the role of coal and nuclear power in electricity generation, to expand the role of natural gas in other markets, to increase the production of oil (and gas and coal) outside the OPEC sources, and to encourage the conservation of energy in domestic and industrial markets.

The Labour Governments of 1974–79 tried to cope with this new situation in a number of ways. In the first place, they pushed for a rapid expansion of North Sea oil exploration and production, aiming for self-sufficiency and net exports. Notwithstanding the establishment of BNOC, and its equity participation in a range of North Sea developments, the dominance of private (predominantly, US) capital was further consolidated by the rapid pace of development. In fact, the Labour Left's agenda for full public control to be accomplished through BNOC, Britoil and the renegotiation of existing licensing contracts was essentially defeated. Rather, rents and revenues from the North Sea were geared to the priorities of stabilisation policy, coming under normal Treasury control, and were thereby denied to the putative strategy of industrial modernisation that was also proposed by the Left (on this, see Ham, 1981). Secondly, the Government adopted the *Plan for Coal* (1974), finding capital expenditure for the expansion of deep-mined coal and the introduction of new mining technology. This was in addition to the continuation of the support that the NCB had tradition-ally received in the form of strict limits on private and open-cast mining, on coal imports and on oil-burning and later gas-burning power stations. Together with the settlement of the miners' pay claim, this had the effect of insulating the National Union of Mineworkers (NUM) from the industrial struggles of the period. And finally, in the case of nuclear power, Tony Benn managed a stalling operation in the build-up of a new round of the programme. But the PWR lobby in private engin-eering and construction companies, as well as in the nuclear industry and in the CEGB, went substantially unchallenged, despite growing evidence of the uneconomic character of nuclear power.

4.4   Energy policy after 1979

By the end of the 1970s, the operation of this policy-making frame-work had introduced a number of tensions into British energy policy, which the incoming Conservative Government decided to deal with in a radically new way. First, there was the problem of supply. The Labour Party had attempted to appease the range of producer interests from the majors in the North Sea, through the workers in nuclear power stations, to underground miners. No attention was paid to where demand for all this fuel might come from, and this simply stored up problems for coal in the future. (The targets in the *Plan for Coal* have been described as based on back-of-an-envelope calculations.) The second set of ques-tions related to the future of a basically corporatist policy framework in the context of increasing private sector involvement in the fuel economy, largely through the North Sea, and a growing differentiation in the potential sources of supply. A third problem was that of financial control: efficiency was secured neither by a system of strategic plan-ning, capable of matching supply to demand, nor by an effective set of market disciplines. And finally, there was the general question of what role could energy *policy* play in the thinking of a government commit-ted to rolling back the frontiers of the state and restoring the centrality of the 'market' in determining questions of allocation and production?

   In response to these problems, the declared energy policy of the new Conservative Government encompassed three major strands. The first of these, the further encouragement of North Sea development, was not really a new departure. In this area, the private sector already played a dominant role, and the principal task of policy was to create as favourable an environment for future growth as possible. Changes to the North Sea tax regime enhanced the returns to investment, thereby stimulating more development and expanding the contributions made to the balance of payments and the state's finances. The major commitment to expand the role of nuclear power in electricity generation did mark a significant departure from previous policy. For, as Secretary of State for Energy (1975–9), Tony Benn had stalled the impetus for an expansion of the nuclear programme, concerned about its economics and the uncertainty over the future design for nuclear reactors. The AGR had proved expensive; its proposed replacement, the Steam Generating Heavy Water Reactor (SGHWR), was abandoned; and the CEGB, officials in the Department of Energy, the merchant bank Kleinwort Benson and the US power company Westinghouse were all pushing for the PWR design. The Conservative Government opted for the latter as the basis of their new support for nuclear power in December 1979.

The final strand of the new energy policy was a general commitment to increase the role of the market. In a speech delivered in 1982, Nigel Lawson, the Secretary of State for Energy, argued that:

> in general ... I do *not* see the Government's task as being to try to plan the future shape of energy production and consumption. It is not even primarily to try to balance UK demand and supply for energy. Our task is rather to set a framework which will ensure that the market operates in the energy sector with a minimum of distortion and that energy is produced and consumed efficiently.

This statement amply illustrates the Government's belief that a combination of liberalisation and privatisation in the energy sector would allow the market to allocate resources efficiently, and thus to bring supply and demand into balance.

Liberalisation was facilitated by a general tightening of the external financing limits of the nationalised industries which, together with the maintenance of the restrictions on competing with and raising capital from the private sector, resulted in the imposition of restructuring packages to meet these new financial disciplines. A more open market was encouraged by the removal of past constraints on the internationalisation of energy supply, as price considerations were privileged over those of security of supply and the balance of payments. This new focus on market-based disciplines was also introduced into the heart of the energy supply nexus through the 'Joint Understanding' negotiated between the CEGB and the NCB, allowing the CEGB to use 'world market' prices to pass productivity increases in the mines into the balance sheets of the electricity generators.

The progressive privatisation of the BNOC/Britoil, the BGC and the CEGB further expanded the role of the private sector and market-based calculations in the energy decision-making process. Significantly, it has only been in the domain of nuclear power that the government has been prepared to suspend market based considerations and to reintroduce regulation in order to protect an uneconomic form of power generation. (Privatisation is only now – in 1995 – being actively contemplated.) Finally, a range of institutional changes – the abolition of the corporatist Energy Commission, a significant shift to using the Monopolies and Mergers Commission to enforce market-based discipline in the public sector, most clearly in the case of coal, and the consequent downgrading of the role of the Department of Energy in formulating overall energy policy – further reduced the capacity of the state to regulate these newly liberalised and privatised energy markets. This process eventually resulted in the Government accepting the advice it received from major private sector energy companies (for example, BP) and 'New Right' think tanks (for example, the Institute of Economic Affairs) to abolish the Department of Energy and to incorporate its residual functions into the less interventionist DTI.

The overall legacy of these developments has been the privatisation of most of the energy supply industries in Britain, a significant assertion of the role of market forces in the determination of future decisions in the sector, and a growing internationalisation of the sources of supply. Some of the major unresolved questions concern the implications of the liberalisation and privatisation of the ESI. What is the future for the UK coal industry in the new environment? What role will natural gas play in the generation of electricity? What are the prospects for nuclear power now that the monopolistic CEGB no longer dominates the electricity supply industry? What role will there be for strategies of energy efficiency and for renewable forms of energy generation? What forms of regulation will apply to a set of increasingly international and European (rather than national) energy markets?

Rather than attempt an exhaustive review of Conservative energy policy, the rest of this chapter will concentrate on its central and most dramatic aspect, the liberalisation and the privatisation of the electricity supply industry. With the gradual shift to a four-fuel economy, and given the essentially private sector character of development in the North Sea, the electricity supply industry came to form the centre of energy policy in the UK. Its radical transformation, indeed its dissolution, thus provides an extremely interesting case-study for the student of industrial policy. For, within the general corporatist framework of post-war energy policy, the most protected 'insider' groups were the NCB, the CEGB and the nuclear power lobby. Yet contained within the proposals set out in the Department of Energy's White Paper, *Privatising Electricity* (Cmnd. 322, 1988), was the systematic removal of this network from the core of British energy policy, with major implications both for the fortunes of coal, gas and nuclear power, and for the ability of the generators of electricity to determine the future pattern of supply. Indeed, it might be argued that the break-up and privatisation of the ESI marks the end of a *national* energy policy for Britain, in however *ad hoc* a form, and the advent of a new context given by the prominence of increasingly international markets, industry-based regulatory authorities and (future) regulation from the European Commission.

4.5 Electricity privatisation and the end of a national energy policy?

In his speech on energy policy quoted above, Nigel Lawson noted some particular features of the electricity supply industry:

Within this overall approach, electricity poses special problems. With the development of appropriate infrastructures, coal, oil and gas can be stored, or traded, to a sufficient extent to provide market disciplines and supply flexibility. This is not true of electricity. For many of its uses, there are no acceptable substitutes and, except for insignificant amounts at the margin, there is no flexibility for dealing with under- or over-supply through trade. So the electricity supply industry, unlike the coal and gas industries, has a duty to ensure that there will be sufficient plant available to meet the top end of the range of most likely demand requirements.

How, then, was the 'market' to be introduced into the electricity supply industry? And, if there could not really be a free-market in electricity, then what would guarantee that supply would match demand in the future? The Energy Act of 1983 had attempted to liberalise the electricity supply industry by encouraging new entrants into the power generating sector and by allowing large industrial consumers to shop around between generators. However, it was widely agreed that this was of extremely limited value. Accordingly, in the Conservative manifesto for the 1987 General Election there were commitments to privatise the electricity supply industries and to play a leading role in the development of nuclear power.

The new Government brought forward legislation for the privatisation of the electricity supply industry in England and Wales and a separate Bill for Scotland. For England and Wales, the Bill involved a wholesale transformation in the structure of electricity supply (given the smaller size of the Scottish industry, a more integrated set-up remained in place). Six major changes were proposed.

(i)   The generating assets of the CEGB were to be distributed on a 70/30 basis between two new private companies, National Power and PowerGen, with all of the CEGB's nuclear commitments going to National Power.

(ii)   The 12 Area Boards were to be sold, becoming private Regional Electricity Companies (RECs).

(iii) The transmission assets of the CEGB, the natural monopoly of the National Grid, were also to be sold to a private company jointly owned by the RECs.

(iv)   The statutory duty to maintain the supply of electricity was to be transferred from the CEGB to the RECs.

(v)   The Government was to impose a non-fossil fuel obligation (NFFO) on the RECs, requiring them to purchase a specified share of their electricity from non-fossil sources (effectively this meant from the nuclear sector).

(vi)   There was to be an official regulatory body as in the earlier privatisations of public utilities, OFFER.

The Bill was immediately criticised by the opposition, by industry analysts and by the Commons Select Committee on Energy, on four main grounds. To begin with, critics noted that the legislation implied a degree of unequal treatment between the coal and nuclear industries.

Coal was to be exposed to full competitive pressures, whereas nuclear power was to be protected behind the NFFO. Next, the duopoly of National Power and PowerGen was seen as too limited a break-up of the CEGB's monopoly, leading to a continued dominance of the generators within the electricity supply industry. Another problem was the issue of security of supply: if the RECs and not the generators were to be charged with providing electricity, and if the RECs were to face a genuinely competitive environment, then how could they ensure that the contracted supply would meet demand? Finally, the Bill was criticised for paying insufficient attention to questions of energy efficiency and support for renewable sources, since little or no obligations were to be imposed on the RECs. In response, the Government denied that coal was being unfairly treated and pointed to the large sums of public money spent on British Coal. The duopoly and the 70/30 split was defended on the grounds that it was needed in order to sustain the nuclear power programme in the public sector, since only a large company could be expected to take over this commitment. The question of security of supply was fudged, as the Government noted that OFFER would have the power to review the situation (but it had no power to compel either the generators or the RECs) and that the Secretary of State would retain directive powers in a national emergency. Lastly, the Government argued that the new market disciplines would force the RECs to pursue efficiency improvements and that renewables would now face a level playing field.

From this brief survey, it is clear that the Bill proposed a major change in the structure of the industry, in that the once powerful CEGB and its associated 'insider' groups of coal and nuclear power were to lose their central position in UK energy policy. The corporatist core of British energy policy was to be broken-up and sold to the private sector, with only minimal public regulation of overall policy. The original thinking was that the regulatory role would be minimal, as real competition would quickly come to characterise the sector. (In practice, regulation has in fact become more intrusive over time.) These arrangements were to have a number of major implications for the future course of decision-making in the sector.

The first casualty of the privatisation of the electricity supply industry was the nuclear power programme to which the Government was also strongly committed. As noted above, the unbalanced generating duopoly was a result of the Government's attempt to transfer nuclear power to the private sector. But as the Bill made its way through

Parliament, the real economics of nuclear power were revealed, and the Government's advisers (the merchant bank Kleinwort Benson) made it clear that, even with the protection of the NFFO, National Power would not be an attractive prospect for the sector. At first, the Government responded by removing the older Magnox reactors from the sale. But in November 1989, the new Secretary of State for Energy, John Wakeham, not only announced the removal of the rest of the nuclear component from the sale but also stated that 'the non-fossil obligation will be set at a level which will be satisfied without the construction of new nuclear stations beyond Sizewell "B"'. The nuclear power stations were to be transferred to a new, wholly public sector company, Nuclear Electric, and the whole civil nuclear programme was to be reviewed again in 1994, the expected date for the commissioning of Sizewell 'B'.

The indigenous coal industry was the second sector to suffer from the new regime. Prior to privatisation, relations between the CEGB and British Coal (BC) were governed by long-term contracts at negotiated prices (known as the Joint Understanding). The expansion of the international trade in steam coal for power generation during the 1980s and falling demand had resulted in low prices on world markets. Although this coal represented only a tiny proportion of world coal production, and is in any case often subsidised, the CEGB was able to force BC steadily to cut prices. To begin with, the full impact of the 'market' was mitigated by the Government's acceptance of BC's case that the competitor fuels were at artificially low and unsustainable prices. The 1989 Monopolies and Mergers Commission Report on the investment programme of the coal industry, *British Coal Corporation* (Cmnd. 550), marked a shift away from this stance, suggesting that BC needed to 'think the unthinkable' with respect to exchange rate movements, competition from alternative fuels, and the possibility of rapid growth in the world coal trade. Moreover, despite large and continuing productivity improvements, in the short term BC could not compete with the current import prices of internationally-traded coal. Thus with the ending of the Joint Understanding and the negotiations with the new private generators in 1993, BC's position was weakened still further. The result was a significant contraction in the market for BC, and a major programme of colliery closures.

These developments were widely predicted by the Government's advisers, and by other observers, including the Commons Select Committee on Energy. In its Third Report, on *The Structure,*

Regulation and Economic Consequences of Electricity Supply in the Private Sector (1989), the Committee noted that:

> One of the most disturbing aspects of the Government's privatisation proposals is the uneven treatment it has given to the coal and nuclear industries. While the indigenous coal industry is left 'wholly or largely exposed to short-term forces in international coal and energy markets, which often do not reflect long-term marginal costs', it is proposed to offer nuclear power a protected share of the electricity market.

The widespread concern that Britain's long-term coal reserves were being sterilised as a result of the short-term operation of a rigged market, and that this might create economic and security-of-supply problems of energy import-dependence in the future, went entirely unheeded by the Government.

Indeed, the position of coal was further undermined by the so called 'dash to gas' undertaken by the new generating industry. The immediate context of the 'dash for gas' was created by the post-privatisation structure of the electricity supply industry. By creating a powerful duopoly between National Power and PowerGen, by taking nuclear power out of the market and protecting it, and by forming a protected franchise market for domestic and small consumers for the Regional Electricity Companies (about 70 per cent of the British market), the Government created a structure in which the RECs sought to protect themselves from the power of the generators by buying into alternative sources of supply. At the same time, advances in the technology of gas-fired power stations, in combination with the increasing environmental concerns about coal, seemed to make gas an obvious choice. To defend their market shares, and perhaps also to push up the price of gas, National Power and PowerGen followed suit. Hence the 'dash for gas'. (In this context it is worth noting that the period since the mid-1980s saw gas overtake coal in British energy production and consumption: in 1985 coal represented 24 per cent of total British fuel production and 30 per cent of consumption, while gas accounted for 16 per cent of production and 24 per cent of consumption; in 1993 coal accounted for 16 per cent of production and 22 per cent of consumption, while gas represented 26 per cent of production and 27 per cent of consumption.)

As in the case of coal imports, many have questioned the longer-term wisdom of allowing a premium fuel with only limited reserve to production ratios to shut out a long-term, indigenous source of supply. But with the deregulation of the UK gas industry, as British Gas has lost both its monopsonist position in respect of North Sea purchases and its monopoly position as supplier to the British market, the proposed creation of an internal market in gas within the EC, the growing concern over carbon emissions from coal-fired power stations, and the shorter construction times and lower capital costs of combined cycle gas stations, gas has (for the present at least) become an attractive proposition to the private sector generators.

The lobby for greater investment in energy efficiency, aimed at reducing energy demand rather than increasing energy supply, and the advocates of support for the development of renewable technologies, were the third interest group to be dissatisfied with the structure of the privatised electricity supply industry. The Government had argued that the RECs, National Power and PowerGen would have an incentive to improve energy efficiency because of their new competitive environment. Now it may be true that the generators faced increased pressures to improve the efficiency of their power stations (though many doubted that significant operating improvements over existing CEGB levels were technically possible), but under the new pricing formula for the RECs over 90 per cent of their profits and assets are tied to the distribution of electricity. Put simply, 'the more units of electricity they distribute the more profit they will make' (Roberts *et al.*, 1993, p. 131). They are under no obligations, and have precious few incentives, to invest in reducing energy *demand*. The ecological case on carbon gases and global warming also went unheard. For the industry and academic consensus is that only very limited reductions of carbon emissions can be expected from changes on the supply side, through alterations in the fuel mix and more efficient generating technologies. The most direct and obvious improvements are to be gained on the demand side, by a general increase in energy efficiency across the whole spectrum of energy use.

Finally, the legacy of the privatisation of the electricity supply industry for the renewable sector appears to be mixed. Under the old corporatist arrangements, with the powerful 'insider' status of coal and nuclear power and the supply-driven character of policy formation, renewables were marginalised. The vast bulk of the Government's R&D budget for energy went on nuclear power, and the Department of Energy even gave responsibility for testing renewable options to the Energy Technology Support Unit (ETSU), located at the UKAEA's Harwell laboratory. (Between 1979 and 1990, total government spending on renewables was some £145 m, while nuclear R&D amounted to about £200 m per year.) This resulted in many claims that ETSU's appraisal of alternative technologies was less than disinterested. In particular, a great deal of controversy surrounded ETSU's assessment of a technology for deriving electricity from wave power (Salter's Duck), and the Department of Energy was later forced to admit that false information had been provided. In this respect, then, the fragmentation of the electricity supply industry has (perhaps only temporarily) reduced the influence of the nuclear lobby. In addition, renewable sources have gained a very small degree of protection under the non-fossil fuel obligation imposed on the RECs. On the other hand, the new investment criteria of the private sector, which demand a shorter payback time and thus a higher discount rate than the public sector, have significant and generally adverse implications for the viability of alternative energy projects. Equally, the greater degree of market uncertainty in generating contracts, together with the continued reluctance of the Government to sponsor adequate R&D for renewables, makes it very difficult for a new technology to establish itself in the market.

In sum, the legacy of the privatisation of the electricity supply industry has been to derail the Government's own programme for a major expansion of nuclear power, to precipitate a large-scale contraction in the indigenous coal industry, to fail to address the problem of carbon emissions in power generation (except by the substitution of gas for coal) and to provide no support for the development of renewable technologies. In addition, the duopoly of the generators, justified by the unsustainable decision to privatise nuclear power, limited the degree of liberalisation achieved in the privatisation process. Finally, the shift of responsibility for supply from the generators to the RECs means that there are no mechanisms for guaranteeing that future supply will match demand.

In contrast to the BGC, which was privatised as a vertically integrated monopoly, the vertical integration of the CEGB was broken up and a more thorough liberalisation was pursued. Regulation of British Gas and the newly privatised electricity supply industry was by means of price cap, RPI-X regulation of their ability to set prices, overseen by OFGAS and OFFER respectively. Such oversight was to recede as competition in the gas and electricity industries advanced. As a leading free-market energy economist has observed: 'the very wide scope of regulation in privatised British utilities is a natural outcome of illiberal privatisation schemes' (Robinson 1993, 31). However, as an authoritative study of regulatory reform has noted, 'the scope, complexity, and

tightness of RPI-X regulation have so far increased over time'
(Armstrong *et al.*, p. 165). Moreover, the Office of Fair Trading and the
Monopolies and Mergers Commission have been routinely involved in
continuing oversight and industry regulation. Alongside price regulation, much of the regulatory activity has been directed towards active
promotion of competition. At the moment the situation is finely balanced, as Armstrong *et al.* conclude:

> The optimistic scenario is that effective and undistorted competition
> will emerge in those activities that are not naturally monopolistic,
> and can then be deregulated, and that the future regulation of remain-
> ing natural monopoly elements will create credible long-term incen-
> tive structures. A necessary (but not sufficient) condition for this is
> that the natural monopoly elements are separated either structurally
> or by very effective conduct regulation. The pessimistic scenario,
> however, is one of ineffective or distorted competition, and a need
> for increasing regulation of investment as well as prices and quality
> of service. At present the prospects are mixed.   (1994, p. 362)

4.6   Conclusions

Together with the abolition of the Department of Energy after the 1992
General Election, the overall result of these developments has thus been
the abandonment of a *national* energy policy for Britain and its replacement by industry-based regulatory authorities. Notwithstanding
significant political opposition to this drift within the UK, the only real
pressures for new forms of regulation in the direction of collective,
social objectives are now coming from the European Commission, with
its agenda of environmental taxes on energy, an increase in direct
investment by the energy industries in energy efficiency, and a shift to
least cost planning for distribution companies. Viewed from the perspective of this agenda, it is difficult to disagree with the assessment of
Roberts *et al.* that:

> Thatcherism developed as a response to the inherited problems of
> the 1970s, the problems of corporatism and overload. The arrival of
> the global environment onto the political agenda has made her ideol-
> ogy as outdated as that of Morrison. For the 1990s, the challenge is
> to find new political and institutional forms which can harness the

actions of individuals and sovereign states to collective purposes.
(1993, p. 191)

Assessed against these criteria, the privatisation of the electricity
supply industry (and of the British Gas Corporation) must be judged a
missed opportunity. On the positive side, however, the ease with which
a determined government was able to remove an entrenched and powerful corporate interest from the centre of UK energy policy suggests
that there are real opportunities for institutional innovation in the
policy-making process. The problem now is to devise ways of regulat-
ing a sector that is increasingly under the control of private capital and
whose markets are increasingly internationalised.

The critical assessment of the privatisation of the electricity supply
industry noted above, of course, assumes that the pattern of institutional
reform could have been done differently and that there can and should
be some kind of continuing public guidance or regulation of the energy
sector as a whole. But while there is little doubt that the break-up of the
electricity supply industry (and for that matter such other changes as
the privatisation of British Gas) could have been accomplished in other
ways, the second proposition is far from self-evident. The Conservative
changes in the energy sector, as in many other areas of industrial
policy, have been driven by the belief that old forms of (quasi) corporatist regulation merely resulted in the entrenchment of increasingly
inefficient producer interests within the policy-making process. The
new subordination to market disciplines seeks to overcome this legacy.
However, the Government has accepted the case (laid out in Chapter 1)
that where the privatisation of public utilities results in significant
market failure, particularly the existence of monopoly power, then there
is a liberal argument for public regulation.

As we saw in more detail in Chapter 1, this liberal stance has been
challenged from both the right and the left. The right have advanced
two rather different kinds of argument. In the first place, theorists of
public choice have argued that government failure is a far more systematic and significant presence than market failure. If this is so, then it
makes little sense to compare the reality of imperfect markets with the
presumed rationality of public actions, even if the latter are insulated
from the political process to the extent that most regulatory bodies now
are. A second line of attack comes from those who question the particular theory of markets underpinning notions of market failure, the neo-
classical theory of general equilibrium. Economists in the Austrian

school see the market not as a process tending towards equilibrium, deviations from which can then be assessed as 'failures' and corrected for by *policy*, but rather as a dynamic process of change in which competition effects the 'discovery' of new knowledge, techniques and practices, and innovations which by definition cannot be known in advance and therefore cannot be substituted for by practices of regulation. The burden of these arguments is that the less public regulation, the better. Policy should aim at lowering barriers to entry into the industries concerned, attending to genuine natural monopolies and to little else.

Critics from the left have argued that market relations need *more* rather than less regulation than the current arrangements allow, and that the environmental agenda in particular cannot be dealt with at all adequately through liberal, market-based solutions. The case for intervention here extends beyond the traditional concern with market failure and starts from observations about the nature of uncertainty much like those of the Austrian school. For the presence of real uncertainty (as opposed to risk) does not necessarily yield Hayekian conclusions about the need to minimise regulation, since it may be perfectly possible to devise alternative forms of regulation which are appropriate to outcomes which cannot be known in advance, such as the environmental impact of energy production and use. Indeed, there is a strong case to be made that, given that many kinds of energy production are irreversible, given that there may be important threshold effects in environmental pollution arising from energy use and given that such impacts are uncertain in the strong sense, only non-market forms of control can guarantee against some socially sub-optimal outcomes (see Dasgupta, 1982, and Perrings, 1987, for detailed discussions).

Thus, notwithstanding the domination of recent developments in British energy policy by the neo-liberal, conservative policy agenda, the debate on the scope and kind of market regulation desirable is by no means closed, either domestically or internationally. However, those seeking further and new kinds of regulation of the newly liberalised and privatised UK energy markets do face formidable tasks both of institution-building, at local, national and supra-national levels, and of empowering new constituencies such as consumers, environmentalists and renewable energy suppliers. The example of the privatisation of the electricity supply industry, supposedly one of the strongest and most protected parts of the corporate state, to say nothing of the near wholesale run-down of the coal industry, shows what is possible. The key questions for future energy policy will turn on whether similar kinds of enthusiasm and forcefulness can be mobilised in a more constructive direction (see Bromley, 1992, for a discussion of some Labour Party proposals).

5 Agriculture

Tom Burden

The focus of this chapter is on the distinctive nature of agricultural policy and the institutions which formulate and implement it. There are some problems in defining what is to come under the heading of agriculture; by convention forestry and fishing are often treated separately though, in reality, forestry is a crop and fish can be 'farmed'. Agriculture is unusual in being a private industry which has been comprehensively planned for the last fifty years. The aim here is to describe and explain the nature and determinants of policy and its impact on the operation of the industry.

5.1 Introduction

The proportion of GDP accounted for by agriculture is declining. Its importance varies from region to region (being high in East Anglia, and low in the South-East, for example). It is, however, a major industry in terms of the size of its output, which accounted for 1.7 per cent of GDP in 1991. There has been something of a neglect of agricultural *policy* in much of the academic literature on farming. Agricultural economics has often ignored the politics of agricultural policy. Agriculture has also been neglected in the context of industrial policy studies. It does not fit the predominant image of industry as involving factory production. In addition, agriculture does not figure in discussions of the role of the Department of Trade and Industry (DTI), the government department most closely associated with industrial policies. Uniquely, agriculture has a separate ministry responsible for policy towards it. It is also unusual because of the family farming tradition and the role played by the household in the work of the family enterprise: in 1985, 58 per cent of the labour input came from family members. It is further distinguished by the relatively small scale of its undertakings. It is also the industry most open to public view, since much of its work takes place in the open air. Finally, unlike most modern industries, it is highly competitive in the sense of having a vast number of competing productive units, none of which exercises anything like a monopoly position.

Farming generally makes heavy use of land, though some recently developed forms of factory farming are an exception to this. The land used is virtually fixed in supply and cannot be moved. Though it çan be improved, there are limits to what can be done given its location and initial state. As an investment it can increase in value even if no income is being generated from it. In 1971, 76.9 per cent of land in England and Wales was used for farming, with another 7.5 per cent used for forestry. The quality of agricultural land also varies regionally; in Wales and Scotland four-fifths of the agricultural land is unsuitable for raising crops compared to only a quarter in England. The fact that agriculture is a user of land, indeed that land is generally a key resource in agricultural production, means that issues concerned with the ownership of land are closely related to the workings of the agricultural industry.

It is worth remembering that throughout recorded history the production of food has formed the principal economic activity of the mass of the population. Much of English agriculture has been highly profit-orientated since the eighteenth century and the 'agricultural revolution'. Indeed, the efficiency of agriculture played an important enabling role in the industrial revolution, since it allowed food output to grow at the same time as the proportion of the workforce engaged in food production was falling. Agricultural policy was also at the centre of political controversy as the industrial revolution developed. In particular, it was in the interests of manufacturers generally that food should be cheaply available to their workers. The commitment to low food prices rather than agricultural protection goes right back to the conflict over the repeal of the corn laws in the 1840s. These laws kept up food prices by preventing the import of grain unless prices rose above a specified level, and their repeal in 1845 was an important victory for the principle of cheap food and free trade in agricultural products. It has also been seen as reflecting the growing political influence of industrial employers.

Cheap food remained an important issue: in the controversy over 'social imperialism' in the Edwardian period, Chamberlain and his supporters argued for 'tariff reform', by which they meant protectionist policies based on import controls. A key element in the failure of this movement was the belief that tariff reform would raise food prices.

The policy adopted towards agriculture is not simply a matter of technical argument over the best way in which to achieve agreed ends. The industry itself is viewed as being possessed of a fundamental social importance which goes far beyond its contribution to material production, important though this is. Agriculture, and the countryside in which it largely takes place and with which it is identified, are important social and political symbols with a powerful resonance. Throughout Europe rural society and the symbol of the family farm have often been portrayed politically as the authentic repository of national tradition, and have formed a base of support for nationalist and populist movements (Goodman and Redclift, 1986, pp. 35–7). Agriculture therefore occupies a special place in political debate and has an importance rather greater than its quantitative economic significance might seem to merit.

5.2   The structure of the industry

The industry is remarkably diverse, with a range of productive units differing in size, capitalisation, product, method of production, topography and soil. Most farming activities are affected by the soil and the topography. Crops are generally sensitive to growing conditions and can only be grown successfully in specific conditions; barley is an exception – it can be grown at high yields under a range of conditions, which accounts for its widespread popularity. Arable farming is concentrated in the south and east, with grassland (often for dairying) in the north and west. Uplands are generally used for sheep, while lower land is used for tillage or grass. Some forms of farming are not dependent on the use of land: the intensive rearing of poultry and pigs, which can be undertaken in barns with concrete floors, can be located anywhere. The increased rearing of animals indoors has also allowed more land to be brought into cultivation in areas where previously it was used for animals. In any particular place the type of farming undertaken is also affected by the proximity of major consumer markets or producer markets, such as food processing firms, for which crops may be grown under contract.

In 1987 there were 254 325 agricultural holdings in the UK. In Great Britain there were 289 000 farmers. The scale of the firms in the industry has changed and farms have grown larger, more capital-intensive, and more professionally managed. The smallest farms in terms of output tend to be found in the sheep and dairying sector. The degree of concentration in any particular part of the industry may depend on the available technology and its minimum efficient scale (how large the production unit has to be in order for costs to kept to the minimum possible with existing technology). For dairying this may be quite small, whereas for poultry, for example, it may be very large, since the advent of massive broiler houses. However, the process of concentration of ownership has been relatively slow because of the high value many farmers place on their independence, and their reluctance to sell out even when their profitability is in decline.

About 25 per cent of farmers farm part-time and thus supplement the family income from other sources. In Britain nearly half of those with additional non-farm incomes obtain them from self-employment. This is in contrast to the situation on the Continent, where wage labour is much more common. In Northern Ireland, where small farms predominate, part-time farming is very common and is often associated with beef and sheep production (which can more easily be undertaken without labour being continuously present).

Around 90 per cent of the land in the UK is owned by private individuals, 8.5 per cent by public bodies and around 2 per cent by City institutions. About 70 per cent of land in private holdings is owner-occupied, with the other 30 per cent let by landlords. Owner-occupation increased in the 1920s and again in the 1950s, with holdings being sold off. The proportion of farmland under owner-occupation has been increasing this century: 10 per cent in 1914, 36 per cent in 1927 and 61 per cent in 1973. The Northfield Committee of Inquiry, which reported in 1979, favoured the encouragement of the system of private landlords with tenant farmers, and justified on it on the traditional grounds of the responsible stewardship of the land that this encouraged.

Farming is an industry based largely on the hereditary ownership, or at least occupation, of land. Landownership occupies a central place in the constellation of interests found around agricultural policy. Though these interests are not as powerful as they once were, they still occupy an important place in British society and in the British economy, particularly when the distribution of wealth is considered. The gentry have declined as owners, though the great landowners remain, but there has been an increase in institutional ownership. Over three-quarters of full-time farmers have inherited their farms or the capital with which to purchase them. Regardless of ownership, those who run family farms are normally able to retain control and pass it on to their successors if they wish. Farmers differ in the extent of their market orientation and the extent to which they are directly involved in the everyday work of the farm (Newby, 1980, p.103). Farmers also differ on the priority they accord to environmental issues and conservation. Agribusiness is generally more ruthless in its pursuit of profit in contrast to the tradition of gentlemen farmers which is based on a more conservative ethic of 'stewardship'.

Legislation gives tenants considerable security of tenure. In the post-war period Labour Governments have tended to increase the security of tenant farmers rather than expand the rights of landlords to dispose freely of their property. The Agricultural Holdings Act of 1948 gave lifetime security for tenants and the protection of an Agricultural Land Tribunal in cases of dispute. An act of 1976 provided further security of tenure. However, statutory successional rights were removed in 1984, after being in force for eight years. The 1984 changes, introduced by a Conservative Government, represent an attempt to free the land market.

Land can represent an attractive investment to the City. City institutions have been expanding their holdings, mainly into prime arable land rather than evenly spread throughout farmed land. Some City institutions buy land as a long-term investment to hedge against inflation, and act simply as landlords without attempting to manage the farming on their holdings. Others have become actively involved in farm management by buying the land from the farmer and then letting it back at a rent. Active involvement may also take the form of a share in profits and providing advice, assistance and sometimes finance to increase profitability. Some City investors believe that owner-occupation is an archaic and inefficient form of tenure which sustains under-capitalisation and an inefficient structure. They believe that ownership needs to be separated from control for maximum efficiency so that those running farms can then be appointed on the basis of competence rather than through inheritance. Naturally this conflicts with the traditional view of the farming community, which is based on continuity of possession and family heritability. This is often ideologically reinforced by the notion of a mystical stewardship exercised by the guardians of rural values and agricultural expertise.

Over the post-war period output, yields and productivity have risen: with productivity increasing at above the rate for industry as a whole. However, British farming is not necessarily more efficient than that of all other European countries. Research in the 1950s and the 1970s, for example, showed that Holland, Belgium and Denmark had better financial and physical returns from farming (Brown, 1991, p. 195). An important part in the development of the industry has been played by the application of scientific knowledge. Indeed, in the period since 1940 agriculture has been transformed by the application of modern scientific knowledge. Government policy has played a role in the promotion of technical progress. The net cost of the Agricultural Development and Advisory Service and of state-financed agricultural research is around £200 m per year. Innovations have also come from developments in industries outside farming. The chemical industry has become a significant supplier, due to the increased utilisation of chemical knowledge in the production of animal feeds, weedkillers and fertilisers.

Farming has always progressed through improvements of livestock by selective breeding to give higher yields of meat and of products such as milk and wool, and to increase rates of breeding. These improvements are now also being effected by the application of bio-technology. Crops improvements, as well, are being sought using genetic engineering. In the past, improvements could only be made through cross-pollination – which meant that plants could only be crossed with close relatives. Genetic modifications mean that genes from a range of different plants, and even from animals, can be incorporated into crops. This has the potential to improve resistance to disease and pests, decrease perishability, and alter flavour and size.

The increased capital intensiveness of farming has brought agriculture into a close relationship with a number of the industries which supply it with inputs and which process its products. These industries include engineering, chemicals, and food processing. Linkages with processing firms can develop beyond simple purchase and sale relationships to various forms of partnership and even ownership. The most extreme form would be vertical integration, though this has not developed to the same degree in the UK as it has elsewhere, particularly in the USA. However, of the money paid out for food, the proportion which goes to farmers has continued to fall. Contract farming for food processing firms has developed substantially and this has further stimulated increased scale and specialisation in farming.

5.3   The policy community

The concept of a policy community involves a modified version of
pluralism. Policy communities are relatively secure and integrated
networks that monopolise policy-making in a particular policy area.
Agriculture has had what has been called a 'closed policy community'
(M. J. Smith, 1989, p. 151). It has been characterised by agreement on
the desirability of continued expansion, and for a long time it was
organised around the annual review of prices.

A range of government bodies has a part to play in the formulation
and implementation of agricultural policy. The most notable feature of
the administrative arrangements affecting agriculture is that the
Ministry of Agriculture, Fisheries and Food (MAFF) remains a powerful ministry in its own right, with cabinet membership for the minister.
This means that agricultural issues occupy a central and continuing
place at the centre of government industrial policy generally.

The main representative body for farmers is the National Farmers
Union (NFU), though more recently the growth of tenant farming
has received special representation with the formation in 1982 of
the Tenant Farmers Association. The NFU was formed in 1908 and
currently represents around three-quarters of all farmers. It provides
services for its membership at county level in dealing with the requirements of a range of government agencies and in getting available grants
from national and EU agencies. Though the NFU exists to represent all
farmers, there are divisions within the industry between large and small
farmers and between arable and livestock producers. Senior positions in
the NFU are generally held by those with a background in arable
farming.

The NFU has considerable influence in MAFF, which sponsors the
NFU by according it sole rights of consultation on farming issues. The
NFU employs a number of technical experts able to offer advice on
the details of policy. The relationship of MAFF and the NFU can be
viewed as a form of corporatism. Alternatively (as with the energy
sector in the last chapter), it may be taken as an example of policy-
making having been 'captured' by those to whom policy is directed.
This kind of relationship has been termed 'clientelism'. One result is
that other interests, such as those of consumers or agricultural workers,
do not have an effective voice in the policy process.

The NFU is an 'insider group' and seldom finds it necessary to
mobilise public demonstrations against the government. The

maintenance of its close relationship with MAFF is a key strategic concern and the NFU has often acquiesced in, and even supported, schemes which involved compulsion on farmers so long as this was organised through MAFF (for details, see Cox *et al.*, 1986, ch. 11). On the Continent, farming is generally on a smaller scale than that in the UK, and the farming lobbies tend to be dominated by the interests of smaller farmers. An interesting point of contrast between Britain and Europe, especially France, is the degree of militant organisation and action characteristic of French small farmers.

The political influence of farmers extends much further than the role of the NFU and forms part of the political framework, though the NFU itself maintains a stance of formal political neutrality. However, the Conservative Party has normally had a strong farming element represented in the party in rural constituencies, in local government and at Westminster. Research in 1967 showed that over a third of all rural district council members were farmers. In the past, rural councils have normally contained a strong farming interest which has been used in part to restrict rural council house building, leaving workers more dependent on tied houses provided by their employers. The re-organisation of local government in 1974 and the establishment of larger units has, however, reduced the power of the farming interest by putting rural areas under the control of councils with a stronger element of urban representation. Members of the traditional landowning class still play an important role in the Conservative Party and many of these see themselves as custodians of the farming interest. The special arrangements under which farming operated used sometimes to be explained with reference to the 'agricultural vote'. This has declined, but it is still significant: in 1959 56 farmers were elected to parliament; by 1983 this had fallen to 31. Over 90 per cent of those elected were Conservatives.

Another important part of the policy community is the Country Landowners Association (CLA). This promotes an ideology of 'stewardship' which depicts landowners as the true guardians of the traditional character of rural Britain. The exercise of this guardianship is portrayed as being best left to property owners, with the minimum of state intervention or constraints on their rights. The CLA has a membership of 40 000. It is a classic 'insider group', working in the corridors of Whitehall on the range of issues of concern to landowners – such as conservation, the taxation of property, and planning regulations (Newby, 1980, p. 58). Much of its prestige arises from the powerful position occupied by this section of the property-owning class in

British society and its continuing political importance – particularly in the House of Lords, where it is powerfully represented.

Other industries which are closely associated with agricultural production also play a part in policy-making. Suppliers of agricultural machinery have a strong interest in the prosperity of farming and in the encouragement of capital intensive methods which increase equipment sales. Modern farming methods rely heavily on agro-chemicals, used as fertilisers and for pesticides and herbicides. There is also a huge market for drugs of various kinds. The volume of City funds now invested in landownership adds a further voice to the claim that agricultural prosperity is of broad national benefit.

Organisations favouring continued expansion of and investment in farming are now confronted by some opposed interests. Consumer interests have had little influence over food policy since accession to the European Community in 1973 and the end of the cheap food policy which existed before that. However, in recent years there have been pressures for a move away from the high-tech methods of modern agribusiness with its emphasis on intensive farming. Alternatives based on organic farming are becoming significant in food retailing. These methods avoid chemical fertiliser, and intensive stock-rearing methods: farm animals are kept outside and untethered rather than in intensive rearing sheds. Schemes to label foods in a way that indicates the processes used to produce them have also been introduced in order to capitalise on environmental concerns about the conditions of food production.

The process of agricultural policy-making is becoming increasingly internationalised. Farm prices and many other aspects of policy are now determined by EU agriculture ministers sitting in the Council of Agricultural Ministers. The deliberations of the council constitute a relatively closed policy forum. The ministers each tend to promote the interests of 'their' farmers. Farm policy is further subject to international influence because the EU is itself a player on the international stage. For example, agriculture was a major issue in the last 'round' of GATT negotiations because of the highly protective nature of European agricultural policy. Agreements made at GATT can themselves constrain future EU policies.

Governments nowadays need to show a concern with environmental issues. The Department of the Environment is concerned with the use of the countryside for activities other than farming and may criticise the environmental damage caused by farming. Other conflicts within the machinery of government may occur. Some organisations acting on behalf of the state may be a focus for the working out of these divisions. The Countryside Commission, for example, has to try to reconcile farming and environmental interests where these conflict. Both the Countryside Commission and the Nature Conservancy Council are major state-sponsored bodies which organise links with a range of other pressure groups interested in their work. The 'policy communities' are large and active. In contrast, however, the groups concerned exclusively with agriculture are small in number and relatively exclusive (the NFU and the CLA) and this assists their ability to influence policy.

5.4   Agricultural policy up to 1947

Following the repeal of the Corn Laws in 1845, British agriculture was open to the world market. From the 1870s agricultural prices declined with the growth of foreign producers of meat and grain, and land prices fell. This produced an agricultural depression which helped to undermine the economic basis of landed wealth. The industry was unevenly developed: the extremes ran from large farms in East Anglia worked by tenants employing substantial numbers of workers, to small-scale, essentially peasant farming, in outlying areas.

Large-scale state intervention in agriculture was first established during the First World War. The system of guaranteed prices and deficiency payments dates from 1917, when guaranteed prices for potatoes, wheat and oats were introduced. When prices fell below the designated level, the difference was made up in Ministry payments to farmers. Following the war, the 1920 Agriculture Act established a widespread system of price support for cereals, but this was summarily abandoned in 1921 in order to hold down state expenditure in the crisis conditions of the time. Throughout the 1920s a largely free market prevailed. Many farmers were strongly wedded to the virtues of free markets, disliked the experience of controls in wartime, and supported the repeal of the 1921 Act. Later however, as prices fell, the repeal came to be referred to as a 'great betrayal'. In the four years after the First World War a quarter of the land in the UK changed hands, as old estates were sold off, bringing into existence a vastly expanded class of owner-occupier farmers. The industry was severely weakened in the inter-war period. Land prices continued to fall and the industry was depressed. Prices did not regain their 1870s level until the 1940s.

Throughout the century, until Britain joined the EC, the role played by protectionism was small. Some attempts to revive and reorganise agriculture were made in the 1930s. At this time the policy community was relatively open and was subject to a range of pressures, including the influence of the imperial dominions and of industry seeking low food prices. Few protective tariffs were imposed on agricultural goods due to the system of Imperial Preference under which goods from the Empire were allowed free entry to Britain. However, import duties were imposed on beef and veal, and there were quotas for bacon and beef imports. The state attempted to manage markets in order to stabilise demand. Acts of 1931 and 1933 set up marketing boards for milk, potatoes and pigs. Price supports for wheat were introduced in the Wheat Act of 1932, again using a system of deficiency payments. Facilities were made available for providing credit, and improvements in the scientific base of agriculture was encouraged through the establishment of the Agricultural Research Council. By the outbreak of the Second World War a substantial array of policy instruments was in place and the agricultural industry was beginning to modernise.

Following the outbreak of war in 1939, state economic intervention was expanded. The authorities were particularly concerned to ensure the maintenance of food supplies. The disruption of trade caused by the naval blockade and the attacks on shipping led to a drive to increase domestic production. The Government was also concerned with the health implications of diet. During the Second World War, mechanisms for the maintenance of working class standards of food consumption included rationing, though at the same time the Government sought through every means possible to increase domestic food output.

Agriculture was totally and permanently transformed by the war. The changes made give an exceptional illustration of the impact of a thorough policy of state control as well as examples of a range of modes of intervention, some involving physical planning controls. County War Agricultural Committees were established. Appointed by the minister, these had around ten members (including one woman and one trade unionist). They devolved authority to about 500 district committees of four to six members, each responsible for dealing with a number of farms. Farms were visited and graded for quality, and assistance was 'given' to those with a low grade. Farmers could be dispossessed if they failed to follow instructions. Targets for ploughing were set; the use of machinery and chemical fertilisers became more widespread; some technical innovations in cropping patterns and live-stock feeding took place; and grants were given for improving land by clearing and draining. Farms had guaranteed prices and guaranteed markets. The Ministry was closely linked with the NFU, which became involved in making and implementing policy (Calder, 1969, p. 424). Because prices were high enough to encourage marginal producers, they produced massive profits for the efficient, and when the government tried to reduce these with the 1943 price review there was considerable protest.

Agricultural wages and farm income increased, as did trade union membership amongst farm workers. The 500 000 male farm workers were supplemented by 80 000 women members of the land army in 1940, over a third of them employed as mobile gang labour. Household agricultural production was also increased substantially, encouraged by the 'Dig for Victory' campaign: by 1944, 25 per cent of egg production came from this source. There was an enormous shift from grassland to crop growing, with the area of arable land increased by 50 per cent and the grassland reduced. Yields also improved and the calorific value of total food production was nearly doubled by 1944 (Calder, 1969, pp. 411–30; Brown, 1991, p. 183).

5.5   Agricultural policy after 1947

Following the Second World War the Labour Government favoured a 'cheap food' policy. Cheap food required a policy of subsidies rather than tariffs, simply because of the high level of food imports and the impossibility of self-sufficiency. Domestically, the policy, in effect, involved a continuation and expansion of the wartime system, though in conditions where trade was restored.

The 1947 Agriculture Act was the central pillar of agricultural policy. The Act took as its aim the:

> promoting and maintaining … [of] a stable and efficient agricultural industry capable of producing such part of the nation's food and other agricultural produce as in the national interest it is desirable to produce in the United Kingdom, and of producing it at minimum prices consistent with proper remuneration and living conditions for farmers and workers in agriculture and an adequate return on capital invested in the industry.   (Hill, 1989, p. 22)

The objectives of agricultural policy in general terms were: to maintain income levels in order to allow an orderly contraction in the number of farmers and farmworkers; to increase efficiency and expand production; to ensure stability in prices and output; and to hold down imports of food.

The 1947 Act employed the system of 'deficiency payments' under which the government designated a price sufficient to ensure profitability. If market prices fell below this, farmers were paid the difference by the state. At the same time, agricultural imports were relatively unrestricted, allowing in cheap food from abroad. An annual price review set prices for the main products. The prices set were used to reimburse most, but not all, of the yearly rise in costs, thus giving an incentive for improvements in efficiency. Orderly markets were encouraged through the establishment of marketing boards, and sometimes quotas were set for the import of certain products to protect vulnerable domestic producers. Subsidies and grants were available to facilitate investment, thus encouraging mechanisation. Policies were also developed to improve the technical quality of farming production. There were controls on farm safety; the use of dangerous chemicals such as pesticides and drugs; crop diseases; animal health and welfare; and measures for controlling pests. The Agricultural Development and Advisory Service (ADAS) was set up to provide free advice for farmers and to encourage 'good practice'. Research on agriculture and food was financed and commissioned by the MAFF.

The stability referred to in the 1947 Act meant adequate incomes for farmers and farmworkers and an adequate return for landowners. However, this meant in practice the maintenance of the status quo: farmworkers in particular gained little from these arrangements and they remained close to the bottom of the wages league.

Until 1954 the Ministry of Food purchased all output and sold it on at lower prices in order to subsidise consumption. Marketing Boards were set up for milk, wool, hops, potatoes, and eggs (from 1957) and these covered 44 per cent of all output by 1957–8. The privileged position of farming was cemented by the Agriculture Act of 1957. This gave farmers the long-term assurance they had always sought. It restricted the ability of governments to alter prices under the annual review: in any one year the guaranteed price of any product could not be cut by more than 4 per cent, the total value of the guarantees could not be cut by more than 2.5 per cent, and livestock prices could not be cut by more than 3 per cent. These provisions led to increasing support costs. In the early 1960s the Government limited the full guaranteed price paid to farmers to a fixed volume of output and reduced the price paid for output in excess of this. However, the costs of agricultural support continued to rise.

Throughout the post-war period a constant underlying theme of policy towards agriculture and the countryside more generally has been a belief in the preservation of rural life. This concern has formed a major component of the ideology of planning which has dominated state policies on land use. It rested on the assumption that the existing pattern of rural life was of benefit to all and should be preserved. This has allowed the maintenance of the traditional relationship between agricultural labour and those who employ it. Land used for agriculture was normally excluded from the requirement to obtain planning permission for development. Even when the planning system was substantially amended by the 1968 Planning Act agriculture was little affected. However, in the 1980s farm building was partially controlled. The general tenor of rural planning has remained preservationist: which means in effect that restrictions on rural development, and on employment opportunities, are maintained to the detriment, in particular, of existing workers who find there is little competition for their labour.

5.6   The impact of EC membership

Since the UK joined the European Community in 1973, British agricultural policy has been determined principally by that pursued by the EC. The main immediate change involved a move from a system based on using taxation to support farm incomes to one based on manipulating the prices paid by consumers. British agriculture occupies a distinctive place in the EC (see Table 5.1). The UK has the smallest proportion of its population in agriculture, 2.4 per cent – in contrast to Greece, which has the largest proportion, at 27 per cent – but Britain has the largest agricultural holdings. The UK receives 8 per cent of EC expenditure on agricultural support through the CAP, compared to receipts of 12 per cent for the Netherlands, 17 per cent each for Germany and Italy and 24 per cent for France.

The Common Agricultural Policy (CAP) is the main form of economic intervention organised by the EC. In the 1970s it took about two-thirds of the budget and made up about 80 per cent of the substantive expenditure, if the money spent on EC administration is excluded. The

Table 5.1 EC agriculture and the Common Agricultural Policy

	EC12	Belgium	Denmark	W. Germany	Greece	Spain	France	Ireland	Italy	Luxembourg	Netherlands	Portugal	UK
% of employed population in agriculture (1987)	8.0	2.8	6.5	5.2	27.0	15.1	7.1	15.4	10.5	3.7	4.7	22.2	2.4
% share of agriculture in GDP (1986)	3.5	2.6	5.1	2.0	14.4	5.6	3.9	9.7	5.2	2.7	4.7	na	3.4
% of household consumption going on food	21.9	21.6	23.8	17.3	40.3	27.6	20.7	43.2	25.2	23.3	19.5	38.6	19.2
% of total EC agricultural land	100	1.1	2.2	9.3	4.5	21.1	24.3	4.4	13.5	0.1	1.6	3.5	14.4
% of EAGGF farm support funds received (1987)		3.5	4.6	17.2	5.8	2.6	24.5	4.1	17.0	—	11.8	0.6	8.2
No. of holding in 1986 (000s)		81.5	88.8	707.8	na	na	1000.0	na	na	3.9	118.9	na	242.4
Average size of holdings in 1986 (Hect)	16.9	16.9	31.71	16.8	na	na	28.2	22.7	na	32.5	16.9	8.9	69.3

SOURCES: Adapted from Burrell *et al.* (1990) pp. 159 and 184.

objectives of the CAP are set out in Article 39 of the Treaty of Rome (Hill, 1989, ch. 2). In the Treaty it is stated that the CAP shall have as its objectives:

(i)   to increase agricultural productivity by developing technical progress and by ensuring the rational development of agricultural production and the optimum utilisation of the factors of production, particularly labour;
(ii) to ensure thereby a fair standard of living for the agricultural population, particularly by the increasing of the individual earnings of persons engaged in agriculture;
(iii) to stabilise markets;
(iv) to guarantee regular supplies; and
(v)   to ensure reasonable prices in supplies to consumers.

The Treaty also required the following factors to be taken into consideration:

• the particular nature of agricultural activity, which results from the social structure of agriculture and from structural and natural disparities between the various agricultural regions;
• the need to effect any appropriate adjustment by degrees;
• that in the member states the agricultural sector is closely linked with the national economy as a whole.

The system of farm support which is the basis of the CAP rests on high tariffs to discourage imports and the maintenance of prices higher than the world market price. The Agriculture Council sets a series of prices around which the policy is organised. For each of the products covered there is a target price, a threshold price and an intervention price. The *target price* is set to give a satisfactory standard of living to a farmer dependent on that product in the least favourable area of the Community. The *threshold price* is the lowest price at which imports from outside the EC are permitted. A levy is imposed to bring imports up to the threshold price. The *intervention price* is the price at which the Commission intervenes to buy up the surplus until the price rises. It represents a guaranteed price for the producers.

The policy often results in the accumulation of stored surpluses. These can be dealt with in a number of ways: they can be sold in the EC if prices rise above the target price; they can be exported at the world market price, with exporters receiving a subsidy; they can be given to Third World states; they can be distributed to the poor or elderly or to hospitals and charities within the EC; or they can be destroyed. The subsidy system is unevenly applied. In relation to the total value of each crop, cereals, milk, sugar and oil seeds are over-subsidised and fruit, vegetables, pigs and poultry are under-subsidised. As self-sufficiency reaches or exceeds 100 per cent in particular products the EU has to store, export (with subsidies) or destroy the surplus. This has given rise to pressure from within the EU to reduce surpluses. Other governments have also protested at surpluses being dumped on the world market.

As a result of the CAP, the EC has become a major 'exporter' of food, though many claim that these exports often amount to little more than 'dumping' – pricing goods for export below the cost of production in order to obtain a market for them. On the other hand, imports of food which would take place in the absence of the external tariff do not take place. This has a favourable effect on the European balance of payments, but has come at the expense of higher prices for consumers, including those who purchase agricultural products in order to feed livestock.

The costs of agricultural support are paid directly by the consumer, and indirectly through the system of community funding. The main 'cost' to the public comes from the external tariff of the EC (now EU) which denies consumers access to agricultural products at world prices. At times during the 1980s world EC prices were double those in the world market. The MAFF calculates the impact as an increase of 8–10 per cent over what they would have been with access to the world market. If we ignore other EC payments of the UK, the net budgetary cost of EC membership for the UK is the difference between UK receipts from the European Agricultural Guidance and Guarantee Fund (EAGGF) for farm support and the payments made into the EC budget. The net cost was over £350m a year throughout the 1980s (Burrell *et al.*, 1990, p. 11). The impact on British farming has been to increase profits, since prices have generally been higher than those set under the system of deficiency payments. The main gainers have been large arable farms; small farms which produce less receive less in subsidies.

Until the late 1970s the CAP was not generally a subject of political controversy. On the contrary, it was seen as proving that national policies could be replaced by harmonised supranational arrangements at

EC level. In the 1980s, however, a more critical attitude began to develop: the CAP was wasteful; it involved over-production symbolised by wine lakes and butter mountains; it was open to fraud; it took up far too much of the EC budget; it violated the principles of the free market; and it encouraged over-intensive and ecologically damaging agriculture.

The Conservative Government elected in 1979 was committed to restraining expenditure under the CAP as well as to support for agriculture. The inconsistency in this stance was reflected in the different views taken by the two key ministries. The Treasury was in favour of cutting public expenditure, while MAFF was pursuing the traditional policy of support for British farming. However, the decisions on agricultural prices were made by the EC Council of Agricultural Ministers, where the Treasury had little influence.

The policy of support for continued expansion of agricultural output continued in the early 1980s along with the increased support prices that this required. Policy appeared to shift in 1983 (M. J. Smith, 1992, p. 140), with more criticism of the CAP and an apparent move away from exclusive concern with increasing output. Expenditure on agricultural research and on capital grants to farmers was cut. The Conservative Party manifesto for the 1987 General Election called for 'radical overhaul of the CAP'. Criticism of the CAP was also a central element in the general critique of the EC developed by the Conservative right wing. At the same time the CAP and modern farming methods were also being extensively criticised by some consumer groups and by environmentalists.

Expenditure under the CAP has always proved difficult to control. Reform was initiated by the Council of Agricultural Ministers. In the 1980s the EC began to attempt to limit farm production by introducing production quotas, and in 1984 milk quotas were brought in. Other schemes have included guidelines for limiting production of cereals, wine, oil seed, sugar and tomatoes. The main effect of quotas has been a shift to other forms of production which themselves were already in surplus – for example, a huge expansion in the production of oil-seed rape in the UK. Subsidies for oil-producing plants rose from 3.6 per cent of the total in 1984 to over 10 per cent by 1990. For some major crops the 'stabiliser' system reduces the price for that part of output which exceeds the quota.

What were claimed to be significant reforms of the CAP took place in 1988. These attempted to redefine the objectives of policy more broadly as part of an overall plan for rural areas, in which EAGGF funds are co-ordinated with those of the European Social Fund and the European Regional Development Fund. However, the extent of 'reform' is debatable, since planned expenditure on agricultural support was budgeted to increase, though by less than the overall EC budget – in effect, it will continue to rise but the other budgets will rise faster. The reforms of the 1980s have had some effect on the overall pattern of EC expenditure: between 1980 and 1993 spending on agricultural subsidies fell from 70.9 per cent of the budget to 49.3 per cent. In the same period expenditure on the European Regional Development Fund and the Social Fund rose from 11.7 per cent to 32.1 per cent.

However, these measures did not lead to a cut in the costs of the CAP, which continued to rise in the late 1980s. This was partly because very expensive export subsidies were used to dispose of excess stocks of farm produce. The reforms of 1988 appeared to set strict limits on CAP expenditure: beef and cereal prices fell and intervention stocks were cut. Farm incomes in Britain also fell. However, by 1990 intervention stocks were increasing again and the EC agriculture budget was again rising. The fundamentals of the CAP – support prices, import levies, intervention stocks and subsidised exports – still remain. Farmers receive prices for their produce which are far above world market levels. Policy is still made in a forum dominated by the interests of producers rather than any other group or interest. Despite its attachment to the rhetoric and sometimes the practice of free market principles, the UK government sought to reform the CAP but not to abolish it.

Further major reforms were introduced in 1992. The MacSharry reforms were portrayed as 'radical' and 'historic'. Designed to reduce the over-production of agricultural produce which costs the EU around £25 bn a year, their stated aim was to bring farm spending under control without making farmers any worse off financially. The reforms involved price cuts of 29 per cent for cereals, 15 per cent for beef and cuts in production quotas for dairy farmers, with quotas for beef and sheep producers. Agricultural export subsidies were reduced by 35 per cent, and medium and large-scale cereal farmers had to set aside 15 per cent of their land.

Set-aside involves paying farmers to let land lie idle. In 1993 farmers who set aside 15 per cent of their cultivated land were paid £200 per hectare. More than £1.1 bn is now being paid to 33 000 farmers, seven of whom will receive over £500 000. Despite the set-aside programme, EU food crop production only fell by 3 per cent, possibly because many farmers increased production in the fields they did use. Farmers can grow non-food crops on the set-aside land: these can include cannabis for paper-making and fibreboard, linseed for chemicals, oil seeds for lubrication, and grain for industrial starch. In the near future biofuels are likely to become an important farm product. Liquid biofuels include ethanol produced by fermenting starches and sugars, and diesel fuel from rape seed oil. However, the environmental benefits are small, since high energy inputs are needed for intensive cultivation, manufacture of fertiliser and harvesting, processing and distribution. The introduction of the set-aside scheme has also involved an attempt to meet some of the concerns of the environmentalists. Farmers can opt for a permanent set-aside lasting for five years or more, and create 'wildlife corridors' around their fields. The 1994 set-aside rules contain instructions on when to cultivate fields in order to protect wildlife, and minimise nitrate run-off and soil erosion.

The UK has been particularly critical of the CAP, partly because in overall financial terms the UK has not benefited from it. In 1989 the UK contributed 14.8 per cent of the total contribution to the EC and received 9.5 per cent of the budgetary expenditure. The entry of Spain and Portugal into the EC exacerbated the problem of surpluses and the pressure for reform became more intense.

Further policy changes in agriculture have been set in train by the GATT negotiations completed in 1993–4. The GATT deal necessitates further reform of the CAP. Between 1994 and 1999 farm product prices within the EC will have to fall by 20 per cent; all import tariffs must be reduced by 36 per cent; the volume of subsidised farm product exports must be cut by 21 per cent; and EC oil-seed farming must be restricted to around 5 million hectares, with a further one million hectares for non-food uses such as biofuel.

5.7 Conclusion

The overall impact of policy is hard to assess, since we do not know what would have happened without support. It is not easy to compare British agriculture with the very different agricultural industries of other states, and neither is it easy to compare it with other industries within the UK. Certainly the industry has survived, unlike some others, though whether the cost of achieving this has been matched by benefits is open to debate.

In terms of policy objectives, farm incomes have been maintained. Viewed another way, however, the state has guaranteed the incomes of inefficient producers. An evident contradiction in policy lies with the attempt to increase efficiency at the same time as supporting small farmers in order to prevent a precipitous decline in the industry. Although not all farmers are equally attuned to purely economic rationality, policy has generally been devised on the assumption that they are. The main 'problem' from the point of view of the state concerns small farms, which are viewed as inefficient and under-capitalised, but which have proved remarkably persistent despite the often low returns received by those who work them.

Agriculture has not experienced the decline in output characteristic of other long-established industries. The returns from agriculture are maintained at an artificially high level by current policies. Farmers also benefit from special tax arrangements: most notably from the exclusion of agricultural land from the rating system, a 'tax benefit' worth £450 m in 1987–8. One major effect of policy, and indeed of the technical changes which have taken place, has been to reduce the degree of risk from the weather. Risks associated with market fluctuations have also been reduced due to price controls. These reductions in risk might be seen as reasons to justify a lower rate of return on assets or at least a reduction of state support.

In so far as increased output and greater self-sufficiency have been objectives of policy, then the outcome could be seen as a success. The degree of self-sufficiency achieved can be indicated by the proportion of food consumption made up of food produced in the UK. In the mid-1950s this was around 55 per cent. In the 1980s it peaked at 62.9 per cent in 1984. The figure has now fallen to about 57 per cent partly due to the vogue for exotic foods and for fresh vegetables out of season. However, around 75 per cent of all food which can be grown in the UK is now produced domestically compared with a figure of 60 per cent in 1970.

The agricultural workforce has declined from 505 000 full-time workers in 1960 to 134 000 in 1986 (Burrell *et al.*, 1990, p. 40). Decline has been greatest in those areas where there has been substantial competition for labour from industry, and there has been an increase in the numbers of part-time and female workers. Both the wages and the range of earnings are low (minimum wage levels are laid down by an agricultural wages board). The consistent replacement of labour by capital and the lack of alternative rural employment, partly caused by planning regulations restricting rural industrial development, have kept the demand for labour down. There has been an increase in the gap between agricultural and other wages: wage levels of farm workers are about 75 per cent of those of industrial manual workers and they are close to the bottom of the wages league. In 1982, 38 per cent of male farm workers had incomes below the poverty line (Burrell *et al.*, 1990, p. 50).

The over-expansion of the industry has certainly resulted in an over-provision of agricultural land, some of which is now unused. There are, however, serious obstacles in the path of smooth adjustment to a more realistic policy. A fall in agricultural land prices would itself destabilise the structure of the industry, due to its effects on debt and City invest-ment in agricultural land. One major impact of the policies pursued has been to confer benefits on the owners of land, a category which now also includes most farmers. More controversially, the issue of landown-ership and of the returns from it has remained absent from the political agenda – an outcome that accords with the aspirations of the CLA, and indeed of the NFU.

In line with arguments about the superiority of unregulated markets, of the kind laid out in Chapter 1, it has often been claimed that the diversion of funds to agriculture has resulted in unemployment else-where. The alternative would be to free agricultural markets. According to its critics, the system of support is expensive and uneconomic: it has reduced employment by encouraging arable farming at the expense of livestock; it has cut off supplies of cheap imported food from outside the EU; and the main beneficiaries have been large farmers. The former head of the Economic and Social Research Council has forecast that if present policies continue, 30 per cent of all farmland in Britain will have come out of agricultural use by 1995–6, with payments of £4–£5 bn to the occupiers of up to 10 million acres. He predicts a rapid move to free-market economics in agriculture and serious dislocation to the present system. This process is also being encouraged by international pressures: the recent Uruguay round of GATT negotiations nearly col-lapsed because of the problem in getting the EU to agree to reduce agri-cultural subsidies.

Some commentators view the system of price support itself as a problem rather than a solution:

The basic mistake, which is older than the CAP, is the belief that stable and adequate incomes for farmers can be achieved through agricultural price support. As historical experience has vividly demonstrated, this instrument is neither effective nor efficient. It is not effective because the development of producer prices has not ensured an adequate level of income for small-scale farmers – which is one of the principal objectives of the CAP – but has generated windfall gains for more efficient large-scale farmers. It is not efficient because aiming at stable and adequate incomes for all farmers has led to output and welfare losses for the economy as a whole.   (Rosenblatt *et al.*, 1988, p. 3)

The shift of the centre of decision-making to the EU has altered the relative influence of the traditional policy community of farming in the UK, and British farmers are now much less in control of policy through their representative organisation than they were previously. However, though this may produce something of a redistribution of benefits, farmers are still the beneficiaries of a policy which channels funds to them largely through the maintenance of high food prices. Indeed, because of the relatively high level of efficiency of UK farming and the fact that the EU policy is adjusted to the 'needs' of much less efficient agricultural sectors, British farmers benefit disproportionately. Overall, in the UK the costs of current agricultural policies appear to be much more widely distributed than the benefits.

6 Labour, Skills and Training

Alan Tuckman

6.1 Introduction

This chapter examines government vocational and education policy (VET) since the 1960s. The availability of skilled labour is one of the main conditions for effective industrial policy, and the support of training for future skill needs might therefore be seen as an important investment. The 1960s are significant since, although the state had long assumed central responsibility for educational provision, it was only then that it began to assume a role in the vocational training system. Before the 1960s, successive governments had paid little attention to work preparation in schools, to the immediate training needs of young people entering employment, or to the needs of existing employees facing changing demands for their skills or longer-term career development. Rather, governments had maintained a broadly *laissez-faire* approach, leaving the design of school curricula to Oxbridge-dominated examination boards, and vesting responsibility for the provision of training in the individual worker and employer. A chaotic, haphazard, and ultimately inadequate VET system was the consequence.

Until the 1960s the training of manual workers remained dominated by systems of apprenticeship which provided entry into the craft trades for a minority of male school-leavers. Though the system constituted the major form of provision of skilled labour for traditional industries, in some cases it involved only a minimal amount of formal instruction within a period of 'time-serving' that extended for between 4 and 7 years, depending on the trade. Some employers of manual workers provided systematic training schemes for technicians and non-craft workers as well, although this was relatively rare, and was confined in the main to large public and private sector employers. Most manual workers received little formal training. Skills were often acquired through mobility within the labour market, supported by courses provided in technical colleges and monitored by a range of examining boards and professional bodies. Recruitment to management positions was rarely on the basis of formal educational qualification at all, but was achieved through on-the-job experience, with many managers picking up supplementary qualifications in the non-managerial professions. British industrial management prior to the 1960s was typically drawn from professionally trained accountancy – which itself shunned graduate recruitment – and not, as in Germany and the USA, from the ranks of professional engineers.

It was not until the 1960s, with the passing of the Industrial Training Act, that there was any government attempt at systematic reform of VET. There then followed three decades of major reforms. First came the establishment of industrial training boards, on which both employers and trade unions were represented, with responsibility for meeting the projected training needs of distinct industrial and service sectors. Next came the creation of the Manpower Services Commission (MSC), with broad responsibility in the 1970s for forecasting skill needs and training provision. The MSC, as an agency of the Department of Employment, also became responsible for a range of job creation and work experience schemes. Paradoxically the ascendancy of the MSC also coincided with the break-up of the post-war consensus, the abandonment of full employment policy, the rejection of corporatist strategies, and the rolling back of the state by the Thatcher Government. In its second, Thatcherite, incarnation the MSC became the instrument through which Conservative ministers undermined alternative interests in training and education, particularly the local authorities and trade unions, and constructed their own agenda on unemployment, and on how best to manage the consequences of the decline of manufacturing and traditional industries. By the mid 1980s the influence and powers of the MSC, no longer concerned with long-term manpower planning, had spread from control of schemes for the unemployed into the shaping of the content of mainstream education. Subsequent reform in the 1990s has seen the devolvement of training management and planning from the MSC to employer-dominated local bodies (Training and Enterprise Councils for England and Wales and Local Enterprise

Companies in Scotland). The three decades of reform have closed with the Major Government claiming a 'training revolution', through the establishment of this new employer-led structure of training provision, and through the creation of a new, unified system of vocational qualifications.

6.2 Training into the 1960s

Well into the 1960s, apprenticeship schemes dominated the training of manual workers in Britain, with profound implications for the development of an overall training policy. For, despite the experience of countries such as France and Germany (where reformed apprenticeship systems have been the focus of government training policies), in Britain apprenticeship effectively allowed training to be kept out of government hands altogether. The apprenticeship system also perpetuated divisions within the labour market: not just between the apprenticeship-trained craft workers and his or her semi-skilled and unskilled colleagues, but also between male and female employment roles. Until the 1970s around a third of boys of school-leaving age entered work through an apprenticeship scheme, compared with only about 7 per cent of girls – virtually all in the service sector.

Rooted in the medieval guild system, apprenticeship remained based on a period of 'time-serving' alongside a skilled worker. Apprentices would learn the 'mysteries' of the trade, the techniques and methods, guarded by craft organisations, of working particular materials. Though not formally examined, the apprentice and journeyman craftsman had to demonstrate proficiency in the work of the craft. In this way, the apprenticeship system reproduced the existing skilled labour force and existing demarcations between crafts, and also socialised the apprentice into the whole culture of work and trade union organisation. As Keep and Mayhew noted, 'the ethos of the apprenticeship was in many respects as much about offering an indoctrination in the ideology of the craft and its union, as it was about the acquisition of skills' (Keep and Mayhew, 1988, p. vi). Apprenticeship, then, defined the craft worker's position within the labour market and his or her relationship with other workers.

But over the post-war period as a whole, apprenticeship became increasingly marginalised, as technological change and mass production by-passed craft methods by requiring predominantly repetitive performance of routine tasks. Within the new semi-automated manufacturing industries, craft workers remained as the maintenance crew for the new production systems. Many traditional crafts also became submerged within the 'sweated trades' where a time-serving apprenticeship became the excuse for a period of low pay. Craft traditions remained in a number of industries – such as engineering, construction and what was left of shipbuilding – which still required workers to perform flexibly on a range of variable, often customised, production processes and products. Beyond these industries, apprenticeship remained as a mode of entry into a number of other trades, like butchering and bakery. But here, other less formal systems of training co-existed with apprenticeship, each requiring new young entrants to the trade to work alongside a more skilled worker, so to pick up methods and techniques. 'Improvers' would work with machine operators until they were capable of replacing them or until a vacancy arose on a similar machine, and so on.

A high level of skilled labour became doubly important in the postwar British context of low levels of investment in new machines. It provided a workforce conversant with the idiosyncrasies of ageing equipment and competent to keep it in operation. It also provided core, experienced, workers able to move into supervision, inspection and quality assurance. Around a hundred National Apprenticeship Agreements were reached in the 1940s, each attempting to enhance the time-serving, on-the-job experience by day release courses for apprenticeship tied to nationally recognised vocational qualifications – principally of the City and Guilds. Although this became the established practice in some areas, it proved far from universal, and in fact

> by the late fifties a fair degree of consensus existed among many commentators, that leaving training to the enlightened self-interest of individual employers under a voluntary system had not in the majority of cases produced much improvement in quality and quantity on pre-war levels and was unlikely to produce manpower planning beyond the short-term dictates of the market. (Lee, 1979, p. 40)

6.3   Government intervention in training 1964–89

By the 1960s it was increasingly recognised in industrial and governmental circles that some form of state action was needed to provide the framework and funding for a coherent training policy designed to meet the long-term demands of the labour market. From models of VET developed elsewhere we can identify three directions that the government might have taken in attempting to implement reform (see Sheldrake and Vickerstaff, 1987, p. 55). Both the USA and Japan depend heavily on *free market* provision of training. In the USA the system is dominated by private provision by training colleges, while Japan has become increasingly noted for the extent of in-house training provided by employers. To some extent it was precisely the failings of British employers to provide or fund a VET system of this kind that led to moves for reform in the 1960s. A further problem in implementing such a 'free market' system in Britain also rests on its apparent dependence on a longer period of secondary education. In both the USA and Japan the school-leaving age remains significantly higher than in Britain, with a far larger proportion of the age group going on to higher education. France, in contrast, offers a highly *interventionist* model, with extensive state provision through state vocational schools funded by a tax on employers, the *taxe d'apprentissage*. Then there is Germany, which not only has a prestigious system of vocational education institutions training engineers and technologists, but has also developed a system of training under *joint regulation* of employers and unions, funded by employers and the state. In the German model, training is highly organised within nationally agreed programmes for each sector, with supervision from a qualified master of the particular trade or occupation.

Until the 1960s Britain had largely followed a 'free market' model, although increasingly this had been supplemented by state-supported training provided off-the-job at further education colleges. Then, in 1964, in a significant change of direction, a Conservative Government introduced – with cross-party support – the Industrial Training Act. The Act established a Central Training Council (CTC) to oversee general training strategy and to deal with issues – such as provision for clerical occupations – which transcended particular sectors. Though the government provided no money for industrial training through the Act, it made provision for tripartite Industrial Training Boards (ITBs). These were given powers to raise a levy, against payroll, to provide grants to defer training costs.

Each ITB was empowered to determine its own levy. In most cases ITBs levied a percentage of payroll: 2 per cent in engineering, with most others less. Some called for a per capita payment. The

Construction ITB levy involved a sliding scale, based on employment category, of between £2 and £45. In all cases, where it was appropriate, exemptions were made for small employers. To a large extent these forms of fund-raising for training reinforced the existing structure and training practices in each sector. Some training innovations did develop, especially out of the Engineering ITB with its introduction of a modular programme for apprentices, but in the main the boards tended to reinforce pre-existing training practices. Some spreading of the cost of existing traditional training was achieved, but little advance was made in developing new training for upgrading adult skills.

Not surprisingly, therefore, the ITB system quickly came under serious criticism. Firms that had been the providers of training complained of the increase in bureaucracy involved in reclaiming their costs, while others resented the imposition of what was effectively a tax on their wage bill. Many small firms – who often gained little from the grants – resented what appeared to be a transfer of their funds through the levy to larger companies. Moreover, much of the training that was provided was specific to the demands of individual firms and not easily transferable within the labour market, even where there was such mobility. Even the modularisation programme within the apprenticeship scheme developed by the Engineering ITB facilitated specialisation to meet individual firms' specific skill demands. In fact, the ITBs worked most successfully in sectors which continued to have well-established systems of craft apprenticeship; and very little reallocation appeared to be occurring in the provision of training or its funding. So, though it could be claimed that the Act focused attention on the problems of industrial training, and heralded an institutional expansion in training agencies, the creation of ITBs did little to affect the balance or composition of skills within the British economy.

By the early 1970s, 28 Industrial Training Boards existed, covering almost 12 million people, or about half the employed workforce, and receiving levies of over £200 m. The 1960s had also witnessed an expansion in off-the-job training through Government Training Centres (GTCs), which grew in number from thirteen in 1962 to fifty-two in 1971 and provided over 10 000 trainee places annually. In 1971 the Department of Employment discussion paper, *Training for the Future*, noted an improvement in training provision since the establishment of the ITBs. It suggested that rising unemployment could be managed by a more strategic manpower policy which provided retraining to areas, both geographically and economically, where skill shortages prevailed.

Its main proposal was for a major expansion in provision of training for the unemployed, through the establishment of the Training Opportunities Scheme (TOPS) with a target of 100 000 places. Except in sectors where there was clear consensus to the contrary, the White Paper proposed that the levy-grant system of funding training should be phased out and replaced with selective grants. Given the limits of the sector ITBs, and the need for a broad co-ordination of the ITBs strategy, the discussion paper also proposed the creation of a National Training Agency.

The 1973 *Employment and Training Act*, based on the discussion paper, introduced the Manpower Services Commission (MSC) to take control of the Department of Employment's training and employment services, the new Training Services Agency and the Employment Services Agency which ran the Job Centres. The new MSC was also to provide manpower forecasts predictive of skill' shortage to inform Departmental training policy. Influenced by trade union pressure and all-party support for the measures, the Commission was established with an executive of ten members: three each from employers and trade unions, with the remainder from education and local authorities. In the post-1973 training regime, the role of providing industrial training remained with the ITBs, while the MSC grappled with the task of creating the first major schemes for the unemployed. As unemployment continued to rise in the 1970s, further funding was regularly injected into its programmes. The annual expenditure on TOPS, the temporary measure established to address youth unemployment, doubled to £100 m, allowing numbers in training to rise from 36 000 to 70 000–75 000 between 1974 and 1976. A vocational preparation scheme for all young people was also suggested by the MSC in 1974, although this was shelved because of conflicts of interest between the Departments of Employment and of Education. The number of GTCs was also increased to provide retraining for the unemployed. Programmes of community service and work experience for both school-leavers and for the growing number of long-term unemployed were also established.

When the Labour Government was replaced by the Conservatives in 1979, the new administration initially had no clearly discernible policy on training – except that training, like all other spheres of government activity, was to be subject to market forces. Since education and training accounted for 15 per cent of government spending, these were likely areas for cuts; especially given that there was also much initial opposition from the new Government to the role and composition of the

MSC – which in all its aspects seemed to encapsulate the very corporatist systems of decision-making, and excessive state activism, to which Thatcherism was so steadfastly opposed.

The MSC had a budget of £563 m in 1979, with £337.6 m being spent on training schemes; these budgets were initially cut by more than £114 m by the incoming government. The MSC saw – for the first time – a decline in its own staffing levels; and also saw its responsibility for funding the ITBs passed across to the employers. This effectively led to the abolition of ITBs in most sectors; sixteen out of the twenty-three were abolished the following year by the Secretary of State under powers given by the Employment and Training Act 1981. But then the MSC began to defend its role and budget by emphasising the possible social consequences of cutting back training and employment programmes in a period of rising unemployment. That defence proved remarkably, and unexpectedly, successful.

For, as unemployment moved towards 3 million, and as the decline of manufacturing industry effectively destroyed the apprenticeship system (between 1979 and 1981 the number of apprentices fell from 21 000 to 12 000 in engineering, and by 54 per cent in construction), the MSC was actually provided with extra funding to expand YOP by 180 000 training or work experience places. A new Community Enterprise Programme, of socially useful work for the long-term unemployed, was also introduced. Though ministers argued that they could not solve the problem of unemployment by 'throwing money at it', they also had to respond to mounting concern about unemployment and its potential political consequences; and significant extra funds were ultimately found to support MSC schemes: £183 m in 1980/81 and £271 m in 1981/82.

Such schemes were, however, only temporary measures to alleviate the immediate problems of unemployment. They did not address the long-term agenda of labour reskilling. At their heart by 1982–3 stood the Youth Opportunities Programme which, since its inception in 1978, had grown to 550 000 places for school-leavers at a cost approaching £400 m. But because it focused on temporary unemployment, YOP had been little concerned with the quality or quantity of training provision. In consequence, much valid criticism was levelled that 'trainees' were being used as cheap labour and that, as trainees and not employees, YOP recipients were not subject to health and safety regulations. Essentially YOP kept young people off the unemployment statistics. In its early years, around 80 per cent moved on to employment or more formal further training, but, as unemployment increased in the early 1980s, around three-quarters of YOP trainees remained unemployed.

To meet this new situation, the MSC prepared to replace the YOP with a *new training initiative*. In a consultative document published in May 1981 it announced the initiative's three main objectives as: more flexible apprenticeship training; better vocational preparation for young people under eighteen, offering 'a period of planned work experience' combining education and training; and widespread opportunities for adult training and retraining. The 'new training initiative' was to bring the MSC to the centre of the Thatcherite project to initiate the 'enterprise culture'. In their history of the rise and fall of the MSC, Ainley and Corney (1990) see the NTI as a significant turning point in the approach of the Commission. Stripped of its manpower forecasting role, it no longer attempted the prediction of skill shortages. Instead it attempted to construct the 'flexible' new workforce suited to the increasingly deskilled jobs that the labour market might offer. In this it could also act to undermine the vestigial power of trade unions through the introduction of new working practices. In the longer term its ambitions appeared to be the construction of a unified system of education and training starting from the bottom-up.

The centrepiece of the NTI was the Youth Training Scheme, replacing the YOP, and intended to introduce systematic training into the youth programme, including a thirteen-week period off-the-job. The immediate cause of controversy concerned the initial recommendation that trainees should receive an allowance of £15 per week while on the scheme. This was considerably less than the £25 wage received on the YOP. Norman Tebbit – the Secretary of State at Employment – justified this by pointing to the increased training offered. He had wanted to go further by withdrawing benefit from any 16-year-old refusing a place on YTS, but failed to get the backing of his cabinet colleagues. In the end, with pressure from the unions, the allowance was raised to £25 per week, a figure still lower than that received at the time by apprentices.

Fifty-five Area Manpower Boards were created to administer the YTS and to monitor local schemes, along with a separate unit to consider schemes presented by large companies. The schemes that developed were divided into essentially two types: mode A which took place on employers' premises, and mode B in training workshops. YTS schemes with an employer became the immediate route for potential recruitment into longer-term employment. Although contested by some unions, YTS also began to replace the initial year of apprenticeship, thus lowering the initial wage. Although the remaining schemes included the relatively prestigious ITeCs – training workshops in computing and information technology – those in workshops clearly offered less chance of secure employment and included training for more marginal groups such as disabled people and ex-offenders. The thirteen weeks of off-the-job training included basic instruction in mathematics, English and computer studies, along with 'Social and Life Skills'. Though the latter tended to be offered by local technical colleges, the Minister by then in charge (David, later Lord, Young) – deliberately challenging the state education system – opened the system to private training agencies and paid them almost £2 000 per trainee to provide training and work placements.

By 1986, when the scheme was extended from one to two years, a quarter of young people leaving school entered the YTS. The scheme, like YOP, remained a state support to employers to recruit low-paid young people. YTS largely replaced existing training in work recruitment rather than increasing the number of places available; it is clearly questionable how much this improved the quality of training. This problem was reinforced by the system of 'additionality' which allowed employers five state-funded YTS trainees, without employment rights, for every two planned young employment recruits. In 1988 benefit was withdrawn from all 16 to 18-year-olds, making YTS effectively compulsory for all school-leavers who did not find alternative employment.

6.4   Vocational education 1964–89

Governments were much slower to move on the question of vocational education. Vocational education had not, of course, been a feature of the classic academic syllabus initially consolidated by the nineteenth-century public schools – just the reverse – and this antipathy to training for work had been generalised within the UK school system, after 1944, by the tripartite division of secondary education created by the Butler Education Act. In that system the grammar schools remained the 'academic' route for those selected for entry at eleven, with most of the remainder within the state sector in secondary moderns. There was provision for vocational, technical, schools which selected for entry at thirteen, but these never achieved more than 4 per cent of the school population. The Education Act also included statutory provision for local authorities to provide places for the vocational education of 15 to 18-year-olds in employment, although funding was never provided for further education colleges.

Not surprisingly, therefore, by the 1960s there was considerable unease – in government circles – about the adequacy of the existing system of secondary and higher education. One early manifestation of that unease was the establishment of the Robbins Committee in 1961 to 'review the pattern of full-time higher education in Great Britain ... in the light of national needs and resources'. Already, in 1958, the Government had given approval for the expansion of the system with the establishment of six new universities to cope with the population growth. Conventionally academic in structure, with some directly modelled on the Oxbridge collegiate system, their main innovation was to place more emphasis on newer disciplines, particularly in the social sciences. Robbins proposed more than doubling the number of students in higher education within the next two decades. The report also noted developments in science, technology, engineering, and vocational education outside the established universities. In 1956, ten colleges of advanced technology had been designated by the Ministry of Education for higher-level work, awarding the Diploma in Technology. These were to be upgraded to universities with powers to award their own degrees. Likewise, Robbins noted the development of higher education within some local authority controlled colleges, proposing that these become polytechnics supporting regional demands for higher education, although without their own degree-awarding powers. There was also some concern shown for the development of management education and training. A few courses in commerce and business administration at undergraduate level were well-established, although – as rather a hybrid, usually based around economics – these did not easily fit with traditional academic disciplines. Nor did undergraduate training in management and business fit the traditional career development that made progression to management the outcome of work experience and promotion through internal labour markets and often mobility between employers. Robbins noted the development of a number of centres – such as Henley – offering post-experience courses and suggested expansion leading to the establishment of business schools in London and Manchester. Less tied to academic tradition, the new universities and polytechnics began to develop undergraduate programmes reflecting a compromise between academic and business specialisms.

Robbins notwithstanding, concern still remained for the secondary school system and particularly for those leaving with no qualification to enter unskilled employment. In 1963 the Newsom Report, *Half Our Futures* (on 'less able' 13 to 16-year-olds), was published. This has been seen as the document most responsible for heralding a move to 'progressive' education in Britain. Balancing concerns for the extension of educational opportunities, it made only tentative suggestions for the extension of vocational training within schools to make the curriculum more relevant to broader individual interests and educational needs:

> for ... the majority of our pupils, courses will need to have a substantial craft or practical element, with an emphasis on real tasks undertaken with adult equipment: this will have important consequences for teachers and for buildings. But we emphasise again that in addition to providing experience in the use of tools and different kinds of materials, and the satisfaction of handling three dimensional objects, the special course work must be made to pay adequate yield in general educational development.   (Ministry of Education, 1963, p. 35)

Moves were also made towards comprehensive secondary education, breaking the division between grammar schools, the secondary moderns and technical schools. This was far from uniform across the country because of the control of education by local authorities. A unified local structure was, in part, intended to widen opportunity and break the division between academic and vocational preparation within secondary education. This ethos was also reflected in the introduction of a new school examination, the Certificate in Secondary Education, designed to be more attractive to employers than the more academic GCE 'O' level. In practice only the highest grade – deemed equivalent to an 'O' level pass – was recognised by employers or in education. This general drift in education away from Oxbridge and grammar school domination led to the mobilisation of opposition from traditional conservatives to what they saw as decline in educational standards. Their production of a number of 'Black Papers' on education proved a focal point for debate and for one wing of emergent 'Thatcherism'. Then in 1976 James Callaghan – the new Labour Prime Minister – suggested, in a lecture at Ruskin College, that schools were failing their pupils through a lack of vocational education. The resulting 'Great

Debate' on education, linked with traditional conservative anxieties reflected in the Black Papers, opened the agenda ultimately to the new vocationalism.

The key moves on vocational education had to wait for the arrival of Thatcher in office and the unexpected flowering of the MSC. For, alongside the establishment of YTS for school-leavers, the MSC began the introduction of vocational education into schools. In November 1982, without any prior consultation with the local education authorities, the Prime Minister announced that funds would become available for a pilot scheme. Like many of the initiatives, there appeared to be no planned, coherent scheme. Although there was no formalised content, local education authorities, short of funds due to government cutbacks and rate-capping, were asked to propose vocational schemes. £46 million was offered to fourteen authorities to run five-year pilot schemes starting in 1983. Behind this was the threat that the MSC might itself set up schools to provide vocational education. Under Section 5 of the Employment and Training Act, the MSC was empowered to provide education for school-age children. Schools and LEAs had considerable autonomy in how they constructed their TVEI schemes, although an important feature was that the contracting process began to permeate the school system through an MSC intent on transforming the culture of education. Schemes needed to be detailed in vocational content as well as individual costing. The contracts with LEAs to run them earmarked the funding to the specific projects and pupils. In 1986, before the end of the pilot schemes, £90 million had been made available by the MSC – from savings from a shortfall in recruitment to YTS – to extend the TVEI to all schools.

MSC control over education was then extended, with it taking over direct funding of all non-advanced work within the further education colleges. Since the advent of YTS, the focus of the work carried out in many colleges had shifted considerably, with weight being given to the off-the-job training provided for trainees in competition with private sector agencies. David Young had been particularly sceptical about the colleges' abilities to meet the demands of local employers and labour markets.

I was becoming increasingly aware of the many defects in the way that the colleges of further education worked.... It is one thing to guarantee the independence of the education system from interference from politicians but quite another if that results in an unchanging, inflexible system. I would visit colleges around the country and time after time I could see that courses were run simply because they were there. ... [young people taking courses] ... Only too late, once they had finished, would they find that the skills they had acquired were in little demand. ...The existing system gave funds for education to local authorities who would then hand them to their own Local Education Authorities. The LEAs would then divide the funds, first between schools and colleges, then colleges' funds would be further divided between advanced and non-advanced, that is work-related, further education. I suggested that we should take part of the funds for non-advanced further education away from Local Education Authorities and give it out from our area offices on a contractual basis. By entering into individual contracts we could be sure that the courses would change to those we thought would be in demand.   (Young, 1990, pp. 117–8)

Young believed that rising youth unemployment was caused by the failings, not of the labour market, but of the bureaucracy and rigidities of both the education system and the LEAs. The latter were also being challenged by major reforms which abolished the Metropolitan Authorities, including the Labour-controlled Inner London Education Authority which had consistently opposed MSC initiatives.

More generally, in the broad sweep of government activity the pattern we see in Thatcherite policy on education and training is one of devolved budgets, with contracts and markets to link 'purchasers' of services to their 'providers'. The Government was intent (as it was in other areas of the public sector) on achieving both a market framework within education and training, and on creating an 'enterprise culture' promoting a positive response to a market order. The pattern of marketisation and the extension of contract relations – initially represented by the establishment of TVEI – developed further in the education system. The MSC became responsible for a further education budget of £220 m, around a quarter of spending on further education. The Education Reform Act of 1988 consolidated the contracting framework, devolving budgets to schools and giving greater authority to governors – the local management of schools – and allowing them to opt out of local authority control. This devolution of financial control went along with centralisation of control over the school syllabus through a national curriculum, national testing and attainment targets. The move out of local authority control extended to polytechnics and higher education colleges, where it was replaced by governing bodies with strong employer representation and a unified funding agency for the whole higher education sector. A scheme, like that with which the local authorities had been threatened with the establishment of TVEI, was also introduced to establish city technology colleges run by independent trusts with funding from industry and commerce.

In 1987 the MSC approach began to permeate higher education, with the 'Enterprise in Higher Education' scheme. Again, like TVEI, there were no clear criteria for the scheme, to which institutions were invited to bid for £1 m that was to become available to each of ten institutions over the following five years 'to develop competencies and aptitudes relevant to enterprise' (cited in Ainsley and Corney, 1990, p. 111). What emerged from all the schemes initiated by the MSC was a transformation of the notion of skill and skill training. Whereas these schemes reflected the idea that failure to gain jobs was due to lack of work experience, they also reduced the skills needed for work to a series of discrete and identifiable competencies, 'core skills' that were required by employers and easily transferable.

Then, at almost the height of its expansion into the education system, it was announced that the MSC – the vehicle for the training revolution of the enterprise culture – was to be abolished. The immediate reason was that trade union representation was withdrawn over a boycott of a new Employment Training Scheme. Antagonism to the growth of this 'quango' had in fact long been on the increase within the government, and their 1987 election manifesto had proposed focusing its responsibilities for employment training by stripping it of responsibility for Job Centres, with its work experience schemes to be taken over by the Department of Social Security. The 1987 Employment Act proposed the establishment of a new Training Commission to replace the MSC. This enhanced employer involvement, ostensibly to reflect the increased significance of tourism, financial services and small business. The framework had been established for a contracting relationship between 'purchaser' and 'provider', with an end to trade union involvement and an enhanced role for employers. As the White Paper *Employment for the 1990s* (which proposed the changes) put it:

it is up to employers and individuals, by their actions, to ensure that the jobs come about; and in re-skilling the labour force there are new partnerships to be created between enterprise, vocational education and training, between delivery at local level and policy and priorities at national level, and between employers and Government, customers and providers.   (cited in Hodgson, 1993, p. 14)

The MSC had done its job, and was then abolished.

6.5   The training state?

There are four interrelated elements to the Major Government's claim
of a training revolution in the 1990s:

- the establishment of the national vocational qualification;
- the devolvement of government responsibility for purchasing training provision on to independent employer-led local bodies;
- sustained employer involvement in training; and
- the introduction of market choice in training provision to school-leavers through training credits.

Within this framework the Government remains central. It both sets
policy targets for training provision and provides funding for specific
schemes; but the implementation of policy is contracted to the local
TECs, who purchase training services from local providers. Within this,
NVQ plays an important role as the measure of achievement both in
contracts and of individual trainees.

(i) NVQ and education

Following the work of the National Council for Vocational Qualifications the NVQ framework has been established to link basic competencies and qualifications across education and in the workplace to
professional qualifications in vocational education and training. This
framework is being constructed to create a parity in the range of
educational and training qualifications, with the hierarchy of vocational qualifications running alongside (and being treated as equivalents of) the existing academic hierarchy of qualifications from GCSEs
through to masters level. NVQs are also the cornerstone of the targets
set by government within training policy and are the measure of
achievement.
   So the NVQ framework performs a number of particular roles within
training, beyond being a unified qualification. It acts to break down

'skills' into identifiable and examinable components which are themselves accredited by superiors – work-based supervisors – or assessors in schools and colleges. It then credits achievement of particular tasks to be reconstructed into a more comprehensive package of credentialled 'flexible work-based competencies'. NVQs are also the measure by which achievements of training policy, and TEC contracts, are themselves measured. They thus provide the basis on which the standards within training can be measured, comparable to the 'quality' standards on which the public sector is increasingly being funded. Skill training itself has become the construction of a matrix of competencies rather than an adaptable and flexible understanding of working processes and practices. Existing qualifications have been adapted to fit into the NVQ scheme, and some short, in-house training run by employers has also been credit-rated to accumulate to new qualifications. A 'new apprenticeship' has been proposed, to be equivalent to the completion of level three of the NVQ, and GNVQ has been introduced in schools as a vocational route equivalent to academic 'A' levels.

The 1990s have also seen a dramatic increase in the numbers involved in higher education, both among 18 to 21-year-olds and among more mature entrants. In 1991 the Further and Higher Education Bill redesignated the polytechnics as universities: at one and the same time creating an apparently unified system of higher education, taking further education and sixth form colleges out of local authority control, and proposing an end to the division between academic and vocational education. Expansion here is clearly connected to continued unemployment levels. Targets were set by the government to expand entrance, bringing Britain up towards the higher education participation rates of most other Western countries; and when the expected rate of growth was exceeded, expansion was halted. Courses have been restructured to fit the vocational training model of flexibility through modularisation and credit-rating. A major characteristic of the expansion has been the move from funding student maintenance from state support grants, which have remained fixed, to loans to be paid back after graduation. Subsidy has already been removed from further education courses which are considered non-vocational.

Elsewhere in the education and training system, a scheme has been piloted, to extend to all 16 to 18-year-olds, to give them training credits. The YTS has been redesignated as 'Youth Training' with a target to make this available to all the 16 to 18-year-olds not entering employment or further education. Employment Training has unified the schemes available for the unemployed over eighteen, giving an allowance of £10 above benefit levels.

(ii) Training in employment

In 1993 the Department of Employment, following the DTI's earlier Enterprise Initiative, launched 'Investors in People',

> promoted as the way to create a training culture among British businesses and manufacturers. It aims to improve performance and have a direct impact on the bottom line of company results by helping employers to reach a high, nationally-recognised standard of training and development for all their workforce. (*Guardian*, 15 June 1993)

Under this initiative, companies and public sector organisations are assessed on their commitment to training. This commitment is judged on the percentage of the payroll being dedicated to training and staff development measured against NVQ standards.

This promotion of employer commitment masks the relatively few employers who invest in skill training. A number of studies in the late 1980s – including one sponsored by the MSC – found that more than half the workforce received no regular, systematic training, while the remaining minority received on average only some 14.5 days per year. The estimated cost of £12 bn for this training is principally accounted for by the wage costs of trainees and in-house trainers (see, for example, Delloitte Haskins and Sells/IFF Research, 1989). Despite three decades of reform, the problem of few employers investing in skill training appears to remain.

(iii) TECs and LECs

Investors in People, along with the range of youth and employment training, are contracted by government departments through the Training and Enterprise Councils and Local Enterprise Companies which were established with the end of the MSC. Within ten days of the establishment of the Training Commission as the replacement for the MSC it was announced that this would be replaced by a network of employer-led Training and Enterprise Councils (TECs) in England and Wales, and Local Enterprise Companies (LECs) in Scotland. The first ten were established in April 1990, with all eighty-eight in existence by

November 1991, two years ahead of schedule. The TECs themselves receive most of their funding through contracts with the Departments of Employment and Industry for the local management of initiatives. A National Advisory Council for Education and Training Targets monitors the TECs in progress towards national training targets, requiring them to produce agreed corporate and business plans. The TECs themselves are not providers of training but act as agents in contracting to local providers for ET and YT, and administering Training Credits and 'Investors in People'.

Tensions were quick to appear between the aim to promote training and Government demands to meet targets and devolve spending back to employers. Within the first year the budget for the TECs was reduced from £3 bn to £2.5 bn. Representatives of the TECs were reported to have warned Michael Howard, the Secretary of State for Employment at that time, that 'the realities of budget cuts, lack of flexibility, and the putting to one side of the world-class objectives bore little resemblance to the vision that attracted businessmen to TECs in the first instance' (*Guardian*, 8 August 1990). One problem the TECs found was that they were expected to develop a three-year strategy and plan to meet targets for training schemes, but the Treasury would only announce their funding on an annual basis. The Government set targets for all 16 to 18-year-olds not in employment or education to be found a place on Youth Training. Increasingly this training would be linked to achievement of NVQ qualifications. With the Treasury squeezing spending, intent on devolving some of the cost to employers, the solution the TECs adopted was to direct their efforts to areas where targets could most easily be met. This was in providing YT for those within what had previously been Mode A schemes and who were likely to have achieved some academic qualifications already. Resources were shifted away from the training workshops, the remnants of the GTCs, and those provided by voluntary organisations.

This shift in resources from training centres led indirectly to a collapse in provision within training centres and workshops, and also highlighted an inherent problem with the management of contracts with government-determined targets. In the period of expansion in training, many charities were able to develop their provision for particularly disadvantaged groups, receiving funding through MSC Mode B to support their schemes. The National Association for the Care and Resettlement of Offenders (NACRO), for example, had become increasingly proficient at developing such schemes. In April 1991 it warned that it was likely to lose 9000 of its 13 000 training places as TECs opted to place contracts with agencies dealing with client groups more likely to achieve their targets, prompting a crisis across the voluntary sector. The TECs were essentially being given the role of divesting the training budget of its welfare role.

Another immediate outcome of the government strategy of funding TECs by results can be seen from events around the remnants of the skillcentres. In 1990 the Government had also privatised its remaining skillcentres – the GTCs. Astra Training Services had taken over forty-seven of the original sixty; and, with an anticipated cut in funding through the TECs of £2.3 m, demanded 230 redundancies from their 1700 employees with a reduction in their protected civil service redundancy terms. In 1993 the collapse of Astra gave publicity to the methods that private contractors could use to meet the targets set by government and TECs, when it was found that they had temporarily taken on their own ex-trainees to achieve post-training employment targets. Complaints about this type of outcome have become more widespread, particularly with contracts to achieve levels of NVQ awards. Criticism has focused on the pressure on contractors (often technical colleges but also private training agencies) to pass trainees in ill-defined 'competencies' in order to fulfil contracts and meet targets that filter through the contracting chain.

6.6 Conclusion

As we have seen, changes in VET are integrally linked to other aspects of industrial policy. Not least, this is through a long-term recognition of the different traditions established by Britain's competitors. Since the nineteenth century the ascendancy of Germany has been pointed to as exemplifying the links between vocational education and industrial expansion. Recent investment in Britain by Japanese firms has also highlighted their apparent emphasis on the training of their workforce. But the recent 'training revolution' in Britain leaves some important questions concerning the reform of VET. First, whether, in the light of experience up to the 1960s, a system based around provision to meet local employer demand will lead to skill training which will meet the long-term demands of the labour market in Britain. Secondly, and to a large extent because the system has been driven by concern about unemployment, can such a system guarantee the extension of skill within the labour market? Since 1960 Britain has witnessed an apparent extension of training provision although, within employment, this has often simply involved a levelling-down in skill, with the disappearance of traditional apprenticeship, alongside the credentialling of the tacit skills and informal learning which had already existed. The very notion of 'skill' has become transformed in the process, reduced to a series of examinable 'competencies'.

All this is adequate only if it is possible to produce a highly skilled workforce from a training structure tied, on the one side, to resolving the economic and social welfare problems of the transition from school to the labour market and, on the other side, to the vagaries of creating generalised 'transferable skills' in a low-wage economy to help to attract industrial investment. But if it cannot, then all these reforms have still failed to create for British industry the training system it so desperately needs.

III LEVELS AND SOURCES OF POLICY

7 Whitehall, Westminster and Industrial Policy

Kevin Theakston

7.1 Introduction

This chapter is concerned with the role of the Whitehall and Westminster policy-making machine and the civil service in the making of industrial policy. A familiar 'declinist' critique identifies deficiencies in the institutions and personnel of the British state as key factors in our economic malaise and industrial under-achievement. This is actually a long-running debate. Many modern arguments for, say, more technocratic officials or for the introduction into Whitehall of private sector business people and business methods actually turn out to echo the pre-First World War campaign for 'national efficiency'. In the inter-war period, and again in the 1960s, there were criticisms that the civil service could not handle new tasks of economic planning and intervention in industry.

Over the last decade or so, commentators of different political persuasions have agreed that the system of government must bear a large share of the responsibility for the state of the British economy. On the right, Sir John Hoskyns – an adviser to Mrs Thatcher – was clear that 'in the long term the machine has a propensity to failure... The cure for the British disease must start with government itself.' In his sights were the culture and style of Whitehall (pessimistic, concerned with performance rather than results) and the small pool of governing talent provided by the Westminster closed shop (Hoskyns, 1983, 1984). In the political centre, David Marquand took the argument on to the deeper issues of political culture and state tradition laying behind the absence of a Japanese or French-style 'developmental state' in Britain. The institutions and conventions of the 'Westminster model' of parliamentary government were, he argued, incompatible with (and had inhibited) the evolution of a proactive and discretionary *dirigiste* state in this country (Marquand, 1988). David Edgerton has given the 'developmental state' debate a new twist by arguing that the British state *has* been 'committed to scientific, technological and industrial modernisation', but its aims have been primarily military and strategic ones. In defence-related sectors of industry, the state has successfully adopted the directive and interventionist approach that critics say should be the general model for government-industry relations (Edgerton, 1991a, 1991b, 1992).

The institutional capabilities of British government can be enhanced, these critics suggest, and some pointed historical lessons are available. Marquand contrasts the irresolute, muddled and defensive state intervention experienced in recent decades with the way in which, in two world wars, an entrepreneurial state apparatus was created and the administrative machine ran the economy with great flair and success. Edgerton argues that the officials working in the service and military supply departments have often been scientific, technological and industrial experts rather than stereotypical mandarin amateurs. And he has shown how the wartime production departments and the post-war Ministry of Supply successfully eschewed the traditional liberal/'hands-off' Whitehall style and intervened actively to 'pick winners' and direct resources.

7.2   The government machine

The fragmentation and institutional instability of the industrial policy community in British government have worked against the development and implementation of a coherent industrial policy. The departmental set-up in the fields of financial and macroeconomic policy has been relatively stable (and marked by Treasury predominance); in contrast, the departments dealing with industry and trade have experienced continual reorganisation and upheaval, with their number, size and responsibilities changing sometimes quite abruptly and for short-term political reasons. As Hennessy puts it, 'success, in terms of sustained growth in the British economy, might have brought stability. Relative failure did not' (Hennessy, 1989, p. 432). Activity, as seen in regular departmental reorganisations, became a substitute for – perhaps even a further barrier to – achievement, as measured in the statistics of economic and industrial performance.

Industrial policy is not something that is formulated and implemented by a single industry department, but instead by a network of government departments (involving also a range of paragovernmental agencies linked to Whitehall, local-level bodies and – increasingly – the European Commission). The main departmental 'players' with industry-related functions include the Department of Trade and Industry (DTI), the Treasury, the regional departments for Scotland, Wales and Northern Ireland, the Department of Employment, the Department of Transport and (until its abolition in 1992) the Department of Energy. In addition, the Ministry of Agriculture (which now has a bigger budget than the DTI), dealing with the farming and food sectors; the Department of Health (the drugs industry); and the Ministry of Defence (industry's biggest single customer, with its Procurement Executive spending around £9 bn a year on equipment for the armed forces), also come into the picture. Other departments' policies can impact on industry too. Wilks gives the example of the Home Office: its 'preference for an annual registration suffix... helps the police identify vehicles. Unfortunately it also distorts the whole pattern of vehicle demand, boosting August sales when factories tend to have reduced holiday production, and allowing continental factories to shift their stocks to Britain' (Wilks, 1990, p. 173).

This pattern of overlapping responsibilities, and the need to secure the active co-operation of a number of organisational actors in order to make progress, produces frequent calls for 'improved co-ordination' but, as Hogwood notes, this is really 'a statement of the problem rather than a description of the solution' (1982, pp. 36–7). The concept of co-ordination is actually very problematic and, in practice, there are a variety of mechanisms through which it can be attempted (with different degrees of success).

(i) The Treasury

The Treasury has long been a favourite bogey figure for those seeking to explain Whitehall's role in economic decline and deindustrialisation. For Pollard, in particular, it institutionalises that 'contempt for production' that makes the government machine 'a powerful contributory cause of our decline' (1982, p. 159). Its responsibility for public expenditure control ensures that it will generally be hostile to increased state spending on programmes directed at industry (looking for cuts wherever it can find them, even if that means sacrificing productive investment). And its macroeconomic management role, it is argued, together with its close links with the Bank of England and the City, invariably lead it to give priority to short-term and financial considerations (the exchange rate, the balance of payments, the rate of inflation), introducing measures (such as interest rate changes) which can affect industry more than any number of DTI 'supply-side' measures.

The Treasury is said to be deeply committed to a free-market approach and sceptical of anything like a positive and interventionist industrial policy. Condemned by the critics for having virtually no direct contacts with or knowledge of industry (in 1993 the top 100 Treasury mandarins were ordered to spend at least one day a year visiting industry – this was presented as a great step forwards), the Treasury nevertheless dominates economic policy-making in government. Although it no longer controls top-level civil service postings, it remains one of the élite departments, powerfully influencing Whitehall's values and culture. It has seen off all challengers, defeating the Department of Economic Affairs in the 1960s and ensuring that the National Economic Development Council was marginalised (and eventually killed off in 1992 at the Treasury's instigation); its power has grown under the Conservative Governments that have been in office since 1979. All this is in marked contrast to the position in other systems, such as France and Germany (where the central economics ministries do not stand back from industrial policy questions) or Japan (where the powerful Ministry of International Trade and Industry has more clout than the Ministry of Finance).

In the mid-1970s it looked as if the Treasury could begin to play a more constructive role in industrial policy-making, with Labour's Chancellor of the Exchequer Denis Healey and official opinion becoming more interested in 'supply side' problems. The Treasury created its own Industrial Policy Group and worked closely with the Department of Industry (after Varley replaced Benn). The inter-departmental Industrial Strategy Steering Group (chaired by the Treasury) shaped the thinking behind Labour's 1975 'Industrial Strategy' and tried to get non-economic departments (such as Education and Environment) to address the industrial implications of their policies. However, the failure of senior ministers to keep up their initial level of interest, and the fall out from the 1976 IMF crisis, meant that the Strategy slipped down the Treasury's agenda; and after 1979, the Thatcher Government's ideological hostility to the idea of an industrial strategy reinforced the traditional Treasury view.

The case against the Treasury should not, though, be exaggerated. Thain (1984) believes that there is only 'limited scope for blaming the Treasury for decline'. He argues that there is no monolithic 'Treasury line', that the Treasury's priorities have been determined by the political decisions of ministers, and that other Whitehall departments and outside interest groups limit its room for manoeuvre. The consensus on foreign economic policy (the 'sterling lobby'), for instance, extended far beyond the Treasury. And the long-term growth in the total of public spending is testimony to the limits on its power. The Treasury is undoubtedly a key player in the economic and industrial policy machine, Thain suggests, but it is not an all-powerful one.

(ii) Defence

The importance of the defence sector in the British economy has long been recognised: it was estimated that 625 000 jobs in industry and services depended on defence expenditure and exports in 1985–6, with the Ministry of Defence (MoD) the dominant customer in the aerospace (45 per cent of output), shipbuilding (30 per cent of output) and electronics (20 per cent of output) industries (Grant 1989, p. 104). The proportion of government R&D funding going to defence – about half – is argued to be higher than in any other major industrialised country, except the USA. With 121 000 staff (1994 figure) the MoD remains Whitehall's biggest ministry, employing more than one-fifth of the civil service, despite the slashing cuts of the 1980s (the department has cut 38 000 white-collar, non-industrial staff and 88 000 blue-collar, industrial civil service jobs over the last fifteen years). The MoD still employs over four-fifths (39 000) of the remaining industrial civil service, and it takes the lion's share of key professional staff groups in the bureaucracy, employing 59 per cent of the scientific civil service, 80 per cent of government engineers and over half of the service's professional accountants (Fry, 1985, p. 49).

The ministry certainly has a close working relationship with the defence industries – critics would say too close, Grant (1989, p. 106), for instance, pointing to 'the inertia that lies behind a mutually satisfactory symbiotic relationship between the MoD and the defence contractors'. Symptomatic of this is the way in which the firms competing for a share of the £9 bn a year procurement budget increasingly recruit former senior 'insiders' – MoD officials or military personnel, more than 2 000 of whom have joined British and foreign defence companies and management consultants – prompting allegations of a 'gravy train' and raising questions about the potential for 'sleaze' and conflicts of interest (*Guardian*, 25 January 1995).

The Procurement Executive was set up as a self-contained agency inside the MoD by the Heath Government in 1972, with Derek Rayner from Marks and Spencer appointed as the first chief executive. Previously, responsibilities in this field had primarily centred on the Ministry of Supply (1946–59), the Ministry of Aviation (1959–67), the aviation group of Labour's Ministry of Technology (1967–70), and the stop-gap Ministry of Aviation Supply (1970–1), though the Navy Department had dealt with the design and procurement of warships and the Royal Ordnance Factories constituted the army's major equipment supplier.

The Procurement Executive aimed to surmount the problems of inadequate cost control, receding delivery dates for equipment, and too great a distance between the users of equipment and its suppliers, that had bedevilled this sector in the post-war period, though in practice its record in these respects has been a mixed one. In the 1980s (as we saw in more detail in Chapter 2) the Thatcher Government sought to instil greater efficiency and value for money in the procurement budget by introducing increased competition for defence contractors in response to continued concerns about overpricing (based on 'cost-plus' contracts) and escalating project costs. A more commercially-minded Chief of Defence Procurement, Peter Levene (an industrialist) was brought in by Michael Heseltine in 1984 in an attempt to impose tighter budgetary control and promote more competition for contracts.

By 1994, however, the MoD was reported to be rethinking its attitude towards competition in defence supply and moving towards a policy of backing 'national champions' able to compete effectively in world markets (the ministry adopting a stance of 'strict neutrality' towards a GEC bid to take control of VSEL, threatening to reduce the number of companies with naval shipbuilding capabilities from two to one) (*Independent,* 29 October 1994). At the same time, shrinking national markets and the ever-increasing cost of developing weapon systems were pushing governments across Europe into searching for more collaborative programmes with the potential for economies of scale on the European level (such as the Future Large Aircraft project and plans for UK–French–Italian warship collaboration). The pretence that Britain has no industrial policy was being exposed, as industrial and defence procurement policies were seen to be increasingly inter-woven (*The Times,* 20 March 1995).

(iii) Trade and industry

Over a long period of time the Board of Trade was one of the central departments dealing with industry. During the Second World War, its officials had developed a clear (and pessimistic) analysis of Britain's industrial backwardness and its post-war competitive prospects, but ministers and Whitehall had balked at creating a full-blown 'Ministry of Industry' to push through some of the radical ideas then being floated (for example, for an Industrial Commission). Instead, the Board's traditional *laissez-faire* or 'hands-off' approach was confirmed and in the 1950s and early 1960s it 'sought to operate industrial poli-cies *neutrally,* giving firms and industries as little special treatment as possible' (Young and Lowe, 1974, p. 27). Industry was to operate on its own within a framework provided by government (for example, legisla-tion relating to restrictive trade practices and monopolies was passed), with the Board of Trade acting as 'a referee rather than a player' (Young and Lowe, 1974, p. 12). The contrast with the attitude and practices of, for instance, the Ministry of Supply and military produc-tion departments is stark, as Edgerton notes.

In the early 1960s, the 'dash for planning' and the establishment of the National Economic Development Council (NEDC) and the National Economic Development Office (NEDO), which had an industrial divi-sion working on sectoral issues, represented the first Conservative moves towards a more active government involvement with industry, but the key developments came, first, after the election of Harold Wilson's Labour Government in 1964, and second, with the arrival of Edward Heath's Conservative administration in 1970.

Labour's ill-fated Department of Economic Affairs failed to break the Treasury's predominance over economic policy, handicapped as it was by an ill-thought-out division of functions between it and the Treasury and by a lack of direct executive powers on key issues, pri-marily because of political decisions giving priority to the defence of the exchange rate which ensured that the Treasury would inevitably come out on top in the inter-departmental struggle. The establishment and subsequent expansion of the Ministry of Technology was a more

successful innovation. Wilson wanted to redirect the national technological effort away from military and 'prestige' (aerospace and
nuclear) projects to boost industrial production generally; and by 1969
he had built up MinTech as a super ministry for industry, transferring
to it responsibilities from the Board of Trade (of which he had a low
opinion) and the DEA, and allowing it to gobble up the functions of
the Ministry of Aviation and the Ministry of Power. The result was
that, by 1970, MinTech had 'wider responsibilities for public and
private industry than have ever been enjoyed by an industry department since' (Grant, 1989, p. 88). According to Edgerton, next to
MinTech, 'Japan's much-vaunted MITI [was] a minnow by comparison' (1991a, p. 105).

Although it was not staffed by a new breed of technocrats, MinTech
was a pioneer in trying to breach the monopoly of the Whitehall generalist, opening up senior posts to scientists and engineers. Young and
Lowe (1974, p. 28) argue that the significance of MinTech was the
'institutionalisation of the principle of discrimination', and the over-
turning of Whitehall's traditionally 'neutral' stance (though, as
Edgerton [1991b, p. 163] points out, this description only makes sense
if the history of the state's role in procurement is ignored). They quote
its permanent secretary: 'from the start the Ministry of Technology
insisted on being selective', and also a former Board of Trade official:
'with the arrival of MinTech, the judgement of the bureaucrat has
replaced the judgement of the market.' Grant's judgement is that

> the MinTech experience... did help to nurture something of an inter-
> ventionist culture among civil servants who were later to occupy
> senior positions in subsequent industry departments. That is not to
> say that they believed in massive state intervention, but they did
> believe in trying to create a working relationship with industry.

But he argues that this period saw 'essentially a reinforcement and
development of an earlier clientilistic conception of government's relationship with industry, rather than a predilection for a replacement of
the market by the state' (1982, pp. 88–9).

MinTech's ministers did not, however, believe that their department
represented any sort of challenge to the Treasury, and they complained
that macroeconomic policy was formulated without reference to what
MinTech was doing (Contemporary Record, 1991, pp. 142–3). It must
be said that whatever its *potential*, MinTech's record in practice was

not impressive, both in terms of shifting technological and R&D priorities and in industrial support and restructuring. Symptomatic of this was the continuation of Concorde, and the conversion of Sir Richard Clarke from being a powerful critic of the project at the Treasury to an enthusiastic and successful advocate for it when he took over as MinTech's permanent secretary.

Wilson also established the Industrial Reorganisation Corporation (IRC) in 1966, giving it the role of assisting and promoting mergers with the aim of creating bigger companies able to compete internationally (and the IRC also acted in a number of rescue cases). Acting as something like a state merchant bank, the IRC's personnel came from the private sector, and it had considerable operational independence (reporting in the first instance to the DEA and later to MinTech), which meant that parliament was able to exercise little detailed control over it (Young and Lowe, 1974). A small, unbureaucratic, active, fast-moving, commercially-orientated body, the IRC's value as a catalyst for industrial development was limited in two ways: first because the government failed to relate its work to any clear and detailed long-term industrial strategy (Young and Lowe, 1974, p. 87); and second, because in its interventions in a number of important cases, 'economic nationalism and social factors seemed more important than any buccaneering pursuit of industrial efficiency', for example its role in the formation of BL and in aiding Rolls-Royce and Cammell Laird (Fry, 1981, pp. 100–1). In the event, however, the IRC experiment was cut off just as it was building up steam.

In 1970, Heath abolished the IRC (it did not fit into his 'disengagement' philosophy) and dismantled MinTech, allocating its aircraft procurement functions (the largest in staff terms) to the MoD and merging the rump of the ministry with the Board of Trade to form the giant Department of Trade and Industry (DTI), bringing together responsibility for industry and for export promotion and trade policy. Hogwood argues that the creation of the DTI provided an organisational container for more coherent policies: 'it removed the organizational excuse for ineffective policies' (1988, p. 219). However, the DTI's very wide policy scope made it bureaucratically unwieldy, with serious problems of internal co-ordination exacerbated by the continuance of different traditions – Trade's free-trade outlook, and on the Industrial (former MinTech) side, a more interventionist impulse. Also, the political and economic crises of the Heath years meant that the Government's approach soon became a reactive rather than a strategic one.

The 1972 U-turn saw the establishment of the Industrial Development Unit inside the DTI (mentioned earlier) and the appointment of a second DTI Cabinet minister (for prices, consumer affairs and trade). Heath's departmental pattern unravelled soon after. A separate Department of Energy had been carved out even before the return of a Labour Government in 1974 saw the DTI broken up to form three ministries – Industry, Trade, and Prices and Consumer Protection – for reasons of party management and political balancing between left and right in the Cabinet (with Wilson particularly keen to deny Benn, whose interventionist ambitions he opposed, a major departmental power base). The National Enterprise Board (NEB), established in 1975, turned out to be a very different creature from that intended by the Labour left, operating as a 'hospital for lame ducks' (Mitchell, 1982, p. 47) rather than spearheading an active, socialist industrial policy. The Department of Industry and the Treasury tried to emphasise commercial viability as the key criterion in government rescue cases in the 1970s, but ministers' political needs could be paramount (Wilks, 1983, p. 141). For instance, the Chrysler bail-out – with the Government trying to shore-up its political position in Scotland – killed off any chance of developing a coherent policy for the motor industry of the sort the Central Policy Review Staff (which took an interest in industrial policy throughout its existence, 1971–83) had sketched in 1975.

7.3   Policy-making machinery since 1979

In 1979, Mrs Thatcher abolished the Department of Prices and Consumer Protection, but kept Trade and Industry as separate departments. However, the DTI's 'common services' (personnel, finance, economics, statistics, legal, accountancy, information) had been maintained after 1974, as were a common staffing structure (permitting cross-postings) and integrated regional offices, a 'shadow DTI' thus existing in the 1974–83 period (Hogwood, 1988, pp. 221–2). In 1983 the Departments of Trade and Industry were merged again, DTI reabsorbing Energy in 1992.

Taking over the Industry Department in 1979, the new Conservative minister, Sir Keith Joseph, handed over a reading-list so that officials could educate themselves in the new thinking about markets and frame policy advice accordingly. His special adviser, David (later Lord) Young, suspected that some officials hoped that the Conservatives would be only temporary residents in government for reasons of institutional self-interest – under a Labour Government there is more money to spend and decisions to take (Young, 1990, p. 46). Sir Keith Joseph was much given to agonised musings about whether his department should be abolished, but there were in fact continuities with the pre-1979 approach, with continuing massive aid to BL, for instance, after the Cabinet overruled its hapless Industry Secretary. Under'his successor, Patrick Jenkin (Industry Secretary 1981–3), the idea that the DoI could play some sort of constructive role surfaced in the support given to the information technology sector (Kenneth Baker being appointed as IT minister in 1981). But the Government's general ideological hostility to state intervention, together with the Treasury's axe-wielding on public spending and pursuit of macroeconomic policies damaging to industry, left the DoI/DTI without much of a role.

DTI staff numbers fell from 16 000 in 1978/9 (in the then-separate departments of Industry and of Trade) to 12 800 in 1987 (falling to 10 886 in 1994), and departmental spending plummeted from over £3bn a year in the early 1980s to £2bn in 1987/8. Other departments made the running on the government's key 'supply side' initiatives: the Treasury on privatisation, the Cabinet Office and Employment on deregulation, Employment on training and small businesses, Environment on inner cities (taken over by the DTI after 1987). Regional policy (long one of the department's main functions) was downgraded and over large parts of its bailiwick – competition policy, regional aid, R&D support, trade negotiations, and so on – the European Commission loomed ever larger as a body to respond to or negotiate with. A series of rapid ministerial changes added to the gloom and the feeling of loss of purpose.

The arrival of Lord Young as minister in 1987 saw an attempt to revitalise and reorientate the department. Young felt that the DTI had lost its way and had become 'a Department of Disasters' and he wanted to change its role and image, putting it back into the political limelight as the 'Department of Wealth Creation' (Young, 1990, p. 237). From being 'the vet's surgery of the British economy' (Hennessy, 1989, p. 431), it would become the champion of free-market competition, the facilitator of the enterprise economy, encouraging small business and trying to change attitudes (the DTI's advertising budget rose dramatically). The talk was of 'an enterprise strategy' rather than 'an industrial policy', the government's line was that 'industry is responsible for its own destiny' (DTI, 1988), and Young dismissed old-style government intervention, the idea of 'picking winners' or the need to give priority to manufacturing industry.

Signalling the new regime, Young abolished the DTI's sponsorship divisionș. Sponsorship divisions provided a point of contact within government for every industry (not all industries falling under the DTI's wing, of course), acting as a channel of communication between the industry and Whitehall and also to some extent as internal lobbyists within the machine for the interests of 'their' industry. Wilks (1990, p. 173) argues that sponsorship divisions (at least in the case of the motor industry) actually communicated badly with companies and that sponsorship was just a 'passive, best-endeavour sort of relationship... involv[ing] no planning and little policy-implementation capability' (Wilks, 1984, p. 194).

The official view was that 'departments need to be critical lobbyists because, at the end of the day, government is interested in total economic performance and a department just acting as a protectionist lobby is unlikely to be contributing to improved performance' (Mueller, 1985, p. 101). Young was adamant that they had to go, however. 'The danger is that "sponsorship" can give the impression of "responsibility" for particular sectors of industry', his 1988 White Paper argued (DTI, 1988, p. 38). He feared that officials who spent a few years in a particular division before moving on would simply end up as the creatures of the trade associations and a conduit for more claims on the public purse (Young, 1990, pp. 240, 257). A National Audit Office investigation of DTI assistance to industry showed that there was something in that suspicion: applications for aid on projects over £2m, vetted by the IDU, resulted in lower percentage level grants than smaller projects examined only by sponsoring divisions. The NAO concluded that the 'shallower investigations' conducted by sponsoring divisions may have led to more aid being given than was strictly necessary to ensure that the projects concerned went ahead (NAO, 1987, pp. 14–16).

'Market' divisions replaced the DTI's sponsorship divisions, focusing on 'the markets for particular goods and services rather than specific supplier industries... [and designed to] tackle broad policy issues affecting all the suppliers and customers in the market in question, rather than dealing with particular industries' (DTI, 1988, pp. 38–9). Grant (1989, p. 93) deprecated the end of the 'sponsorship' function: other countries saw the value of specialist industry divisions as a source of expertise and a means of keeping in contact. He also

detected a 'hidden agenda': destroying part of the administrative apparatus that a future interventionist government would need. In the event,
the vertically organised market divisions did not last long, Young's
successor, Nicholas Ridley, replacing them with 'horizontal units, for
example, 'manufacturing technology', responsible for delivering DTI
services of a particular kind to many types of businesses', though
responsibility for some industrial sectors – vehicles, aerospace, shipbuilding – was located in units called 'Business Task Forces'
(Connelly, 1992, p. 36).

The arrival of Michael Heseltine after the 1992 General Election
saw further changes. 'Sponsorship' divisions were now revived, with
the aim of encouraging closer contacts with industry (the DTI was
apparently not in touch with 60 per cent of Britain's companies), but
the minister indicated that he did not want them to be channels for
special pleading and ruled out the return of subsidies and bail-outs
(indeed, the DTI's budget was set to fall further) (*The Sunday Times*, 7
June 1992; *Guardian*, 4 July 1992). Private sector secondees were
brought into the DTI to work on export promotion and in the department's Innovation Unit. As we saw in more detail in Chapter 2,
Heseltine – styling himself President of the Board of Trade – tried to
combine the rhetoric of free enterprise *and* that of selective intervention. However the sight of the Treasury flexing its muscles and scoring
a point against Heseltine by abolishing the NEDC (a body which he
thought the Industry Minister should chair), together with the fiasco of
the pit closures programme announced in late 1992 (when the
Employment Department was not kept informed of what the DTI was
planning), hardly augured well for this new-style industrial policy. So
the DTI's institutional weakness within government remains very real.
'Whitehall watchers' will have noted that Heseltine was denied the
chairmanship of the Cabinet's industrial policy committee set up in
1992, that role going instead to the 'neutral' Lord Privy Seal. The
DTI's budget – already smaller than that of the Department of
National Heritage – looks set to fall further as a result of a Treasury-
led 'fundamental review' of its spending over the next 5–10 years. The
frontier between the DTI and the Employment Department remains
unsettled, with evidence of duplication, confusion and civil service
infighting; a merger of the two departments could not be ruled out
(Kelly, 1994). It is not surprising that employers' groups continue to
complain that the DTI is not the effective and forceful champion that
industry needs.

7.4   The Whitehall culture

The character of Britain's mandarin élite is a favourite target of 'declin-ist' critics. It is no accident, they suggest, that the civil service took on broadly its modern form at the same time – the end of the nineteenth century – as Britain's economic decline set in. The public school/ Oxbridge anti-industrial culture was the breeding ground for the new corps of administrators who were 'almost without exception lacking in scientific, mechanical, technological or commercial training or experi-ence' (Macdonagh, quoted in Wiener, 1981, p. 24). The mandarins were 'essay-writers rather than problem-solvers', in Correlli Barnett's (1986, p. 215) dismissive phrase. 'The ethos of the British senior civil servant is that of the adviser-regulator, not of the original-thinker-doer', according to Peter Hennessy. This meant that 'the British Civil Service in similar conditions could not have done what the Japanese or, particu-larly, the French bureaucracies did so brilliantly after the war on the economic and industrial fronts... because [it] was not designed for the purpose' (Hennessy, 1989, p. 717). Hennessy in fact contends that Whitehall's failure after 1945 to fashion the peacetime equivalent of the army of 'irregulars' – the businessmen, scientists, engineers and other 'temporaries' who had helped to make the wartime civil service 'a world-beating bureaucracy' – represented 'probably *the* greatest lost opportunity in the history of British public administration' (see Hennessy, 1989, chs 3 and 4).

Wilks' (1990, p. 173) view that 'higher civil servants have little training in, familiarity with, or, one suspects, sympathy for manufac-turing industry' is one that is widely shared. The mandarin who con-fessed that it had never occurred to him to visit a factory – 'What were they like?' – was not the fictional Sir Humphrey but a real-world senior official quoted in the *Financial Times* in early 1993 (21 January 1993)! There is indeed a wide gulf of understanding between Whitehall and the private sector, arising from a difference in culture, a merchant banker seconded for a spell into the DTI told Hennessy (1989, p. 523): 'the civil servant is thinking of his public duty, his responsibility upwards to ministers, whereas the private sector person is thinking of how to get their company to survive in a competitive environment'.

'Ruthless and single-minded maximisers of world market share or gross national product' are not the civil service ideal, Correlli Barnett (1986, p. 221) complained, a view shared by Tony Benn in his 1960s technocratic phase: 'our present Civil Service is not interested in growth. It is geared to care and maintenance' (Benn, 1987, p. 264). Whitehall just does not understand the profit motive, argue some critics. Lord Chandos (a Conservative minister in the 1950s) believed that 'civil servants regard with suspicion and distaste illiterate and vulgar men who have made a lot of money' (quoted in Theakston and Fry, 1994). An official who had been out on secondment to business confessed: 'civil servants often have bad feelings about contractors – they are viewed as "money-grabbing" and that is seen as contemptible. I now realise that making money is alright so long as abnormal profits are not being made' (Gosling and Nutley, 1990, p. 52).

Sir Leslie Murphy (who was chairman of the NEB 1977–9, and who had experience of both Whitehall and private business), agreed that 'civil servants had no industrial experience and did not understand industrial problems'. But his was not a blanket condemnation:

> civil servants were not good at running a large state industrial holding company or dealing with large businesses like BL and Rolls-Royce. However, they were better at handling requests [for financial assistance] under the Industry Acts where social and other considerations had to be taken into account.   (Murphy, 1981, pp. 26, 28).

This balancing or arbitrating role is, of course, the classic 'generalist' function. Within the DTI itself the generalist ethos dominates: officials' 'career moves might well take them from active involvement in the affairs of a sector of manufacturing industry to a post concerned with tourism or the recondite formulae of the General Agreement on Tariffs and Trade' (Blackstone and Plowden, 1988, p. 129).

However, the generalist's lack of in-depth expertise is a key factor in the reactive and arm's-length administrative style marking government's relations with industry. Abromeit's work on government and the British Steel Corporation led her to link lack of expertise with government passivity and policy inertia:

> Frequent changes leave no incentive to civil servants to enter wholeheartedly into the problems they deal with in each position, nor do they allow for commitment to programmes, or for a sense of responsibility for programme results. Instead, civil servants tend to define their tasks in very limited terms ('administering the statutes') and, because of the limited base of knowledge they operate from, to take

the 'safe course' of avoiding risks and postponing decisions – hence to cling to the status quo. (Abromeit, 1986, pp. 95–6).

Generalist mandarins seem particularly vulnerable to the charge of 'amateurism' when dealing with high-technology projects, perhaps one reason why government's role has so often been that of a 'milch cow' in that field (Dell, 1973, p. 165). How else can one explain the behaviour of the Ministry of Aviation official who, faced with the original estimate of £60m for Concorde, cheerfully added another £40m 'for the sake of not getting things wrong'(Bruce-Gardyne and Lawson, 1976, p. 13)? A case-study of the Alvey project also revealed 'the limited ability of non-expert officials in central departments to assess high technology proposals' (Keliher, 1990, p. 67). A Treasury official described his department's approach:

> We often subject what the DTI submits to us by way of these key technology proposals to a 'Red Jelly Test'. If we can substitute 'Red Jelly' for, say, opto-electronics without any damage to their case, then we don't think DTI has presented a very good case because it doesn't discriminate between one technology and another... It's a good exercise to go through because you come up with statements like 'We should support Red Jelly because the Red Jelly producers are risk averse' or 'There are fantastic externalities from Red Jelly'. Bullshit. We want to know precisely what it is you are claiming for this technology as opposed to any other technology.

But another Treasury mandarin explained, 'we wouldn't ask much about the technicalities because we wouldn't be able to judge even if someone told us' (Keliher, 1990, p. 69).

Former Labour minister, Edmund Dell, has similarly noted the way in which the reluctant attitude of the civil service to government intervention in industry, together with lack of substantial experience of industry, has conditioned the form of that intervention when it has occurred:

> Civil servants will know from bitter experience that politically intervention is more likely to be an embarrassment than a triumph. Therefore their protective attitude to ministers as well as to the government service will recommend caution... Where the political risks are so grave and the possibilities of national advantage so

questionable, why get involved? If one has to get involved, why get involved too deeply? Why take management responsibility that can reasonably be left to others?... A rescue operation by the government may bring in a political dividend. But why get involved voluntarily? Why convert what sometimes may be a reluctant necessity into a positive policy of intervention, when the dangers are so great and prospective gains so doubtful? (Dell, 1973, pp. 159–60)

Benn, in the 1970s, declared that 'the idea that somehow you could solve the problem by having more qualified civil servants is rubbish. If I had ten thousand PhDs in Business Studies in my Department of Industry, it would contribute absolutely zero to our productivity' (Benn, 1989, p. 242). Whitehall, however, *has* made efforts to improve its economic and industrial expertise, but deep-rooted attitudes and practices are not easily changed. There is, though, a sense in which it cannot win because closer links with industry fuel left-wing suspicions of a political bias in the civil service in favour of business values (seen in the reactions to retired officials taking jobs in business).

Amazingly, there were only about a dozen professional economists working in Whitehall in 1960 but, following the creation of the Government Economic Service in 1964, the number was almost 200 by 1970 and about 400 by 1976, though the 1980s saw major cutbacks in the government's economics capability: the Economist Group was just 116 strong in 1988 (seven of these in the DTI), growing to 183 (sixteen in the DTI) by 1992.

Attempts have been made via secondments and exchanges to give civil servants direct experience of industry and to fill the skills gap in government by bringing in outside expertise. However, these programmes are not large-scale (280 outward/189 inward movements in 1986, for instance), involve the financial sector and consultancy firms more than manufacturing companies, and departments often waste the experience officials gain by posting them to unrelated jobs on 're-entry' (Gosling and Nutley, 1990). The DTI in particular has acknowledged that the formulation and implementation of industrial policy can require expertise not available in Whitehall (it accounted for 82 of the total of 469 interchanges in 1986 noted above – the Ministry of Defence accounted for 204). Industrial advisers have been brought in on short-term contracts since the 1960s. The Industrial Development Unit (IDU) formed in 1972 to appraise projects and handle applications for selective financial assistance was, from the start, staffed predominantly by secondees from accountancy firms, banks and industry. The Alvey directorate, established in 1983 to fund IT research, brought together civil servants and managers loaned from IT companies. But the scale of this influx must be kept in proportion: DTI staff totalled over 11 000 in 1992, secondments thus involving less than one per cent of its personnel at any one time.

7.5   Parliament and industrial policy

Parliament has not so far loomed large in this chapter because it does not loom large in industrial policy decision-making in Britain. The contribution of parliament as an institution to the making of industrial policy is discounted in most orthodox accounts of the process. The 'policy communities' view focuses on executive-group bargaining, with parliament shut out from the politics of 'bureaucratic accommodation' that ensues. At most, on this view, parliament legitimises policies formulated elsewhere and has an indirect influence as ministers have to calculate what they can get through the Commons (particularly what their own backbenchers will wear). Similarly, in the 'adversary politics' model, what matters is not parliament *per se* but its domination by the Government and the malign effects of ideological polarisation and swings in party support.

Edmund Dell's experience as a minister and MP in the 1960s and 1970s was that parliamentary control of the executive was particularly weak over the making of decisions in the field of industrial policy which discriminated between companies, industries or regions. He believed that governments had to work much harder to justify their interventions in industry to their international partners than they were ever likely to have to do to win parliamentary support (Dell, 1973, pp. 120, 198–9).

'Major industrial policy legislation has been little altered in its passage through Parliament', Grant (1982, pp. 38–9) observed. 'Control of secondary legislation which is often necessary to implement selective assistance schemes is even less satisfactory'. The 1972 and 1975 Industry Acts, for instance, gave ministers wide discretionary powers to provide financial assistance to industry. Under section 8 of the 1972 Act only selective financial assistance over £5m needed authorisation by a House of Commons resolution: Benn gave the Meriden co-op £4.95m and in 1973 Norton Villiers Triumph received

£4.8m, depriving MPs of the opportunity for debate. Parliament is in any case often presented with a *fait accompli* in such cases, with ministers pleading 'commercial confidentiality' as grounds for refusing to make available full details of a company's situation and the Government's rescue package.

The general problem of pinning down responsibility for policy in situations where a number of departments and/or ministers are involved in decision-making is also encountered in the industrial policy area. Harold Wilson refused to allow Harold Lever, Chancellor of the Duchy of Lancaster, to give evidence to a select committee on the Chrysler rescue on the grounds that he was not the responsible departmental minister, though he had in fact been a key figure in the relevant negotiations. The accountability issue was raised in an even more problematic way in the case of the NEB. To operate successfully the NEB was held to require considerable autonomy in its day-to-day commercial decision-making. But holding ministers at arm's length also meant holding Parliament at arm's length. MPs could not question ministers in detail about the NEB's activities, including its expenditure of large sums of public money (a similar difficulty had arisen in the case of the IRC in the 1960s).

There is in any case the frequent complaint (from the CBI, the Hansard Society, and others) that, like the Whitehall mandarins, MPs do not understand the problems of industry and lack that direct personal experience that might act as an antidote to an overly-ideological approach. Judge (1990, ch. 4) concludes that the House of Commons is indeed 'not a microcosm of the composition of British industrial society' and shows that there is in Parliament limited collective experience of major sectors of industry, though the proportion of MPs with pre-entry experience of productive industry is not, he contends, as low as some critics think. He gives the following figures for MPs' primary pre-entry occupations in 1983.

The 'talking classes' dominate the House of Commons: in 1983, 16 per cent of all MPs were lawyers and 13 per cent were from the education sector. More than two-thirds (71 per cent) of MPs were drawn from the service sectors of the economy, compared to 59 per cent of the working population employed in those areas. But Judge points out that the position has been little different at other times in this century: the percentage of MPs coming from the 'productive' industries was 23.5 in 1918, 30.2 in 1923, 15.5 in 1931, 21.1 in 1935, 22.8 in 1945, and 17.9 in 1951 – an average of 23.4 per cent over the whole century. Judge detected a basic divide between the older heavy industries as the

Table 7.1 *MPs' occupational backgrounds*

	% of MPs	% of working population
'Productive' (manufacturing, production, construction, transport)	25.1	38.7
Business services (banking, finance, legal, retail)	34.2	31.8
Other services (education, military, police, media)	37.2	27
Agriculture	3.5	2.5

SOURCE: Judge, 1990, p. 88.

mainstay of Labour's parliamentary representation (with Labour MPs predominantly representing the workforce/unions) and the 'newer' sectors (including the data industry, electronics, and so on) having greater Conservative representation. It is arguable that those criticising MPs and Parliament for being too remote from industry make too much of this sort of biographical data and confuse sociological with political representation. Party ideology and constituency interests count for more in understanding MPs' attitudes and activities, and Parliament's major limitations are surely of an institutional nature (its subordination to the executive, its deficient internal mechanisms and resources).

In a number of ways Parliament may have become a rather more significant actor in the industrial policy field since the 1980s than before, although this development should not be exaggerated. First, there is evidence that MPs seemed to be more active as constituency lobbyists, trying to defend local industries facing job losses or closure and also trying to promote new industry (seeking public assistance, grants, government contracts, and so on). As Wood described it:

Constituency economic lobbying by MPs is not confined to interventions with ministers. MPs lobby and are lobbied by the head offices of firms with plants or offices in their constituencies, as well as firms that might be enticed to make a move into the area. Local authorities, local business groups, trade unions and individual firms often turn to the MP for help in convincing a central government official to make a favourable ruling on a matter of concern to them. (Wood, 1987, p. 399)

The greater attention paid to lobbying MPs and Parliament, argues Judge (1990, p. 221), reflected manufacturing industry's belief that its voice no longer carried the weight that it previously did at the Whitehall level.

Parliament's improved scrutinising capability was the second significant development of the 1980s. The National Audit Office, Parliament's public spending watchdog, has savaged the DTI's procedures for dispensing aid to industry, for instance. The department, it found, 'appeared to have no formalised system for surveying the industrial field to ensure that they identified problem areas and to identify priorities for assistance'. Assistance had not always been as well-targeted or as cost-effective as possible, and the absence of clear and quantified objectives made the assessment of value for money difficult (NAO, 1987). The House of Commons Trade and Industry select committee, established in 1979, has played a monitoring and information-generating role. It has attempted to operate in a bipartisan fashion which, inevitably, means avoiding contentious policy issues (the pit closures inquiry being something of an exception here). The government's central policy objectives and its major strategic decisions have not been something over which the committee has had much influence. From ministers' point of view, the select committee may sometimes complicate the decision-making process or embarrass them, but it is not a body that alone can deflect them from the course they choose. Similarly, the House of Lords' select committee reports on manufacturing (the 'Aldington report' 1984 and the 'Caldecote report' 1991) turned out to have minimal influence upon government policy.

Judge's view (1990, p. 221) is that the House of Commons after 1979 became both more and less capable of influencing the direction of industrial policy. At a *micro* level, he argues, where MPs have accepted the general framework of government policy, they have often been successful in influencing the details. But MPs have had very little influence over the government's *macro* policy aims (privatisation, monetarism, the free market, the move away from industrial policy).

7.6 Conclusions

Making sense of Britain's economic and industrial travails requires a multi-causal, not a mono-causal explanation. 'The state is not primarily responsible for Britain's economic decline', argued Peter Hall:

'however it has not been an innocent bystander' (Hall, 1986, p. 67). Walter Williams (1989, p. 251) agreed that 'an ailing machinery of government is not the primary cause of Britain's problems. Exogenous facts beyond the control of British government no doubt dominate all controllable factors'. William Keegan and Rupert Pennant-Rea (1979, p. 9) made the point more vividly: 'the economic policy machine of ministers and officials has given the impression of permanently trying to run up the downward escalator'.

Quizzed by Peter Hennessy, the economist David Henderson rather pooh-poohed the idea that a country's economic success depended crucially on the quality of its civil service:

> I'm not sure that in the British case it's been a major influence on economic performance. In so far as it has been, it has been to do with ideas that were held outside the Civil Service as well ... The British Civil Service has something to answer for in its closed nature and the way it has not reacted to evidence. But it's very easy to overdo the extent to which you can blame economic performance on the administrators   (Hennessy, 1989, p. 688)

But as Sir John Hoskyns has argued, it is not the individual bits and pieces of the British system of government that matter so much as the system as a whole – 'the total "configuration"'. A few adjustments with a spanner, so to speak, are not enough. The British state has developed, historically, as 'a "Pontius Pilate" rather than a "Bismarckian" state' (Wilks, 1986, p. 40) – more *liberal* than *developmental*, as we observed in Chapter 1. Its permanent officials are remote from industry and their traditions are of arm's length regulation rather than interventionist and discriminatory. Its politicians react to short-term crises rather than articulating long-term modernisation strategies. Its administrative machinery gives a greater priority to financial and macroeconomic policy than to any sort of co-ordinated and coherent industrial policy.

Not surprisingly therefore, there have been many calls for change. Peter Hall has argued that 'a state can transform the operation of its economic system, but first it must transform itself'(Hall, 1986, p. 68), citing the French experience in the post-war period (but the French, of course, had the advantage of a deep-rooted *dirigiste* state tradition). Walter Williams cautioned that modernising the British government system did not 'guarantee the curing of the British disease', but nevertheless believed that without 'an institutional great leap', the 'continuing pre-modern anti-modern British central government seems likely to doom the nation to economic decline and political instability' (Williams, 1989, pp. 251, 259). Wilks too (1986, p. 45) was clear that Britain 'does not require a policy, it requires an upheaval in the institutions of economic life ... The need is for basic reform of the institutions, policy-making processes and some of the traditional features of economic structure.'

But Britain cannot simply transplant a Japanese-style MITI and a French-style breed of technocratic officials. The traditions, constitutions and political environments of French and Japanese government are very different from those of Britain. It is also clear that administrative reform is not something that involves a 'big bang' implementation of a critic's blueprint but is instead a process of piecemeal adaptation, as seen with developments since the 1960s – in terms of personnel (civil service reform) and machinery (the emergence of the DTI). The problem is, of course, that change at this pace is probably not enough to arrest, let alone reverse, economic and industrial decline quickly, and that will make the task much more difficult and politically perilous. If what one leading civil servant once called 'the orderly management of decline' is no longer a viable long-term option – not least because it cannot be kept a politically and socially orderly process indefinitely – we are still a long way from developing the political and governmental apparatus that may be a necessary but not sufficient condition of economic regeneration.

8 Local and Regional Economic Development

Ed Gouge

8.1 Introduction

The effects of industrial change on the wealth, social character and politics of local areas are intense, particularly where a locality has been dependent on one or two major industries. It is not surprising, therefore, that both local and central government, and even local business, have created policies to try to deal with local economic problems. In addition, there has been a long-standing imbalance in economic development between the regions of Britain which has required government attention.

This chapter will look first at policies designed to correct regional imbalances, from their adoption in the early post-war period to their decline in the 1980s and at the recent revival of interest in regional questions largely stimulated by the European Union. The second part of the chapter will examine the development of economic intervention by local authorities and other organisations in their areas and by central government and its agencies in localities.

8.2 Regional industrial policy

Variations in unemployment between regions, related to the decline of heavy industry, had appeared in the inter-war period, but public intervention to deal with this was limited. The experience of the Second World War and the election of a Labour Government in 1945 provided the conditions for a more interventionist economic policy. The wartime Coalition Government saw the preparation of ideas for the reconstruction of the economy and society of Britain to produce a better standard of living for the working class as essential in order to inspire the population to tolerate current deprivations and keep up the war effort. The 1944 White Paper on Employment Policy outlined two ways of trying to prevent the levels of unemployment which had prevailed during the 1920s and 1930s. First, to use macroeconomic policy to reduce unemployment due to lack of demand, by stimulating consumption subject to other objectives such as maintaining a balance of payments surplus. Second, to deal with 'structural' unemployment in those regions where traditional industries had been in decline before the war by means of a programme of taking industrial jobs to the workers in those areas. The Labour Government, with a high proportion of MPs from these regions, if not such a high proportion as at present, could be expected to ensure that a regional policy was carried out.

The new Government chose not to use the local authorities as the main vehicle for policies on structural unemployment. This was despite the involvement of many local authorities in their local economies since the late nineteenth century. In 1899, for example, Luton Council, alarmed by the effect of foreign competition on the straw hat industry, began a programme to attract new firms. Derby set up a development committee in 1906 to look at how its economy could be diversified away from overdependence on railway and related engineering (Ward, 1990). Larger towns regularly promoted the advantages of their locations for manufacturing firms, while seaside towns did the same for their tourist industry. The onset of the depression in the 1930s led many authorities to subsidise firms with cheap land or electricity and even to carry out industrial building themselves. Labour councils had seen the improvement of wages and conditions of work as an objective and applied standards to their own manual workforce and to that of firms to which they contracted work.

Central government in the 1940s, however, was confident of its ability to control its reform programmes from the centre. Whitehall had successfully intervened to run the war economy. The Board of Trade had administered, fairly efficiently, a system of licensing of new building to ensure that supplies were channelled towards the war effort. It had managed the reorganisation of production in existing factories. In the words of Hugh Dalton, the President of the Board of Trade, there was a feeling that in many areas of policy 'the gentleman in Whitehall really does know best'. Central government had also since 1934, in designated areas with high unemployment, given loans and grants to incoming industry and carried out factory building and infrastructure improvements. The Local Government Board, the ministry responsible for supervising local authorities, had not been keen on local authorities' independent industrial promotion and development initiatives before the war, and so there was an established civil service resistance to creating a programme that would be developed locally.

The pattern of policy was now set and the existence of a Labour Government only modified its form. It was a policy based on financial incentives to manufacturing firms to move to designated Development Areas accompanied by central government investment in infrastructure and sites. This was accompanied by a variation of the wartime licensing system in the form of Industrial Development Certificates (IDCs), required before planning permission could be given by local authorities to any development of over 5000 sq.ft in those parts of the country outside the Development Areas. The two parts of the system were run from Whitehall by the Board of Trade, while local authorities designated sites for industrial development in the land use plans that they were now required to produce. The system was regional in scale but essentially local in impact. The Development Areas were a collection of the localities that had seen high unemployment before the war and areas gained or lost status as their local unemployment rates changed. Policy was concerned with individual investment decisions involving manufacturing industry. There was no attempt to study local or regional economies as a whole, or to integrate firms with each other, or with wider aspects of their surrounding economies.

There was broad political agreement surrounding the new industrial location policies. The main political parties had agreed many of the construction plans during the wartime coalition, and the post-war Conservative Party had leaders such as Harold Macmillan, who had seen the effects of unemployment as a young MP in the North-East, determined to modernise the party by accepting the welfare state and management of the national economy. The policies also appeared to have an immediate impact. By 1947 the Development Areas with 10 per cent of Britain's population had received 50 per cent of new manufacturing industrial development and had a large supply of advance factories.

Despite this early success, regional policy was soon in abeyance. The cuts in expenditure following the balance of payments crisis of 1947 led to a reduction in the programme. By the early 1950s there was economic growth across Western Europe, but industrial production in most other European countries was only just beginning to overcome wartime devastation and so Britain's heavy industries, traditionally the mainstay of the Development Areas, found a captive market, and unemployment in these areas fell to the national average. Equally, there was enough growth to maintain the strong manufacturing base in the inner parts of the big cities while also allowing investment to move to the Development Areas and to the new and expanded towns that had been started during this period.

The apparent disappearance of regional economic disparities led the Conservative Government to reduce spending in the Development Areas from the £8.1 m that they had inherited in 1951 to £4.8 m per annum between 1951 and 1958, to end advance factory building and effectively to suspend the operation of IDCs. Grants for capital expenditure to firms locating in the Areas remained automatic.

The winter of 1957–8 saw the first slight economic downturn since the war and the return of rates of unemployment above national levels in the Development Areas. The reaction of the Conservative Government illustrated that regional policy had become a means of managing local unemployment rather than part of any broader national or regional strategy. Expenditure in the Development Areas was increased to £11.8 m by 1960–1. The Distribution of Industry (Industrial Finance) Act, 1958 and the Local Employment Act, 1960 extended the scope of financial incentives to firms and concentrated help on smaller Development Districts defined more clearly by unemployment levels and, at first, to areas with high unemployment outside the existing designated areas; and IDC control became effective again.

During the period 1958–1979, regional policy was consistently applied by both Conservative and Labour Governments. The objective was still to manage unemployment, which was gradually increasing throughout the period, in local areas. The Development Areas were politically important to both parties. For Labour they were the source of their parliamentary majorities, while the Conservatives began to lose ground there (the Conservatives had a majority of Scottish seats in 1955 but only 20 by 1983) and were concerned to reverse this. Both parties were being challenged by the Scottish and Welsh nationalist parties, which had startling by-election victories at Hamilton (1968) and Carmarthen (1967), respectively. The appointment of a Minister for the North-East illustrated political concern for that area. There was also a broader argument in the economic boom of the first half of this period that growth in the Development Areas would reduce some of the inflationary pressure caused by labour shortages in the South-East.

The policy remained one of industrial development controls in the prosperous areas and provision of infrastructure and incentives to industrial investment in the depressed regions. The bias towards the encouragement of manufacturing was to a small degree corrected with the creation of a Location of Offices Bureau in 1965. The London office boom illustrated the increasing importance of service employment and the Bureau was to encourage firms to move away from London, where Office Development Permits were required for new development. Public sector offices, such as vehicle licensing, were also decentralised.

The period also saw an attempt to push policy in a different direction. Development Area policy was designed to alleviate problems in the areas of worst unemployment. The Toothill Report in 1961, the result of a committee of business, trade union and academic members set up to look at the problems of the Scottish economy, proposed that the areas with the most potential for economic growth in the depressed regions should receive the most government spending, rather than the areas with the most problems. Growth pole theory was attracting academic support and, though it remained rather poorly defined, its supporters agreed that concentration rather than dispersal of investment would produce economies of scale, and that growth would become self-sustaining and spread wealth to the surrounding poorer areas. The Conservative Government took an interest in the idea, but the election of a Labour Government in 1964 brought back to office Douglas Jay, who had been the minister responsible for regional policy in the 1940s and who showed no interest in innovation. Nevertheless, the idea influenced the creation of a second wave of New Towns, mainly in the Development Areas, and could be seen in the proposals of the advisory regional planning strategies that were commissioned by central government or developed by the Regional Economic Development Councils, created by the new Department of Economic Affairs in 1965. The Scottish Office showed more enthusiasm for regional planning and supported a Falkirk/ Grangemouth growth zone. The returning Conservatives incorporated growth zones in their 1970 White Paper on Regional Policy, but a sudden increase in unemployment in 1971 pushed them back into supporting any locality with high unemployment.

Apart from the growth pole ideas and the effects of the debate over Scottish and Welsh devolutions in the mid-1970s, regional policy varied in detailed operation rather then in basic objectives during the 1960s and 1970s. The range of areas assisted was extended beyond the traditional heavy industrial locations to include rural areas, for example in south-west England, the big northern cities, and seaside resorts and also the north Midlands. Three categories of area were created, making the system more complicated. Special Development Areas were created in 1967 with extra levels of assistance, and Intermediate Areas were introduced with more limited assistance mainly for building and land clearance. The types of incentives were also changed. At various times firms received grants towards new building, plant and machinery, training, operating costs and even a direct subsidy related to the numbers employed. The Regional Employment Premium, which had the advantage of being directly related to employment, was intended to make goods produced by firms cheaper. There were also cheap rents for factories, free depreciation on plant and machinery, and a rebate on Selective Employment Tax. Labour was keener on IDCs than were the Conservatives, who were suspicious of direct controls on industry, and in 1964 Labour reduced the size of new development that needed an IDC to as little as 1000 sq.ft.

By the mid-1970s the centrally directed local economic policy aimed at depressed regions that had been in operation in some form since the 1930s was beginning to look obsolete. The policy depended on mobile manufacturing industry generated from the southern half of Britain but this was no longer forthcoming. From the 1960s, British manufacturing came under increasing pressure from world competition, resulting in falling profits, and when demand fell in the recessions after 1973, 1980–1 and 1991–3, significant proportions of it did not survive. Employment in manufacturing fell from 1966, even in the newer, consumer industries.

Firms cut costs by introducing more capital-intensive methods, by concentrating production in fewer plants and by relocating to new areas where cheaper labour could be used. The effects of the restructuring of manufacturing industry on local areas was dramatic. The factories which were closed were generally the older ones where the physical layout would make it difficult to introduce new machinery, or which where located in high-wage and unionised areas where labour costs were higher and where there would be more resistance to new practices that would worsen working conditions. These factories were largely in the inner areas of big cities which had been the powerhouse of British manufacturing in the 1950s. Increased traffic congestion in cities was also a factor and some firms sought locations with a better environment to attract the skilled staff that were needed with the adoption of new technology. The Development Areas were also highly vulnerable, as they had a strong history of labour organisation. The Development Areas lost employment and there was much less mobile industry to be attracted. After the mid-1970s it is estimated that regional policy made little impact, though parts of South Wales did gain new investment. Further rationalisations in coal, steel and shipbuilding worsened the situation. In general, firms moved to new factories, or concentrated production on existing factories in small to medium-sized towns in Southern Britain, the Midlands and East Anglia, employing many more women and at lower wage-rates. Central Government reacted slowly to these changing regional economic patterns, but in 1977 gave the inner cities equal status to the Development Areas for economic development resources.

In Scotland the increasing ineffectiveness of regional policy and the possibility of using North Sea oil to revive the Scottish economy if it could only be freed from British control was an important factor in the success of the Scottish National Party, which received its peak support in the October 1974 General Election. The Labour Government reacted to the situation by setting up the Scottish Development Agency (SDA) with a new approach to regional economic development, and a similar organisation in Wales. The SDA was a regional industrial development body with a versatility that has not been seen before or since in Britain. It was created when the Labour Government still had enthusiasm for an industrial strategy. The SDA was seen as a regional version of the National Enterprise Board, with powers to provide an advice and consultancy service to firms and provide finance though loans, grants and equity provision, as well as to attract investment and to carry out factory building and environmental improvement. Whereas the NEB gradually lost the support of the Labour Government, the SDA was seen as essential to its political strategy in Scotland and had the support of the Scottish Office. The SDA developed the whole range of its powers, including the development of relationships with the financial institutions to provide management and financial help to small and medium-sized firms, and the encouragement of joint ventures between Scottish and foreign companies. It also attempted to create strategies for what it identified as growth sectors in the Scottish economy, such as electronics, health-care, energy-related industries, and production engineering, and for some traditional industries.

As we saw in more detail in Chapter 2, the Conservative Government taking office in 1979 had a different view of economic development from that which underlay the traditional policies of regional aid. Neo-liberal economic theory argued that the market would equalise economic factors between areas over time. However, restrictions on the workings of the market, for example national wage bargaining, prevented this. A second strand of market ideas was the view that there had to be an enterprise culture that would produce entrepreneurs with new ideas for products and services and encourage the setting-up of small firms. There was considerable interest in the idea that a supply of small firms provided the basis for future company growth and job creation. The Development Areas and the inner cities were seen as particularly lacking in the base for this enterprise culture.

These two strands ran in different directions, the first towards deregulation nationally and locally, and the second towards government intervention to create the enterprise culture. However, political considerations also pushed the Government towards intervention. Public focus on the inner cities and the riots there in 1981 and again in the mid-1980s strengthened the hand of ministers such as Michael Heseltine, Secretary of State for the Environment from 1979 to 1983, who believed in a stronger government role. The Secretaries of State for Scotland and Wales were faced with the problem of retaining political support in parts of Britain with less confidence in the Thatcherite experiment, and so the Scottish and Welsh Development Agencies survived to carry out major interventionist programmes. The Welsh Development Agency was less ambitious, but even as late as 1988 Peter Walker, the Secretary of State for Wales, was able to announce a public sector-dominated revitalisation package for the South Wales valleys. Nevertheless, the SDA was gradually steered away from strategic intervention to local and small-firm initiatives, culminating in its redesignation as 'Scottish Enterprise', which was broken into local area teams.

The Government gradually reduced the significance of regional policy. In any case academic opinion had concluded that it had had little success in attracting mobile industry after 1976, while in 1980 and 1981 the closure of branch plants in assisted areas accelerated (Townsend, 1987, p. 230). In 1980 the areas covered by regional policy were reduced from 47 per cent to 28 per cent of the working population, and standard grants were no longer to be mandatory in Intermediate Areas. Office Development Permits and Industrial Development Certificates, which restrained growth in more prosperous areas, were abolished.

In 1984 the Government was forced to grant Intermediate Area status to the West Midlands conurbation because of the collapse of manufacturing industry in that region, and to restore assistance to Greater Manchester and Sheffield. The map of assisted areas now covered the conurbations of Britain, excluding London, rather than particular regions. By the mid-1980s expenditure on regional assistance was about half of what it had been in the mid-1970s and ministers now perceived it as having a social role in relieving unemployment rather than any economic policy role. A final change in 1988 ended Regional Development Grants as automatic grants, and resources were concentrated on selective assistance, with more concern for service industries, the adoption of new technology and small firms.

The run-down of national regional policy was made easier by the existence of the European Regional Development Fund (ERDF), which had been created in 1976. Local authorities in all areas except the South-East and East Anglia received some funding between 1975 and 1987. The ERDF monies were meant to be additional to those allocated by national governments to poorer regions, but in Britain, and in other countries, central governments kept control over them and saw them as a substitute for their own spending. Grants from the ERDF did not allow local authorities to spend above the limits of expenditure on infrastructure work that central government imposed, but provided cheaper finance than the capital markets. Reform of the EC regional policy in 1988 provided more resources and still covered most of the regions previously funded. The EC Commission has been concerned that the Single European Market will adversely affect the less competitive regions and so is seeking to expand the Regional Fund further.

Regional aid is now seen as a minor part of policy. However, the depression of the early 1990s particularly affected service industries in the south of England and so the Government extended Development Area status to the Isle of Thanet in Kent and Intermediate Area status to a range of seaside areas in the South-East and to parts of London. The depression has also meant that much larger areas, including those in the south, became eligible for EU aid. The opposition parties have shown an interest in a system of regional government with economic development powers, similar to those that exist in other parts of Europe, and a different result in the 1992 General Election would probably have seen some sort of initiative. The Government showed no interest in elected regional government or devolution to Scotland, but during 1993 moved to create a civil servant with responsibility for the

overall co-ordination in the regional offices of those ministries that
have an economic role.

8.3 Local economic development

One of the major features of industrial policy in the last twenty years
has been the range of initiatives developed by local authorities in order
to stimulate economic growth in their areas. There remain limitations to
the powers and, more seriously to the resources available to local
authorities, but nevertheless their activity has been significant. We have
seen above that local authorities were largely bypassed by post-war
regional policy. Their main involvement was under the new powers,
given by the Town and Country Planning Act, 1947 to produce development plans which would allocate land for employment, and to
control development. Local authorities in Development Areas were
involved in advertising and in providing premises and infrastructure to
meet the needs of incoming firms. Similar work was done in the new
towns, designated by the Labour Government in the 1940s and 1960s to
receive overspill population and manufacturing industry from the big
cities, but here by Development Corporations run by boards appointed
by central government. The Conservative Government after 1951 preferred Town Expansion Schemes – largely organised by the big cities,
which were exporting people and jobs.

Local economic development in the period 1945–70 was therefore
largely concerned with managing the physical implications of manufacturing growth. There was little or no analysis of the local economy
as a whole. The creation of the trunk road system and the national electricity grid in the 1930s had created the idea that almost all light manufacturing firms were highly mobile and could easily be attracted to new
locations. The exception to this pattern of growth was in the rural areas
of Britain. Many of the small industries there had closed down because
of competition from larger firms in the towns, and this, combined with
a depression in agriculture since the 1880s, had produced rural depopu-
lation. The Development Commission, a government agency set up in
1909 to carry out projects to help agriculture, now began to provide
loans and grants to small firms in rural areas.

From the mid-1960s increasing unemployment and the decline of
British manufacturing led local opinion to focus on new policies. The
falls in manufacturing employment in the major conurbations were

dramatic, though not fully appreciated at the time. The West Midlands lost 369 500 jobs between 1965 and 1981, some 40 per cent of its total; while Greater London's manufacturing employment declined from 1 453 000 in 1961 to 680 600 in 1981 (Buck *et al.*, 1986, pp. 62–4). By the 1970s unemployment rates in local areas of these previously prosperous conurbations were as high as in the Development Areas and the local authorities began to lobby for Development Area status. Central government reacted slowly to the inner city economic problem. The issue were seen as social during the 1960s and early 1970s and, in particular, the result of the adjustment of immigrant populations to the cities and the loss of skilled labour to the new towns. The new towns programme was ended, even though its contribution to decentralisation of industry was limited. However, continued increases in unemployment rates and the work of the Community Development Projects and Inner Areas Studies commissioned by the Government, which documented the collapse of manufacturing industry in their areas, forced a realisation of the problem. The 1977 White Paper, *Policy for the Inner Cities*, gave the inner cities equal status to the Development Areas in the allocation of economic development resources.

(i) *The development of local authority initiatives*

Central government in the 1970s remained largely preoccupied with the national economic issues of inflation, wages policy, major industrial closures and national unemployment figures and, apart from the slow development of inner-city economic policies after 1977, took limited interest in local economic policy until the mid 1980s. It abandoned demand management as a means of maintaining full employment and its regional policy became ineffective. Local authorities therefore began to look for their own solutions.

Four types of local authorities became involved in economic development. Authorities in the North-East, Scotland and Wales found that regional policy was having less effect as mobile investment declined and even the branch plants set up by large firms taking advantage of regional assistance were closed. Traditional manufacturing areas such as West Yorkshire or Lancashire which had not experienced the problems of the hard-core Development Areas now had rapid job loss. Local authorities with an inner-city area overlapped with the first two categories, but included the London Boroughs and the West Midlands authorities which had previously been seen as a source of industrial jobs to be exported elsewhere. Finally, the more remote rural areas were too isolated to receive firms decentralising from the cities, and were losing jobs in agriculture.

It would be wrong to see local authorities acting entirely independently and on their own initiative. The Labour Government coming into office in 1974 had ideas of a National Industry Strategy and created a National Enterprise Board. The Department of the Environment, in a 1977 Circular, encouraged all local authorities to provide enough industrial land and to be sympathetic to industrial firms in areas of mixed or residential land uses, even if they created some environmental problems.

Central government concern with unemployment in the inner cities led to discussions with local authorities in the inner cities and the passage of the Inner Urban Areas Act, 1978. This gave powers to local authorities in designated urban areas to improve their older industrial estates, give loans and grants to firms and more easily acquire land for industrial development. It picked up on policies that were already being carried out by pioneering local authorities (those in the North-East had promoted the Tyne and Wear Act, 1976 to obtain extra powers) and pushed them at all councils in metropolitan areas. Partnerships of central and local government and other public and voluntary bodies with extra resources were designated in London Docklands, Hackney–Islington, Lambeth, Newcastle–Gateshead, Manchester–Salford, Liverpool and Birmingham to tackle the range of economic and social problems. Other public organisations became directly involved in local economies often in co-operation with local authorities. Coal and steel closures led the nationalised industries to set up NCB (Enterprise) Ltd and BSC (Industries) Ltd respectively to help the areas affected. The latter attempted, in towns such as Ebbw Vale and Consett, to encourage new firms to diversify the local economies that depended almost entirely on the steel works. The Scottish and Welsh Development Agencies worked in partnership with local authorities, and in Scotland the SDA was very much the dominant partner to the smaller authorities.

Local authorities reacted in two, rather contradictory, ways to the shortage of mobile industry. On the one hand, they decided to compete more fiercely for the small supply of mobile firms and on the other, they looked to their existing local economies and sought to help firms to expand or become more efficient and to encourage the creation of new small firms. They argued that small and medium-sized firms were tied to local economies, in contrast to large firms that might take local authority help and later shut down local branch plants if they needed to rationalise.

Although local authorities turned towards their local economies, they had little experience in either analysing how they worked or in dealing with the problems of individual firms. It is not surprising therefore that they tried to adapt their existing skills to the new problems. Local authorities, especially in the Development Areas, become more ambitious in promoting their areas to potential investors. Advertising in national newspapers and trade journals, mail shots to firms in growth areas, and attendance at national and international trade fairs and exhibitions were the main methods. Although some of this was in co-operation, for example via the North of England Development Council for local authorities in the North-East, disillusion began to set in by the late 1970s about the effectiveness of promotion. Success in promotion depended on being able to offer regional assistance, and increased pressure was put on central government by local areas to gain assisted area status or to move up from lower to higher categories of assistance.

Secondly, local authorities sought to lower costs for new or expanding manufacturing firms by providing ready-serviced industrial land, by giving grants and loans for new building and plant, and by allowing rent-free periods or cheap rents on local authority estates. As manufacturing industry declined, the property market showed less interest in factory building and more in retail and office development that provided higher returns. Local authorities became involved, in many cases for the first time, in advance factory building. In the North, Scotland and Wales this was for medium-sized and small units, and elsewhere mainly for small units, as a market hardly existed in these types of property. The provision of small units became a major local programme, one supported by central government, and gradually became more innovative – with councils providing pooled services such as typing for firms in clusters of small units.

Thirdly, local authorities sought to increase the efficiency of existing firms by encouraging the improvement of older premises. Rochdale pioneered the idea of Industrial Improvement Areas on older industrial estates where improvements to premises, better access and environmental enhancement would help firms already operating there, and make the area more attractive to new investment. The Government incorporated new powers for inner-city authorities to declare Industrial Improvement Areas with funding for the work and grants and loans to firms. By 1984 over 200 had been declared, mostly to cover older industrial areas or estates but including some commercial areas as well.

Finally, the local authority became the central point for information on available premises and on the range of grants that could be obtained. Already a range of central and local bodies were involved in local economic development, and this complexity of organisation has been one of the distinguishing characteristics of policy in this field. Central government encouraged local authorities to provide a named officer to carry out this industrial liaison.

Undoubtedly newer and better premises provided benefits to firms and helped them to adopt new working methods and expand. Even in the mid-1980s some 18 per cent of industrial buildings had been built before 1919 and a further 22 per cent between 1919 and 1965, and early post-war property was now becoming obsolete (Fothergill *et al.*, 1987, p. 20). Small firms were facing difficulty in finding suitable and cheap premises. There is, however, no guarantee that premises in themselves create lots of new jobs. The provision of new premises may merely move firms from one place to another and even encourage firms to shed labour by the adoption of more capital-intensive methods. The rate of local authority factory building could never keep up with the huge numbers of jobs lost by the closure of manufacturing firms. Even by 1979, therefore, more adventurous authorities were moving beyond the provision of premises. The desire to generate change in the indigenous economy led to an interest in the impediments to the creation of small firms, where problems of finance, marketing, or management could be more important than a shortage of premises. Local authorities began to look at whether they could provide a wide-ranging advice service to potential and existing new firms. The Manpower Services Commission was created by central government in 1973 to tackle the problems of unemployment, and the expansion in its activities led to local training projects with which local authorities became involved.

This development of a greater variety of local economic policies by local authorities came up against a number of constraints. Local authorities in Britain have to have sanction from an Act of Parliament to carry out any function. Local authorities had had for some time possession of legal powers in relation to land and development, while locally sponsored legislation and the Inner Urban Areas Act, 1978 supplemented this. Extension to policy areas such as direct support to the everyday operations of firms or training raised questions of the legal powers available. Councillors and officers responsible for economic development began to look to Section 137 of the Local Government Act 1972 (Section 83 of the Local Government (Scotland) Act 1973 in Scotland) which allowed local authorities to spend a 2p in the £ tax on any purpose that they considered to be of benefit to their inhabitants. The amount raised was limited (£38 m for the largest local authority, the Greater London Council) and other types of projects competed for the funds.

The widening of policy created problems for local authority organisation. Work on factory development and improvement could be reasonably well handled by officers with planning, surveying or architectural qualifications in established planning and estates departments. An extension into business advice and the assessment of firms for loans and grants, into training or into analysis of the local economy, required skills not found in local authorities. Local authority committees were not geared to taking the quick decisions which firms often wanted, and so separate economic development committees were set up. Neither officer nor councillors in the 1970s really came to grips with the idea of a comprehensive economic strategy and policy largely consisted of a package of industrial projects.

(ii) The rise and fall of the radical model

After 1980 quite new policies were attempted by a number of Labour-controlled authorities. These policies were also intended to be part of a wider strategy that looked further than just the relief of unemployment and the building up of the local industrial base. The new strategy was gradually undermined by central government restrictions in the late 1980s, but has had a continuing effect on local practice and especially on the debate about future local economic strategies.

A number of changes in the 1970s came together to influence the new approach. Radical ideas in the late 1960s emphasised the need for people at the grassroots level, whether in the workplace or the community, to come together and organise in order to change society. In the 1970s there was an expansion of local groups concerned with the improvement of their neighbourhood and of professional community workers employed to help stimulate this activity. Marxist ideas were used to examine local government, previously largely ignored by academics, and certain writers developed the idea of the 'local state', the network of public organisations including the local authority, which could be used either to support the operation of capitalism or to modify it to help the working class locally. Trade unionists in firms threatened with closure, such as Lucas Aerospace, drew up alternative production plans using the existing technology in their factories to produce new products. The 'new left' achieved more power in the Labour Party generally and as local councillors replaced older councillors in safe Labour authorities and on the metropolitan county councils which Labour won in 1981. Finally, the new Conservative Government's policy of a strong sterling and higher interest rates led to a sudden rise in unemployment in 1980 and 1981 and the closure of an exceptionally large number of factories through company collapse. The need for a local economic policy seemed more important than ever.

The new policies were not widespread, even among Labour councils. Furthermore, there was no clear division between radical and non-radical councils in economic policy, although councils in the core Development Areas tended to keep to their existing policies. A new approach was pioneered by the Labour leadership in the London Borough of Wandsworth, in power between 1974 and 1982; and, after 1981, the Greater London Council, the West Midlands County Council and Sheffield City Council were. each in different ways, leaders in the field. The seven metropolitan county councils, all Labour-controlled after 1981, had the resources and particularly the staff to experiment. However, the ideas were adopted to some degree by many Labour councils and spread through the local government professionals to influence even Conservative-controlled authorities. Wandsworth, controlled by an increasingly right-wing Conservative group after 1982, continued to have active economic policies, while Kent County Council adopted some of the initiatives pioneered by Labour-inspired enterprise boards. Councils adopting new policies still continued to some degree with 'traditional' policies of industrial building, promotion and encouragement of small firms.

At the heart of the new model of economic policy were two approaches. The first was the view that one of the major problems of British industrial performance was a particular failure of the market which public financial help to firms could correct. The second was that Labour local authorities should use their powers and resources to intervene in the local economy to improve the position of workers as against that of employers. There was always, however, potential for conflict between the objective of helping firms to be profitable and that of strengthening labour.

The first approach stemmed from the argument that Britain's orientation towards international finance had meant that the banks and other investors had ignored the needs of manufacturing industry. This might be true even of large firms, although national policy would have to deal with that, but it was certainly true of small to medium-sized firms not quoted on the Stock Exchange, who were starved of funds to modernise. For local authorities, concentration on the funding of this sector had advantages, because these firms were normally locally owned and so would not take public investment and then move out as the multinationals in the Development Areas had done. Local Labour politicians did not pretend that with the resources available to them they could have a major or rapid effect on the local economy, but believed that they could demonstrate the success of intervention. This would give credibility to a national policy of reflation, part of the Alternative Economic Strategy adopted by the national Labour Party.

If the first approach would help capital to restructure and become more profitable, the second approach was designed to strengthen labour. Investment in firms would have strings attached, unlike most previous local authority and regional funding. For example, firms would have to recognise trade unions, pay reasonable wages and adopt policies of health and safety at work. The local authority would also use its own power in the marketplace as a major purchaser to get similar commitments from the firms that supplied it. Trade unions and groups of workers opposing the restructuring and closure of factories would be given resources to develop alternatives more advantageous to the workforce.

Another element of the radical approach was to relate social objectives to economic development. This had been in evidence to some extent in inner-city policy but had been absent from property-based approaches, apart from a general desire to help the unemployed. Local authorities would now seek to help groups disadvantaged in the labour market, such as women or black workers, both through the local authority's own employment structure and by its intervention in the market. Many projects would be aimed specifically at the poorest communities and encourage people in these communities to become involved in organising the projects.

These broad objectives led to a range of policies which are discussed below. They also required new styles of organisation. The active authorities created employment departments – the first was in Sheffield in 1981 – with some staff from outside the built environment professions that had dominated local economic policy before. The new officers had expertise in community organisation or financial and economic analysis or in trade unions and industry. They also tended to be politically sympathetic to the new approach, mirroring the much greater role of councillors in leading policies rather than simply relying on council officers.

The main vehicle for intervention in industry in many radical local authorities in the 1980s was the *enterprise board*. Enterprise boards were still under political control because they still had councillors on their management boards, received funding from the authority and often had the outlines of their annual work programme laid down by the authority. However, their semi-independent character meant that they were able to be more flexible and take decisions more quickly, although despite these advantages some councils such as Sheffield and Nottinghamshire preferred to keep control within the council and did not set up boards.

Boards were able to give loans and even take a share of the ownership of firms to give them capital to expand, and they were ready to be involved in financial restructuring, mergers or management buyouts. A combination of private and public funds was mobilised for these purposes on the basis that profitability could be achieved as a result of the funding. Capital was given primarily to medium-sized firms to meet the funding gap in this sector, rather than to very small firms which were often seen as poor employers. It was soon found, however, that medium-sized firms also suffered from poor business planning and marketing or from limited use of new technology and so boards began to help with advice on these.

The West Midlands and Greater London Enterprise Boards related their interventions to a broader view of the local economy by means of sector studies. Strategies were drawn up, for example, for the foundry industry in the West Midlands and the food processing industry in London, while Lancashire intervened to rationalise the fishing fleet at Fleetwood. The GLC, in particular, related some of these studies to new arguments about flexible specialisation. A number of writers, most notably Piore and Sabel (1984), have argued that computer-programmed industrial production allows firms to make rapid changes in the specifications of the product marketed in order to react quickly to changes in consumer demand, and that small and medium-sized firms were in a better position to take advantage of this than large firms. These firms also divided parts of the production process between them and clustered in an 'industrial district' to allow easy contact. Although there has been considerable controversy about these ideas, the view of some economic development officers was that public technological, financial and other support could help to create these new areas of industry and influence them.

Despite these attempts to create a wider strategy, most interventions by enterprise boards were opportunistic. Although the boards showed returns on capital that were as good as comparable private sector investments, and better cost per job ratios than most central government job creation programmes, they also became involved in short-term rescues of firms on the brink of collapse as much as in longer-term planning. The funds available were limited. The GLEB was spending £55 m per year compared with £500 m per year by the Scottish Development Agency for a similar population. Hopes of using trade union and local authority pension funds faded in the face of the strict financial criteria that these were required to meet. Although the GLC did include the cultural industries as one of its sector studies, interventions concentrated on manufacturing industry to try to restore jobs lost rather than attempt to influence the expanding service sectors.

The intention of the radical approach was also to strengthen labour. Councils sought to do this both by improving the position of workers in private sector firms and by promoting new types of industrial organ-isation. Agreements were concluded with firms benefiting from enter-prise board investments to ensure such things as minimum wage commitments, health and safety at work statements and trade union recognition, until the 1982 Employment Act made the last of these impossible. Similar requirements were placed on firms through contract compliance where firms carried out work or supplied goods to the council. The firms rarely seemed to find the conditions difficult, although it is not certain how rigorous the monitoring was to make sure that they were applied in practice. The GLC's concern to involve the workforce and unions directly in firms' managerial decision-taking caused more problems and often had to be abandoned. The biggest threat to workers, however, was from large firms that were restructur-ing their plants, rather than the medium-sized firms that were involved with Enterprise Boards and contracts. Councils developed 'early warning systems' by monitoring what was happening to major local employers and gave trade unions resources to develop alternative plans involving fewer job losses and new areas of work. The most spectacu-lar initiative was by the GLC, which joined with local authorities in France, Belgium and Ireland to bring together Kodak workers to discuss the major changes proposed by the multinational firm.

Radical local authorities sought in three ways to develop new types of industrial production. The first was support for co-operatives, and this was popular even among councils that did not attempt other radical policies. Some authorities set up Co-operative Development Agencies, attracting finance from the Co-operative Bank, the Co-operative Retail Society and Industrial Common Ownership Finance Ltd. Second, encouragement was given to community businesses to run local services such as taxis, laundries or gardening, and the benefits for the community of these justified, if necessary, a continuing subsidy. Thirdly, the council itself was used to run municipal enterprise. Sheffield, in particular, followed this approach rather than investment in the private sector, and created horticultural services and educational materials production to avoid buying them from outside. In most local areas the local authority is easily the largest employer and its employment policies have a major impact on the local area. These initiatives were all expected to provide better quality employment and were related to ideas of 'socially useful production', by which products for which there was a need in the community would be sought and new technology applied to develop prototypes.

Local authorities sought to achieve social objectives in their employment programmes. The distinction between social and economic is in any case never clear, and local authorities have sometimes emphasised profit-making investments to the detriment of social benefits that cannot be quantified. The social objective most rigorously pursued by councils adopting the radical model was that of equal opportunities. In both their own employment and through contract compliance and investment, councils sought to monitor the recruitment and promotion of female and ethnic minority workers. Left councils were suspicious of very small firms because they often provided poor wages and conditions, but support was given to small ethnic minority businesses.

A range of other policies with a social dimension was followed. Councils developed their own training programmes in craft, managerial and technical skills. Leeds monitored the operation of the Government's Youth Training Scheme to ensure that the temporary jobs provided were of a reasonable quality, while Sheffield topped-up Youth Training Scheme wages to union rates. Councils supported unemployed workers' centres and funded council or outside staff who could give advice on employment and welfare rights. West Yorkshire and Lancashire sought to push spending in their employment programmes to the poorest parts of the counties.

Although elements of the radical approach still remain, as a strategy it had come to an end by 1987. The Conservative Government was hostile to the interventionist and social policies of the radical Labour councils, and a virulent campaign in the national and some local newspapers helped raise the temperature. Nevertheless, action by central government was gradual. A review of local economic programmes was commissioned in 1980 and the resulting Burns Committee report showed much more activity than the civil service had expected. The Government wanted to cut local authority expenditure on economic development to a 0.5p in the £ rate to be used to help small firms, but backed down against opposition from the local authority associations and the House of Lords at a time when, with rapidly rising unemployment, it could hardly be seen to be preventing job creation projects. In fact the Local Government (Miscellaneous) Provisions Act, 1982 clarified the ability of local authorities to fund economic development programmes.

The most serious impact on the new policies came from the abolition of the metropolitan counties in 1986, as this removed several of the main innovators. By the late 1980s central government was also beginning to exert more control over local expenditure by putting an upper ceiling on the local taxation levels of a number of Labour councils. Contract compliance was made illegal and the 1989 Local Government Act, although it established economic development as a function of local authorities, severely restricted the role of enterprise boards. The successive Conservative general election victories also demoralised the radical left. The radical model had been in operation for only a short period and with limited resources and only marginal effects on the level and quality of employment. Nevertheless, it had had a considerable impact on ideas in local government and convinced the Labour national leadership, who were originally rather suspicious, that some version of it would have to be incorporated in future Labour programmes.

(iii) The Conservative Government and the enterprise strategy

We have seen that the view of the Conservative Government of 1979 was that the operation of the market would correct imbalances of economic growth and employment, and that the Government would need some programme of action to stimulate the enterprise culture, especially in the inner cities. Past public policies and local authority attitudes were blamed for restricting the market and discouraging local enterprise. There was also the pressure of events, notably the inner-city riots of 1981 and the rising levels of unemployment, which led the government to feel that it had to provide an immediate remedy. A desire to by-pass the local authorities, especially as they became increasingly controlled by the opposition parties, also led central government to intervene more in local economies in the 1980s than it had in the 1970s.

In the same way that post-war regional policy had reacted to levels of local unemployment, inner-city policy under both Labour and Conservative governments concentrated on small parts of cities with high levels of unemployment rather than looking at the economies of cities and regions as a whole. The Conservatives continued to fund the Urban Programme and the Partnerships begun by Labour, though with a little more emphasis on projects intended to create jobs rather than with only social objectives. The main force of policy, however, shifted to a mixture of deregulation and subsidy. The main vehicles for this were Enterprise Zones (EZs), Urban Development Corporations (UDCs) and the Urban Development Grant (UDG; later renamed the City Grant).

In all, twenty-five EZs were declared between 1981 and 1984, mostly in the inner cities, but some in other areas that had suffered industrial decline, such as north-west Kent, Corby and Hartlepool. The zones varied in size from 50 to 450 hectares and largely comprised areas of derelict industrial land. Early ideas of suspending employment protection or health and safety protection were abandoned, but no planning permission was required by firms locating there. More importantly, firms were subsidised by removing the need to pay local authority taxes for 10 years and by 100 per cent capital allowances on industrial and commercial buildings.

The Local Government Planning and Land Act, 1980, gave the Secretary of State for the Environment powers to designate UDCs run by boards whose members were appointed by central government. UDCs in Liverpool and London Docklands were created in 1981 and nine others, for Cardiff Bay, the Black Country, Teeside, Tyne and Wear, Trafford Park, Bristol, Sheffield, Leeds and Manchester, during 1986–8. The UDCs were able to take over land in their areas and were given considerable funding to prepare land for development and carry out infrastructure works. Land was sold relatively cheaply for development and with a generally relaxed land-use planning regime. Finally, a system of Urban Development Grants was created in 1982 to provide a subsidy to private development projects in inner-city areas that would not otherwise have been profitable. These were organised through the local authorities, as were the EZs, but in 1987 they were replaced with a similar system of City Grants whereby central government dealt directly with the private sector. Derelict grants were similarly geared to private sector investment rather than public projects. The government also created six Freeports in which firms were exempt from customs formalities and duties but, given the developing EC and international free-trade regimes, these had little impact.

The Conservative strategy for inner-city economies became, whatever the original intentions, one that was property-led. EZs, UDCs and UDGs subsidised property development rather than firms producing goods and services – it was assumed that this would change the image of the areas affected and attract new economic activity and that the benefits of this would 'trickle down' to the unemployed in the designated areas and the surrounding parts of the inner city. The property boom of the mid-1980s, partly stimulated by these policies, helped to ensure that a considerable amount of development took place in EZs and UDCs, most notably in London Docklands. Only a small amount of the new development stimulated by the new policies was in factory building. Corby EZ had 90 per cent of its new firms in manufacturing but this was unusual. The EZs mainly attracted warehousing and retailing, in particular the huge Metrocentre in the Gateshead EZ, as retailers looked to move to cheaper locations with surface car parking outside town centres. The UDGs stimulated commercial development and helped to create a market for owner-occupied housing in the inner cities. There was almost no attempt to ensure that firms occupying the new developments provided jobs for the local unemployed, and the extent of 'trickle down' during the 1980s appears limited.

The Government's policies were evaluated in terms of overall expenditure, costs per job, amount of private sector investment 'levered' by public investment, and whether the private sector investment would have gone ahead anyway. Evaluation was carried out methodically by research organisations under contracts from central government, by the National Audit Office (NAO) and, in a more general and investigative way, by Parliamentary Select Committees. The EZs saw an increase of 1.5m sq. of floorspace and 13 000 new jobs between 1981 and 1986, but were very expensive in costs per job and there was evidence that much of the development would have otherwise taken place elsewhere. The government announced in 1987 that there would be no general extension in the number of zones, although it did declare two more later to lessen the impact of shipyard closures in Sunderland and the closure of the Ravenscraig steelworks in Scotland. The UDG has also levered considerable investment in property, although a proportion of this would have gone ahead without grant.

The London Docklands Development Corporation (LDDC) was spectacularly successful in attracting offices and luxury housing in the half of its designated area near to the City and in developing some cheaper owner-occupied housing. It was, however, criticised for remoteness from local communities and the lack of any clear strategy for transport to service the new developments. The NAO criticised a general lack of any clear strategy by the Government for the UDCs. The LDDC illustrates a basic problem with a strategy that was property-led: it depended on a buoyant property market and in those areas, especially the North of England and Scotland, where the market was very patchy, development depended more heavily on public sector subsidy. When the property market collapsed everywhere, the strategy collapsed with it, leaving behind projects, such as the huge office complex at Canary Wharf in London Docklands, which are difficult to let and other projects abandoned with no obvious means of reviving them or of providing alternatives.

The other major arm of the Conservative Government's approach was to involve the private sector as a participant in local economic policy and not as simply a receiver of it. This was closely related to ideas of the enterprise culture and the creation of small firms as the seed-bed of future economic growth. The approach developed partly out of the reaction of some managers in large firms to the local impact of industrial decline, and partly from arm-twisting by government ministers in their day-to-day contact with business and at special seminars on the issue.

In 1978 Pilkington's, the Lancashire glass company that dominates St. Helens, set up an Enterprise Trust with directors and managers seconded from the firm after Pilkington's had decided to reduce their local workforce. It gave advice to potential entrepreneurs and worked to ensure that premises were provided. By mid-1983 over 100 such private sector trusts and agencies had been set up, though local authority involvement and funding was also considerable. Chambers of Commerce looked beyond servicing their members to provide small business advice. The CBI sponsored 'Business in the Community' to get the major companies interested in inner-city investment, and Michael Heseltine took the major investors around Liverpool after the 1981 riots to impress on them the need to take the inner-city problem seriously. New legislation required local authorities to consult private sector organisations and business people found places on the governing boards of the UDCs and other public bodies.

Many Enterprise Trusts and Agencies expanded beyond support for entrepreneurs and small firms to development projects and training. By the end of the 1980s there were over 250 such trusts and agencies, but little detailed evaluation of their work had been carried out. There was now a range of organisations providing help to small firms; a 'Business in the Community' survey in 1986 suggested that 78 000 jobs had been created by the Enterprise Trusts and Agencies, although it is difficult to say how many of these jobs depended solely or even primarily on their advice. Although some funding and secondments were obtained from the private sector, the trusts and agencies still depended heavily on local authority financial and other support. A strategy of using large firms to help develop small firms might be successful where a tradition of setting up new businesses existed, but was much more difficult in some declining industrial areas where there was only a small private manufacturing sector in the first place. More fundamentally, although the social conscience of managers in large firms produced ameliorative programmes such as this, major decisions about investment in new plants and plant closures were taken as market decisions. Pilkington's budget for its Enterprise Trust in St. Helens was tiny compared with its expenditure on its new plant in Kent (Moore and Richardson, 1989, pp. 147–8).

The other area of concern for the Government was that of the rural areas. A number of studies pointed to the existence of poorer groups in rural areas and the continued problems of unemployment in the remoter rural areas. The Conservatives faced increased competition for votes in the rural areas, particularly in south-west England, from the Liberal Democrats. In addition, EC agreements led to a reduction in agricultural subsidy. The framework of Rural Development Areas and the work of the Development Commissioners was continued and local authorities were encouraged to reduce the planning restrictions faced by small firms in rural areas. Support was made available to farmers who wanted to diversify into new types of business.

8.4 Conclusions

During the late 1980s the Conservative Government created what it considered would be an adequate framework for local economic development. The Local Government and Housing Act, 1989 provides a clear, though discretionary, power for local authorities to be involved in economic development. Section 33 of the Act gives spending powers and requires local authorities to provide an annual Local Economic Development Statement if it uses those powers. Local authorities have to balance business or other needs and consult local business interests on their statements. The Act also increased control over local authority policies of which central government disapproved. It was not possible to prohibit the creation of companies by local authorities as these powers were needed for other purposes, but the powers of Enterprise Boards were severely limited, particularly by controls over the size of their investments.

The Government also extended central control over local policy by the creation of Training and Enterprise Councils (TECs) in England and Wales, run by boards appointed by central government. As we saw in Chapter 6, the 82 TECs were given a bundle of responsibilities drawn together from existing bodies, in particular the training functions of the Training Agency (formerly the MSC) and the function of helping small firms from the Department of Employment. This has given them no clear strategic role locally and a rather uncertain relationship with the Enterprise Agencies and Trusts and the local authorities, who have all developed similar functions.

The Government has continued to see the UDCs as the main vehicle for economic regeneration in the inner city, even though the poor state of the property market has limited their scope. A new UDC for Birmingham was created in 1992, though in this case at the request of the local authority. Indeed, the setting up of the Urban Regeneration Agency in 1993, with powers to intervene to improve derelict land and encourage projects in local areas across the country, suggested a sort of roving UDC. Enterprise Zones, by contrast, were seen as an expensive experiment and there was no attempt to create new zones to replace those coming to the end of their ten-year period. Central government funding of local economic projects has become more uncertain and competitive. A City Challenge fund was created and local authorities were invited to bid for it, and then this and the Urban programme were ended and were replaced by a single regeneration budget (about £100 m in 1995–6) for which local authorities have to submit proposals.

Involvement in economic development had by the 1990s spread to more local authorities, particularly those in rural and suburban areas.

Many more authorities have become Labour and Liberal Democrat-controlled, with the unpopularity of the Government between general elections, and new administrations often produced an extension of the economic development role. The depression of the early 1990s had a much more severe effect on the South-East than other areas in the post-war period. By the mid-1990s only a few authorities in Surrey with large areas of green belt had no significant economic development programme. The provision of serviced land and premises, especially small workshops, has remained an important part of local initiatives, but has nowhere near the dominance that it had in the early 1980s. Local authorities are now heavily involved in advisory services, mainly to small firms, including such areas as marketing advice. The 'radical' model has been in eclipse because of a loss of powers, budgetary restrictions and the general retreat of left-wing ideas. There now appear to be fewer differences in the political direction of policy. One aspect of a developing consensus is the concept of 'partnership', with local authorities working with the private sector, bodies created by central government and the EU, to progress schemes. The effect of this has also been to concentrate efforts on individual projects instead of the development of an overall strategy for the local area.

The hostile relationship between local authorities and the first two UDCs has settled down to one which involves co-operation. The London Borough of Newham in east London worked with the London Docklands Development Corporation in the late 1980s to promote a major retail development which would also secure commitments on the number of local jobs created, although the state of the property market prevented the scheme from taking place. The second round UDCs have worked more closely with local authorities and have been more conscious of their social objectives, especially as the limitations of the trickle-down strategy became evident. The best example of partnership has been in Birmingham, where the local authority created Birmingham Heartlands Ltd in 1987, with ownership predominantly by private developers but shared with the City Council and the Chamber of Commerce. The company promoted a mixture of commercial development and social projects such as childcare and the improvement of council housing. The arrangements met with central government approval and at the City Council's request the Government created a UDC to succeed the company and provide extra resources, but with half the members from the local authority, unlike the other UDCs.

The continued decline of manufacturing in the large cities and the success of service industries in the consumer boom of the late 1980s led local authorities to switch their economic development projects away from a concentration on manufacturing industry to look at other sectors. The largest cities, such as Manchester, Edinburgh, Cardiff and, of course, London have considerable advantages as centres for the higher level managerial functions of firms and related services such as publishing and advertising, and as centres for 'consumption' in retailing, the arts and other entertainments (Bianchini, 1991, pp. 36–8). The range of culture and the quality of the environment are thus seen as key factors in attracting economic activity and the idea of competition between cities to attract these sorts of jobs has become stronger. Glasgow was successful in its bid to be designated European City of Culture in 1990 and used the period to promote itself, and Birmingham began to transform its image with new public spaces and cultural facilities. London, by contrast, has had no overall body to carry out similar policies and has been falling behind in comparison with 'rival' cities such as Frankfurt and Paris. All local authorities have promoted tourism and retailing as growth sectors, even though jobs in hotels, shops and catering are often low skill and low paid.

The range of organisations involved in economic development has now moved to a new agenda and beyond the mainstream activities of land and premises and advice to small firms. The creation of the Single Market in the EC and Britain's continued poor trading performance has produced a national discussion about the ability of Britain to compete, given its generally unsatisfactory levels of post-school education and skills training, and considerable agreement has developed about the need for improvements. Local authorities developed a wide range of initiatives in this area during the 1980s. As we noted earlier, by the 1990s training programmes had become the responsibility of the TECs, supervised by the Department of Employment, who now run national training schemes, though work has often been contracted back to local authorities and the latter often still have training policies of their own in priority areas.

The extent to which the TECs have gone beyond the standard schemes varies considerably, but many have concentrated on the problems of particular groups and commissioned studies of the structure of their local labour market. An important constraint, however, is that their future budgets are related to success in placing trainees, and so there is a danger that they will concentrate on the least disadvantaged

groups that can be most easily trained and found work, leaving the rest
to local authority schemes. Some UDCs have also entered this area,
sensitive to criticism that local people had not found jobs in their developments. Labour market policy by all organisations has gone beyond
merely trying to meet shortages of particular skills to looking at the
policies of employers in entry, recruitment and promotion. Problems
such as the labelling of particular parts of cities as undesirable and from
which no one would be employed, or the attitudes of recruitment agencies or access to training while at work to allow promotion, are beginning to be tackled.

Another area of development, mainly by the larger local authorities,
has been an extension of the sector studies of the 1980s, though now
without any expectation of major direct intervention to restructure
firms. The approach is now limited to encouraging connections
between firms and developing support services. Wolverhampton, for
example, developed a strategy for its clothing industry, involving the
upgrading of technical and managerial skills, the creation of networks
between firms and retailers, the provision of units for individual design-
ers, the encouragement of better working practices and the adoption of
new technology. Labour councils have remained concerned with the
problems of low pay and poor employment conditions. The cost of
sector analysis and the advantages of a national or regional perspective
have led a number of local authorities to come together to carry out
industry-wide work – for example, MILAN, the Motor Industries Local
Authority network, and Local Action for Textiles and Clothing based in
Huddersfield. The most impressive was SEEDS, the South East
Economic Development Strategy, which looked at twenty sectors in the
region and tried to provide a context for trade unions and issues on
which to lobby central government.

An important development has been the recognition of the importance of information for local economic development and the new technology related to it. The cost of this technology and the information
collection that was necessary threatened to create a division between
information-rich, large firms who had a clear picture of market
changes, technological developments, sources of finance and so on, and
information-poor medium and small firms, trade unions and community organisations. Some major local authorities, already large users of
information, have developed systems to which others could have
access. The Manchester HOST system was developed in 1991 with
funding from the Urban Programme and British Petroleum sponsorship,

and provided a local and commercial database for small firms, community groups and the public sector. Edinburgh has sought to expand its financial services sector with a relevant information system. Systems have also been developed by some rural agencies, such as Highlands and Islands Enterprise, given the special problems of access in remoter areas.

The early 1990s have also seen the recognition of a relationship between local economic development and the environment. The Government's international commitments in relation to 'sustainable development' as defined by the Bruntland Report have begun to filter into its advice to local authorities on new development, while an EU directive now requires that an environmental assessment is carried out on all major new developments before planning permission is given. A number of local authorities have produced Green Plans to outline the environmental implications of all of their policies and there has been some encouragement to firms to undertake environmental audits of their operations. The London Borough of Greenwich has produced plans for one of its major development areas to encourage firms with good environmental practices and include those involved in recycling. However, little real thought has been given to the relationship between current economic development policy and sustainable development. For example, the increased emphasis on specialisation and competition between localities is likely to lead to a considerable increase in the use of transport and therefore of energy as more goods are exported and imported between areas.

Local economic development has now become an established activity, though carried out by a range of organisations. TECs, local authorities, Enterprise Agencies, Enterprise Boards, Urban Development Corporations and Chambers of Commerce may or may not all be pulling in the same direction, and the relationships between them will be a problem. There is now considerable consensus over the policies which are to be followed and a more expert economic development profession has been created, but there is hardly a clear strategy for the local level. The success of local economic development in solving the basic economic inequalities between the inner cities, poorer regions and remote rural areas and the more prosperous parts of the country, and its contribution to contributing to national economic revival, remains uncertain.

9 Industrial Policy and the European Union

Christopher Lord

9.1 Introduction

It is often argued that Britain's membership of the European Union puts the padlock on any prospect of a meaningful industrial policy and throws away the key. The theme of this chapter is that this is not so. Rather, EU membership creates a new matrix of possibilities, constraining some choices but enlarging others, producing options for a supranational policy framework in parallel with a national one, with the latter in some ways shored up in its potential effectiveness by the European relationship.

9.2 Britain and the European Union

Britain was not one of the founder members of what used to be called the European Community. This was formed in two waves between 1950 and 1957. In 1950, Benelux, France, Germany and Italy agreed to pool their coal and steel industries under a single authority, later known as the European Coal and Steel Community. In 1957, the Six signed the Treaty of Rome, the defining agreement in the construction of the modern European Union. A principal feature of the new treaty was a customs union in which industrial products would move freely across internal political frontiers, while the economies of the Six were subject to a common tariff against outsiders.

The Union has thus always been intimately concerned with the development and sustenance of industry in Western Europe. However, its ultimate goals were always overtly political: to create an ever closer European union with economic integration serving as the means and motor to the political project. It was to this that British Governments of the 1950s, both Labour and Conservative, objected. None the less, if political integration was unacceptable, so was economic exclusion, and the extent to which UK Governments always sought to avoid this has not yet been fully appreciated in the historical literature. In pursuance of Churchill's axiom that Britain should remain 'with' even if it was not 'of' Europe, an association agreement was negotiated with the new Coal and Steel Community, while the Eden and Macmillan Governments proposed that the new EEC should be contained in a free-trade area embracing the whole of Western Europe. When this proved impractical, Britain nevertheless went ahead in 1959 with a European free-trade area (EFTA) that linked the UK with several of the smaller countries around the outside of the original EC: Austria, Denmark, Switzerland, Sweden, Portugal.

However, the ink was scarcely dry on the EFTA agreement before the Macmillan Government decided that there was no substitute to full membership of the EC itself. An application was announced on 31 July 1961. As was usually the case at the time, British policy was dominated by diplomatic, rather than industrial, considerations. However, the latter were not absent from the rethink of UK relations with the new Community. The formation of the Community served to highlight the success of the Western European economies in achieving a growth rate that was, on average, twice that of the UK in the 1950s and 1960s.

Between 1960 and Britain's eventual accession to the Community on 1 January 1973, the Confederation of British Industry (CBI) developed and refined arguments that pointed to the necessity of UK membership. Most of these implied that industrial competitiveness rose with the size of the productive unit: that it was about beating rivals to the economies of large-scale production. The 1971 White Paper on British entry to the EC thus pointed to the importance of 'selling into markets perhaps five times as large as present. For advanced industrial countries, the most favourable environment is one where markets are large'. John Davies, Trade and Industry Secretary in the Heath Government and himself a former director of the CBI, argued that Britain 'had to break out of its industrial confinement...it had been seeking to sustain its historically acquired scientific and industrial attributes from too narrow a base' (cited in Lord, 1995). The European Commission agreed with this analysis, arguing in its 1968 appraisal of British entry to the EC that many industrial projects had been initiated in the UK over the last fifteen years only to be abandoned as orders could not match development costs in Britain's restricted national market. In answer to the objection that Sweden and Switzerland had shown an alternative route to growth through specialisation in small-scale niche markets, the CBI argued that Britain had already sunk its capital and trained its labour in volume manufacture. Of course, in many sectors, British firms could still operate with full economies of scale if key industries were concentrated into the hands of just a few producers. But this implied an oligopolistic industrial structure, an arrangement that was seen as oscillating between stagnation and instability, while always imposing welfare costs on the consumer. Each of Britain's twenty largest industries was already 50–90 per cent owned by between three and five producers. Davies thus urged EC entry to overcome the dilemmas of 'needing size' in Britain's productive units 'yet fearing it'.

Other arguments pointed to the advantages of technological collaboration between Britain and the economies of the EC. The National Economic Development Council argued that on British entry would depend the question of whether the world was divided into two centres of technological development or consisted of just one, the USA. Wilson's proposal in 1967 to combine British entry with a new technological Community reflected a belief that the UK could still take a lead in projects confined to Europe while partnerships with US producers would only syphon off Britain's accumulated knowledge and its best scientists. In 1963, the R&D of just the five largest companies in the USA had equalled that of Britain and the Six put together. Heath likewise saw European co-operation in R&D as the only alternative to political dependence on the USA and 'industrial flaccidity'. Both Conservative and Labour Governments between 1961 and 1974 thus suggested that British accession to the EC should be accompanied by the further development of an active and European dimension to industrial policy; and that it would not be enough just to rely on private sector responses to the giant market created by the EC. Technologies were clearly identified as in some sense special to the economic base and as requiring a degree of collaborative support and cultivation through Community institutions.

Between 1973 and 1985, British expectations of EC membership were to be largely disappointed. The pace of UK deindustrialisation continued without any significant impact from EC entry. Expectations had always been inflated by the belief that higher economic growth would somehow and mysteriously be an automatic prize of EC membership, when, in reality, everything was always going to depend upon the quality of governmental and private sector responses to the new context. In any case, entry coincided with the downturn in the world economy induced by the 'oil-shocks' of 1973 and 1979. Under the pressure of economic stagnation, the large market on which so many hopes had hung, was re-fragmented as member states simply substituted non-tariff barriers for the tariffs outlawed by the Treaty of Rome. Recession also induced a paralysis in the Community's decision-making process. Institutional stalemate in the EC interacted unfavourably with the problem of the UK's contributions to the Community budget. Britain was faced with having to make net payments into the budget of one per cent of its GNP, an arrangement that represented a significant worsening of the balance of payments constraint on UK industrial growth. This was not sorted out until 1984.

The period 1973–86 also revealed a series of political patterns that must now be reviewed as background to any discussion of Britain, the Union and industrial policy. British Governments always expected to take a leading role in the EC, at the very least as part of an inner triumvirate of France, Germany and the UK. However, in practice the Franco-German side of the diplomatic triangle has proved stronger than any British connection with the other two sides. As a result, Paris and Bonn have tended to determine the goals, timing and detail of new Union initiatives since 1973. In part, this is a reflection of the very different domestic politics of the three countries. Where, at least until recently, European unity was a source of domestic consensus in France and Germany, it is an issue that cuts across the party divide in British politics, thus limiting UK participation to EU measures that minimise splits in the governing party at Westminster. Nor is there a robustly and reliably pro-European public opinion on which to base UK participation in all schemes of European integration. The Eurobarometer series of opinion polls reveals that UK support for the EC and its further development is erratic and somewhat schizophrenic, with a strong desire to participate in any material pay-offs from the Union co-existing with a reluctance to accord the EC the means to deliver in the shape of new policies or strengthened institutions. Though it does need to be said that public approval for remaining in the EC by a margin of 2 : 1 in a referendum in 1975 has served to legitimate EU membership in British politics.

This is not to suggest that there are not deeper problems of political culture in Britain's relation with the EU. In particular, it has proved

especially difficult to fit a system that stresses the absolute and inalien-
able sovereignty of its national parliament into a transnational political
enterprise committed to the goal of an ever closer political union. There
has also been a marked reluctance to accept the notion that Britain is a
'European state', as opposed to a diplomatic entity with an equal sense
of attachment to the USA or even the British Commonwealth.

The experience of 1973–93 shows how all of this may limit the use
of the EU as a context in which to develop industrial policy. British
Governments have tended to favour three kinds of policy development
for the European Union.

- They have preferred 'negative' to 'positive' integration: the
  removal of restrictions to the cross-border economic activity by
  private actors to the construction of common policies at the
  European level with a view to producing some other set of outcomes than would flow from the autonomous operation of markets.
  Into the first category we might put the removal of tariffs and
  quotas under the Treaty of Rome of 1957 and the further work of
  the Single Market initiative of 1986–92; into the second, we might
  place the technology policies of the Union, its structural and
  regional policies and maybe even plans for social and monetary
  policies.
- Where British Governments have had to concede new policies or
  institutional change, they have preferred the inter-governmental to
  the supranational model. In other words, they have argued that
  things can be managed through the intimate co-operation of veto-
  holding governments, rather than through the transfer of power or
  initiative to supranational institutions. Connected to this has been a
  desire to ring-fence the political implications of new EU initiatives:
  to resist the notion that there is some 'spill-over' dynamic of
  European integration with further initiatives being required if previous achievements are to be protected; to insist that Britain's agreement to whatever are the policies of the moment entails no
  commitment to go any further towards full integration.
- British Governments have been eager that the policies of the Union
  should be open to the outside world. This clearly implies opposition
  to some of the more protectionist forms of industrial policy.

However, the problem that British Governments have continuously
faced is that the dynamics of European integration are not entirely

under their control. They are scarcely in a position to object to other countries choosing to use their sovereignty as they see fit, even if this means forging ahead of the rest of the EU. The possibility that Britain might be left behind thus has to be weighed against the ideological and domestic discomforts presented by European integration. British Governments have to consider the danger that other members, by integrating faster, might pre-empt for themselves a disproportionate share of the benefits of European co-operation and still create pressures for Britain to make a belated entrance to a policy regime. The clearest example of this kind of pressure came in 1985 when President Mitterrand and Chancellor Kohl threatened to introduce a Single Market between their two countries alone, unless Margaret Thatcher agreed that a new internal market for the EC required a raft of further policy commitments and some reform of the Community's institutions. It is to the Single Market that we now turn.

9.3 The Single Market programme explained

As a result of the Single Market, much of the regulatory framework of British and other EU industry is now split between two levels, the nation state and the EU. This section sets out the main features of the programme and argues that it reflected a growing belief in the 1980s that the European state provided an inadequate political context for successful economic performance. However, 'classic arguments' about economies of scale outstripping the size of national markets do not provide a sufficient explanation for the Single Market programme. For this, we need to look to the way in which the European state had by the mid-1980s subverted its own role as a credible regulator of markets by itself becoming a source of comprehensive market distortion, and to more 'contemporary' arguments about the importance of producers being as free as possible to form networks – even across political boundaries – in pursuit of competitive advantage. The arguments here echo issues raised in Chapter 1, in the discussion of different forms of state–market relationships.

(i) The state as a source of market distortion

The Single Market programme entered public consciousness as a promise to create a frontier-free Europe for business by 1992.

However, this was always something of a slogan, designed to set a clear target for political decision-making and to stimulate private sector responses. In reality, a fully integrated market was never going to be achieved in one burst of political commitment between 1986 and 1992. Although the EU has already enacted more than three times as many measures as originally anticipated, there are many further steps that it could take towards a Single Market. If we were to define such a market as a situation in which it is as easy to trade across the political boundaries of the member states of the EU as within them, it soon becomes obvious that this is an ideal that is never likely to be perfectly attained.

The Single Market programme can be seen as an attempt to shift the Union's policies into the mainstream of contemporary European economic life, based mainly around industry and services. It might seem strange that this was considered necessary. After all, the Treaty of Rome of 1957 had promised industrial free trade in exchange for protected agriculture. However, as explained above, the first half of this arrangement had fallen away in the 1970s, leaving the Community over-concentrated on an agricultural policy that was dysfunctional, as well as marginal in terms of the sectoral balance of European economics.

The erosion of industrial free trade in the 1970s suggested that open markets could no longer be created by just removing tariffs and quotas. By the 1980s, all Western European state were major taxers and spenders – typically to the tune of 50 per cent of GNP. There were clearly many ways in which states could use all the millions of daily transactions in which they were involved to favour domestic over foreign producers. To combat this covert fragmentation of European markets, the European Community would have to become involved to an unprecedented degree in detailed microeconomic regulation, in myriad relationships between states and producers. Where the removal of tariffs and quotas was concerned with economic transactions as they crossed political boundaries, the Single Market was more heavily geared to the more intrusive task of providing a common regulatory framework for what was going on inside European societies.

A raft of examples will illuminate the point. The Cecchini Report (Cecchini, 1988) for the European Commission itemised a series of non-tariff barriers that it estimated were adding up to 30 per cent to the cost of trading goods and services between member states. To favour their own producers, member states fixed a bewildering array of incompatible trading standards, forcing those who wanted to serve the European market to the unnecessary cost of adapting their production lines to the different requirements of each EC country. In many high-tech industries there was (and is) a tendency for convergence on international industry standards, such as IBM compatibility in the case of computing. It was unlikely that European producers would win the international race to secure the substantial pay-offs that come from setting such standards, so long as political factors encouraged the fragmentation of the European market into a mosaic of different product regulations.

Another especially restricted area before 1986 concerned financial services and the movement of capital. On the one hand, this meant that industry faced added costs in financing itself. For example, bank loans were up to three times as expensive in some EC countries as others. On the other hand, industry faced restrictions in the ease with which it could move funds around the Community. This was a serious problem as business conditions increasingly favoured the formation of corporate alliances, or what has come to be known as intra-trade transactions between subsidiaries of the same company located in different countries.

Governments also showed a marked bias towards their own producers in public procurement. It has been estimated that in 1985 public purchasing of final goods and services accounted for around ECUs 600bn or 15 per cent of EC GNP. However, only 2 per cent of public contracts were awarded to producers from another EC country (Commission of the EC, 1993). This sheltered inefficient local producers, prevented others from reaping full economies of scale and specialisation, and increased the cost of government policies with consequent crowding out of private sector activity. Finally, frontier controls themselves enforced delays and costs – for example, through the need to deduct the Value Added Tax already paid to the exporting state and substitute the Value Added Tax due to the importing state. It is also worth noting that all the extra costs of pan-European transactions mentioned here were far greater for small and medium-sized enterprises, which, in turn, meant that the benefits of integration were not properly enjoyed by a sector that is often an important source of industrial change.

It is essential to note that the Single Market programme resulted from a deliberate reappraisal of how to ensure Western Europe's competitiveness in a changing international political economy. It was not a chance indulgence in European integration. Much of the impetus came from lobbying of individual governments and the European Commission by industry itself. The main theme of this campaign was that the so-called 'national champion strategy' into which EC states had lapsed since 1973 had failed. Many of the non-tariff barriers itemised above were being used for a very specific purpose: to maintain particular companies that represented a country's continued presence in a certain industry. For some of the larger member states, this bordered on a belief that the national economy should have something of everything, regardless of the financial losses and misallocations of resources that were involved in maintaining particular companies. This was blamed for a condition known at the time as 'Eurosclerosis'. After years as one of the more dynamic centres in the world economy, the EC had experienced minimal trend growth over the period 1973–86.

A broad consensus developed among European industrialists that they would be better off with freedom to restructure themselves across frontiers than looking to a regime of undiscriminating subsidy within national economies. This argument also reflected an important shift of philosophy since the 1960s and 1970s. The main argument for market integration had ceased to be primarily about the economies of *scale* and came to be much more concerned with the *scope* of companies of all sizes to network across political boundaries.

(ii) On the importance of networking

P. A. Geroski shows that size is no longer the issue in European market integration. Of the industries studied by the European Commission in 1988, 89 per cent had a 'minimum efficient scale less than 10% of the Community market'. What is more, their cost curves were shallow, suggesting that even if, in some cases, they were being forced by restricted markets to operate at slightly less than efficient scale, the extra costs were insignificant and possibly even less than the managerial diseconomies of forming themselves into larger units (Geroski, 1991, pp. 30–1).

If size is less important, new theories of competitive advantage stress the importance of large and small companies being able to assemble a great variety of strengths, most of them external to the firm themselves (Delors, 1994, p. 21). Often these clusters of productive advantage are to be found in geographically concentrated areas. However, one or two missing ingredients will almost always need to be sourced at a distance and, in any case, the name of the game is to lock into a whole series of criss-crossing networks. These allow firms to maximise opportunities for shared research, production, marketing and distribution – not to mention the circulation of new ideas and innovations (Porter, 1990). A Europe of nationalistic regulation simply limited the degrees of freedom with which such networks could be formed across political boundaries and raised the costs of transnational networking even where this was possible.

9.4 The Single Market and national industrial policy-making

Having explained the Single Market, we can now go on to ask how far it constrains national industrial policy. This we shall do by looking at the Competition policy that has grown up around the Single Market programme, in order to police the activities of member states. A careful examination of the arrangements for state aids, monopolies and mergers, ownership and foreign direct investment reveals that the EU is by no means uniformly hostile to national industrial policy. There are even circumstances in which it encourages and empowers it.

(i) State aids to industry

Two patterns emerge from any inspection of the figures for state aids to industry within the EU. First, the level of such aids has not been significantly reduced since 1986. Second, substantial variations remain in the degree to which the EU's constituent states provide financial support for industry. Figures on the proportion of gross spend on R&D undertaken by national governments show that the average for the EC as a whole was 41.2 per cent in 1990 and the range between lowest and highest was 35.1 per cent to 49.5 per cent (see Table 9.1).

Table 9.1 *Proportion of national spending on R&D by EC Governments*

	1986	1990	1991
France	52.5	48.3	48.8
Italy	55.3	49.5	52.0
Germany	35.3	35.1	37.2
Netherlands	44.0	45.1	44.9
UK	41.5	35.8	34.2
EU	43.7	41.2	40.9

The Single Market programme, in fact, always sought to redirect state aids, rather than abolish them. To a degree, the continued variations in the extent of national supports for industry is a sign that the programme has still some way to go in rationalising and redirecting state subsidies. However, they also indicate the different degrees to which member states have chosen to avail themselves of the continued opportunities for national industrial policy, even under the aegis of the Single Market programme.

A blanket prohibition of state aids to industry would have been the easiest solution to enforce. However, the Commission has argued that such an undiscriminating position might only reduce the competitiveness of European producers in the world economy. First, it has pointed to the 'theory of second best' to show that if markets are already distorted, which is almost always the case, it does not follow that the best reaction of public bodies is to carry on with a policy of non-intervention as if nothing had happened: 'in the presence of market distortions adequate public subsidies may actually restore efficiency' (Commission of the EC, 1991b, p. 29). Second, some state aids may create or improve, rather than misallocate and crowd-out valuable factors of production. A key consideration is the need to avoid falling behind in new technologies whose benefits diffuse widely throughout the economy and do not accrue exclusively to those who carry the risks and costs of development. The Commission thus recognises the case for state aids to make up some of the gap between private and social returns on innovation.

However, failures of the market to provide adequate investment in the sources of competitive advantage are not limited to the capital side. Western Europe contains marked variations in levels of regional development. These can largely be traced to the very different histories of each region in respect of the embodiment of skills in the local workforce. In a well-behaved market, the problem would be self-correcting: it would pay entrepreneurs to train the pockets of unskilled labour until the workers of all regions were perfect substitutes in a calculation of the marginal productivity of labour times the marginal cost of employment. That this does not happen is once again down to externalities: no employer can be sure of getting the full benefit of investment in training and, in any case, a large part of the productiveness of any single company is often determined by its location in a regional cluster of fellow-producers, with the implication that it makes less sense for one firm to set up shop until others do. What all this points to is the logic of allowing member states to continue to use regional policy to support those producers that invest in local skills, to promote infrastructural investment and to encourage the formation and development of localised clusters of competitive advantage.

Moreover, the problem is not confined to areas that have never been fully developed. Modern economies are clearly exposed to demand or supply shocks that can render economically useless the skills in which a large part of a regional workforce has been trained. Indeed, the creation of the Single Market may increase the probability of such regionally concentrated shocks. In the absence of mobility of labour and in the presence of some capital market failure, there is a clear argument for public policy to share in responsibility for retraining and restructuring. The clearest example of where this kind of state aid has been allowed – and even welcomed by the European Commission – is in the massive support that the German Government has provided to the Treuhandsanstalt's efforts to retool former East Germany.

Far from eliminating state aids, the whole drift of EU policy has been to subject them to commonly agreed principles and disciplines. The Commission has been eager that member states should not support industries in ways that produce over-capacity or waste scarce development resources through the duplication of scientific research. It has also been keen that aids to some of the more advanced regions in the EU should be limited in order to sharpen the effectiveness of efforts in the more backward areas. To this end, member states are required to keep to maps that show the areas they can aid.

It is even arguable that the Single Market programme has had the paradoxical result of sharpening the cutting edge of national industrial policies in the area of state aids. EU disciplines may have ensured that aids are more sharply targeted, better protected against interest group capture, and less likely to lead to waste and duplication as a result of policy inconsistency between EU states: 'a substantial proportion of the public expenditure channelled into state aid could be wasted where the effects of such aid are cancelled out by similar aid in other member states' (Commission of the EC, 1992). The last few years have, in fact, seen a considerable increase in the notification of state aids to the Commission. As Sapir and his colleagues have shown, member states have found it in their own interests to maintain a system that allows them to see what others are doing and to avoid contradictions and duplications between individual national policies (Sapir *et al.*, 1993).

(ii) The regulation of monopolies, mergers and collusive practices

As industrial concentration had been all the vogue in the 1960s, many sectors of national economies were dominated by just a few companies. One of the expected benefits of the Single Market was that firms that were oligopolies in the national context would be part of a larger and more competitive pool of companies in a more integrated European economy. On the other hand, the Single Market was also supposed to lead to a good deal of transnational restructuring through mergers, takeovers and joint ventures. There was a clear danger that this might lead to the reintroduction of a cartelised economy, only on a European scale. The Single Market was thus always seen as requiring a strengthened competition policy at the EU level, an option that was made more attractive by the advantages of giving companies involved in transnational restructuring a 'one-stop shop', rather than a whole series of legal regimes to regulate takeovers and joint ventures (Commission of the EC, 1989, p. 179).

European Union competition policy creates a series of boundaries between national and European responsibility for market structure. On the first point, the Commission has jurisdiction over 'all concentrations with a Union dimension'; in other words, if the aggregate world turnover of the companies in question is above ECU 5bn; or, if the aggregate EU-wide turnover of at least two of the undertakings is above ECU 250m; or, if each of the undertakings does at least a third of its turnover in a second state of the EU. Although there is some controversy as to whether the EU's own policy allows sufficient flexibility for companies to form clubs to apportion the costs and benefits of research that would not otherwise be conducted between themselves (on this, see Hay, 1993), it would presumably be possible for national competition policies to encourage such arrangements within the parameters set out above.

(iii) Ownership

The Treaties are silent on the issue of ownership, and EU countries are all different in which of their industries are owned publicly and which privately – and several have carried out nationalisations since joining the Union. None the less, the Commission has recently begun to encourage privatisation. It is thought that this would: lessen political pressures on states to provide illegal aids, which would risk a round of retaliation between governments that would be potentially disastrous to the Single Market; improve the allocation of resources in the European economy and consolidate the efficiency gains of the Single Market; give management greater freedom to innovate, restructure and finance their operations as they see fit; and encourage the formation of transnational partnerships, particularly in utilities and communications where networks need to be made inter-operable and generally adjusted to a European economy of intensive cross-border transactions.

(iv) Foreign direct investment

The British Government has sought to marry its industrial policy with the Single Market programme in a very specific way. Its goal has been to turn the UK into a prime location for direct inward investment for companies outside the EU seeking a production base inside the Single Market. The figures do, indeed, show that the Single Market programme has stimulated a considerable increase in direct investment in the EU by producers from the Far East, North America and EFTA.

The Single Market programme has attracted foreign direct investment (FDI) by adding to the privileges enjoyed by 'insider' over 'outsider' producers and, so long as a non-EU company located in the UK includes a minimum of local content in its exports to the rest of the Union, it has the same legal status as an indigenous producer. Various terms such as 'tariff-hopping' or 'bridgehead investment' have been coined to describe this process. However, the formation of the Single Market has also led to 'rationalisation investment' by outsiders (Greenaway, 1993, p. 103). As Union policies are substituted for national frameworks, it becomes easier for non-EU producers to concentrate different activities in different parts of the EU.

It is no exaggeration to describe Britain as the major beneficiary of the Single Market's magnetism for FDI. Britain may also have benefited from some redeployment of capital within the Union. As we saw in more detail in Chapter 2, the prominence of Britain as a destination for FDI is apparent in terms of both stocks (cumulative totals) and flows (new additions). In the five years to 1993, FDI accounted for more than £40bn, or one-fifth, of all new capital formation in British industry. The proportion of industrial assets in Britain owned by foreign interests likewise rose from 13 per cent to 20 per cent (*Financial Times*, 13 October 1993). Most famously, Britain has become a base for the Japanese car industry in Europe. As if to confirm the importance of promoting localised clusters of productive advantage, the arrival of the Japanese car companies has, in turn, given the UK a new competitive advantage in whole series of industries producing car components.

Some commentators have looked to this FDI to restore a manufacturing base reduced by two recessions; and to give Britain an adequate capacity to produce tradable goods, without which there can be no solution to the balance of payments problem, or a long-run return to a situation in which the warranted growth, the maximum possible given a balance of payments constraint, matches the underlying capacity growth, the minimum growth needed to ensure full employment.

Nevertheless, the use of the UK as a prime location for FDI directed at the Single Market is not without controversy. It would be naïve to claim that the flow of FDI to Britain has not in part been policy-directed. Indeed, as we argued in Chapter 2, attempts to offer Britain as a production base for outsiders wanting to get into the Single Market was a key element in the Government's industrial policy in the late 1980s. However, the EU countries need to avoid wasteful competition in their efforts to subsidise inward investment. A discriminating attitude is also needed to distinguish those occasions when FDI can cause more problems than it solves. On the plus side, it can help the diffusion of technologies and cope with the problem of factor immobility by bringing industry to a relatively immobile pool of labour. On the minus side, it can be a means: of abusing market power to secure monopoly rents and block new sources of international competition; of promoting 'social dumping' by playing states off against one another to reduce the social costs of employment; and of retarding the diffusion of technologies by locking host countries into downstream production, while sourcing, or syphoning off some of their valuable skills and technologies.

Among the fifteen present members of the EU, Britain has been the main sender as well as the main host of direct investment. Both of these patterns might well be economically beneficial. However, they must qualify some of the more extravagant claims observed above about the potential role of FDI in re-industrialising Britain. Indeed, together with the growth of mergers and acquisitions, FDI adds to the definitional ambiguity of the British economy. Do we define the latter as British companies, even though so much of the capital stock located in Britain is owned by companies domiciled abroad, while, conversely, so many foreign assets make up the balance sheets of British firms? Do we define it as the stock of labour and human skills that are relatively more rooted to the national territory, even though the economic opportunities of the population are increasingly governed by the ways in which individual lives are commingled with international capital? Such questions are not part of an idle intellectual parlour game but penetrate to the heart of what our industrial policies should be and who should conduct them. Some (such as Garrett, 1992) may argue that it is sufficient to concentrate on policy targets, such as labour training and physical infrastructure, that remain amenable to national policies. However, the whole analysis above, with its emphasis on externalities in technologies and industrial clustering, would suggest that policy also needs to be directed towards internationally mobile companies and capital. Only transnational political processes like the EU can meet the latter challenge. It is to a survey of how far the Union has begun to develop an industrial policy of its own that we now turn.

9.5 The industrial policies of the European Union

In this section we shall look at four areas in which the EU goes beyond market liberalisation to make more proactive industrial policies: that is to say, policies that are not market neutral, in that they inevitably affect the nature and employment of the factors of production, the balance between sectors of the European economy and the location of productive activity. In Section 9.3 we encountered the possibility of market failure and showed how it might justify a continued role for national industrial policies, even in a Single Market. However, national policies may need to be supplemented where market breakdowns are transnational in nature. Where failures spill across boundaries, individual states will not always correct them. They may lack the incentive to act where the profits of distortion accrue to their own producers and the costs are borne in other countries, or even the capacity to act, for negotiating clout and advanced administrative infrastructures are qualities that are unevenly distributed across the EU. Each of the four areas in which the EU has developed an industrial policy of its own – the nurturing of technologies, the management of excess capacity in particular industries, commercial policy and regional development – involve problems of transnational market failure.

Before examining these areas, it has to be noted that the EU has yet to develop a political consensus on how precisely to develop industrial policy – there is continual tension between national policies, ministers on the Council, and even Directorates General of the Commission, as to the most desirable balance between market liberalisation, rigorous enforcement of competition law and Union or national support for particular sectors and producers. The second and third Delors Commissions (1989–95) saw some heroic bureaucratic battles between DG–IV (Competition), DG–III (Internal Market and Industry) and DG–XII (Science and Technology). In the college of Commissioners, Leon Brittan was often pitched against Delors and his formidable Cabinet. Arguments within the Commission became increasingly entangled with shifting coalitions within and between the member states to define the EU's contribution to industrial policy. For instance, in the critical months leading up to Maastricht, Michel Rocard was replaced as Prime Minister of France by Edith Cresson, who was determined to raise the position of industrial policy on both the national and transnational political agenda (Dinan, 1994, p. 179).

(i) Technological development

One case of market failure is provided by the existence of 'positive externalities'. This is where producers do not receive the full benefits of their activity, with the result that something of value is under-provided. A classic example is the development of new technologies, where even rigorous patenting laws cannot legislate against the development of all kinds of derivatives from the original innovation. A typical policy reaction is for the state to provide some financial support to close the gap between the private cost of research and its social pay-offs. But if the benefits of research are likely to diffuse throughout a Western European economy made even more transnational by the Single Market, no single member state is likely to provide the optimal level of support for R&D for fear that neighbouring states and producers will just free-ride on its efforts.

With the exception of Euratom, the EU was until recently little involved in the politics of technological collaboration (Sharp, 1993, p. 202). Things changed in the 1980s when European governments and industries were faced with the challenge of an entirely new generation of technologies: a challenge that they did not seem to be meeting well on the evidence of heavy deficits in the new information and biotechnologies. This raised awkward questions: was an international division of labour in which Western Europe exchanged consumer goods and services for high technology a neutral and optimal outcome of market forces, or was it more institutional in origin – a reflection, perhaps, of the fragmented political structuring of Western Europe compared with Japan and the USA? Would gaps in the EU's technological base trigger an industrial decline, forcing Western Europe to exchange low for high value-added goods and services, excluding it from some of the more lucrative rents in the international political economy, and forcing it out of the high-growth club in which some countries perpetuate their lead from one economic cycle to another through high capital surpluses, continuous product innovation and the steady skilling of their population? On such questions would ultimately depend the very affordability of the expensive consumer and welfare societies of Western Europe.

Under the Single European Act of 1986, the Union was given the task of 'strengthening the scientific and technological base of European industry and to encourage it to become more competitive at an international level'. However, new programmes with exotic names such as ESPRIT, COMETT, RACE, EUREKA and PROMETHEUS had been developing steadily throughout the 1980s, Technically, only the first three are Union projects, with the last two being umbrella organisations for co-ordinated use of national R&D funding in relation to specific projects. However, the various programmes do exist side by side to the extent that the Union initiatives are heavily weighted to pre-competitive research whereas the inter-governmental ones are much closer to the market (Sharp, 1993, p. 214).

As far as the former are concerned, Sharp explains that the Union initiatives of the 1980s were able to draw substantially on the lessons of disappointing collaboration between specific Western European states in the 1960s and 1970s. Much of the EU work is to do with 'match-making' between potential collaborators, with the aim of turning the somewhat randomised scattering of technological talents of Western Europe from weakness to strength. An emphasis has been placed on linking industry to the considerably under-acknowledged strengths of European university research, on linking large to small companies and, of course, on transnational alliances.

The EU projects have also sought to minimise the dangers inherent in officials attempting to pick winners. Not only has research tended to be pre-competitive; political decisions have been confined to choosing broad areas of research, with invitations being extended to potential groups of collaborators to frame the specific proposals and bid for funds. Funding has then been based on a 50 : 50 division between the EU and the companies participating in a project. This has the advantage of exposing the companies themselves to some risk in the event of the research being misconceived, while also allowing some compensation for the disincentive to indulge in R&D, given the difficulties of internalising all benefits.

Indeed, the 50 : 50 division would seem to be broadly compatible with empirical estimates of how the private and social returns from many forms of pre-competitive research break down. The Union programmes, however, make further provision for participating companies to internalise the benefits of their research. All members of a specific project are allowed equal access to the results of the research and to use them as they feel fit; and, if a company is part of one EU-based project, it may have preferential access to the results of other EU-funded research (Sharp, 1993, pp. 209–15). These arrangements are clearly designed to shift the balance of incentives to lessen the free-rider problem and give companies a motive to contribute at some point to the overall pool of research. Geroski makes the interesting point that public policy-makers may not need to do much to tip the balance of incentives in such a way. Against the incentives to free-ride, companies know that if they are to benefit from technological diffusion they have to preserve the complementarities between their own technologies and those of other producers, and ensure that they are sufficiently involved in R&D of their own to remain on the learning curve needed to absorb other people's technologies (Geroski, 1993).

The various Union initiatives are drawn together into four-year framework programmes that set out the EU's overall priorities for technological development and assign a total budget. As yet, the Union is a relatively small player in terms of resources available to fund technology. The 1992 budget, for instance, was only ECUs 2450 m, though this is planned to increase to ECUs 4200 m by 1997, or by 11.5 per cent a year in real terms (Scott, 1993, p. 76). Although there are many different problems in interpreting the meaning of a balance of payments deficit in one particular sector, it should be noted that, in spite of national and EU efforts, the EC's deficit with the rest of the world in information technologies actually quadrupled from $5bn in 1980 to $21bn in 1991 (Sharp, 1993, p. 218).

The 1990–4 framework programme shows an interesting shift of priority for Union support towards the development of environmental technologies. The Union is a potentially valuable framework to combat industrial pollution. Left to themselves, member states are likely to establish a sub-optimal trade-off between industrial development and environmental sustainability, given that each country can externalise some of its pollution costs in an interdependent and crowded European environment. EU policies may also facilitate wider international agreements to reduce emissions of CO_2 and CFCs. Apart from promoting and diffusing pollution-saving technologies, the structural funds can compensate the poorer members of the EU for the relatively greater burden of investment in a sustainable environment, though more radical ideas, centring on a hydro-carbon tax introduced by all members at the same time so that none lose competitiveness, have not yet been taken up. In terms of self-interest, it has also been suggested that Western Europe's indigenous conditions put it in a good position to become a world-leader in environmental technologies, thus offsetting some of its competitive disadvantage in information technology.

(ii) Capacity management

This function goes all the way back to the original Coal and Steel Community of 1952. Markets may not eliminate problems of excess capacity where an industry is dominated by just a few companies and the policies of more than one government. Geroski and Jacquémin have suggested that one reason why Western Europe has been relatively sluggish in its ability to adapt to periodic economic shocks is that its political economy does not promote the easy entry and exit of firms to and from product lines. They remind us that entry is an important source of innovation, as well as competitive pressure; and that exits are needed for the old to make way for the new. However, there are many ways in which established companies can abuse their established position to pursue entry-deterring strategies. In an area like the EU, in which challenger and challenged may well be companies located in different states, the competition-destroying strategies of individual companies may be reinforced by the protectionist behaviour of governments, with entries and exits from markets coming to depend on an institutional distribution of power, not on economic strengths alone (Geroski and Jacquémin, 1989).

Of course, the Single Market programme should restrict such abuses. But, as we argued above, market forces might still be insufficient to ensure the optimum management of capacity in key, oligopolistic, sectors of European industry. So long as companies are covering their running costs, they may remain in a line of production even though they are making a loss when their capital costs are taken into account.

This is because their capital costs are sunk: they have already been incurred. However, such an outcome may not be rational for the economy as a whole, in so far as it denies market share to an entrant who might be able to make a return on capital. There may also be an inertia in the process of exiting from a market with excess capacity. Imagine a handful of companies, each located in a different EU country, all making a loss because of excess capacity and only one having to leave the industry for all the rest to return to profit. It may well be that no company moves to scrap or restructure capacity, in the belief that it only has to wait for one of the others to exit for its own activity to recover profitability. Not only may such delays produce mis-allocations of resources that last for several years; eventual outcomes may depend more on poker skills than productive efficiency (Geroski and Jacquémin, 1989).

An example of how the EU can contribute to the co-ordinated management of such capacity problems is provided by the steel industry. The problem of inertia in capacity closure/restructuring was clearly illustrated in 1982 when steel production in the EC fell to just 110m tons of an available capacity of 197m tons. In 1993, the EU is once again having to broker capacity reductions between European steel producers who would otherwise face aggregate losses of ECUs 4bn a year (*Financial Times*, 17 September 1993). Apart from the inherent value of any co-ordinating function, the EU has some leverage in the form of refusal to allow state aids unless these are accompanied by sustainable restructuring, and in the form of grants from the Union's social funds to support retraining.

(iii) Commercial policy

One of the problems of international trade theory is that productive advantage is always, in part, politically created (Gilpin, 1987). Even if some players in the international trade system believe that everything should be left to market forces, they have to recognise that this is patently not so in other trade centres. Part of the burden that falls on the EU is one of managing the interface between its constituent economies and the wider international economy. This arrangement is supposed to give the EU a certain bloc solidarity in which it can deploy its collective negotiating strength as the largest single trading area in the world economy.

There are some examples of the EU using its commercial policy to protect particular EU industries, the most famous of these being the ceilings it has negotiated on Japanese car imports to the Union and its membership of the multi-fibre agreement, which effectively creates a cartel for the textile industries of developed economies. However, the actions of the EU have essentially been limited to easing problems of adjustment for old industries that are in trouble; it has not, as yet, formulated a strategic trade policy, designed to give new sectors a breathing space from external competition during key periods of their development (Tsoukalis, 1993, p. 296). The main reason for this is that a political consensus does not exist for such an approach between the main member states. The result is that the EU's commercial policy tends to be a mixture of the defensive and reactive – for example, strict anti-dumping codes – with the hope that it can head off the need to develop a strategic trade policy of its own by using the former GATT (now WTO) process to limit the ability of other states to give their own producers a head-start in new sectors. For example, the EU looked to the recent Uruguay round of GATT talks to replicate many features of its own Single Market programme, such as competitive access to public procurement contracts, at the international level.

(iv) Regional development

In addition to setting a framework for the regional policy of member states, the EU has various regional policies of its own. The most important of these – the Structural Funds – are not directed at Britain. Britain is, however, as we saw in Chapter 8, eligible for disbursements under the ERDF.

Deployment of ERDF funds gives an interesting insight into what the EU considers to be some of the issues in creating localised clusters of productive advantage. A recent grant of £630m to Merseyside was only confirmed after the British Government agreed a plan that included 'concentration on training and human resources', the 'encouragement of knowledge-based industries' and 'technology transfer' between Merseyside's two universities and industry, greater graduate retention in the locality, and the 'preparing of sites' and infrastructure for inward investors. The Commission had also taken two steps to maximise the multiplier effects of its aid. First, it insisted that the British Government should match EU contributions pound for pound, thus eliminating a risk that EU efforts would only be a pretext for the national authorities to do less. Second, it has invited clearing banks to make loan capital available via a special investment fund, where interest rates will be subsidised by using the EU's own credit rating to back projects and thus reduce risk premia (*Financial Times*, 25, 26 June 1994).

The creation of the Single Market may well have had the effect of increasing mutual engagement between the EU and local and regional tiers of government. The sharpening of the competitive environment brought about by the Single Market has made it all the more important that each locality should have a clear niche in the productive process, and that it should have adequate political institutions to ensure that physical and educational infrastructures are well matched to the needs of the local economy. The creation of a Committee of the Regions under the Maastricht Treaty was, in part, a response to demands by regional government for direct access to EU decision-making, unmediated by the need to work through national authorities.

9.6   Conclusion

Pointers to the future are usually deceptive. However, the Maastricht Treaty of 1991 and the Delors Report, approved by the Heads of Government in December 1993, may allow us to draw some of the threads of this chapter together into an overview of how the EU sees its role in industrial policy developing from here.

Industrial policy was not a main priority of those who negotiated the Maastricht Treaty. None the less, the Treaty contains several clauses that could become the basis of industrial policies of varying scope and ambition, depending upon the consensus from time to time within the Union (for details, see Lord, 1993 b). Under Article 130 of the Treaty, the Union is supposed to 'speed up the adjustment of industry to structural change'; 'to foster the exploitation of industrial policies of innovation, research and technological development'; and to ensure 'policy consistency between national and EU efforts in these areas'. Article 129 gives the Union the task of 'contributing to the establishment of transeuropean networks in the areas of transport, telecommunications and energy'. Article 198 gives legal personality to the European Investment Bank and empowers it to borrow from the financial markets in order to fund projects associated with less-developed regions, modernisation and cross-border collaboration.

The Delors report seeks to operationalise these clauses of the Treaty. However, the two events were separated by a recession, which concentrated minds on how Europe could best make its living in the world, and a political crisis of support for the EU, which inclined its friends to search for issues most relevant to the life chances of the citizenry. Turning to specifics, the report identifies three main problems in Western Europe's economic condition.

- There is a technology gap, measurable in terms of a balance of payments deficit with North America and the Far East in sunrise technologies. As seen, the problem here is that societies that lag in their absorption of new technologies or their development of new products can too easily become embedded in a disadvantageous position, as skills and infrastructures, which take years to change, come to be geared to downstream production (Delors, 1994, pp. 111–12).
- Transport, energy and communications networks, which form the arteries of Europe's economy, and shape the productivity of its industry, are subject to gaps, bottlenecks and problems of interoperability created by different national policy regimes and traditions.
- The evidence of the last two or three economic cycles since 1973 is that Western Europe is capable of achieving respectable increases in GNP without employment growth. Part of the problem is hysteresis – unemployment makes people unemployable because they lose their skills and motivation. But, whatever the cause, endemically high levels of unemployment in Western Europe produce problems of social incorporation, political consensus and human waste.

Implicit in the Delors report is that these problems are neither created, nor curable, in the market place alone. The report adopts the eclectic position – typical of the EU for most of its history – that good economic performance requires a mixture of competitive markets and effective public institutions. On the one hand, it calls for further privatisations and for greater flexibility in the labour market; on the other, it argues that modern competitive economies should not take human and material resources as given, that their companies and public authorities need to work together to improve the qualities of the factors of production, promote their mobility and increase the flexibility with which they can be combined into new sources of competitive advantage (Delors, 1994, p. 108). Among specific rationales for mixing institutional action with market responses, Delors makes the following points.

- Technological lags, in relation to Japan and the USA, are caused by a malign combination of a relatively lower spend on R&D with the region's political and cultural fragmentation. This calls for transnational action to avoid duplication of R&D effort and speed diffusion and application.
- The 'wealth of nations depends more and more on the creation and exploitation of knowledge'. This places a special burden on the member states as the main providers of education.
- The issue of networks has arrived on the EU's political agenda at the same time as the US Administration is concerned to secure the maximum competitive advantage from information 'super-highways'. Even discounting some of the wilder talk of a second industrial revolution, it will be essential for each centre in the world economy to achieve the right mixture of public and private actions for these new technologies to be successfully incorporated into their productive base; and the EU will have to be the site of some of the public policy-making, given the transnational nature of the infrastructures in question.
- There is a one-off opportunity to combine the restructuring of transport and infrastructures in Western Europe with the reintegration of Eastern Europe into the economic life of the continent as a whole. There are political imperatives here, of avoiding the reappearance of an excluded, resentful and unstable eastern periphery. This might well justify EU funding of connections with the east.
- Problems of hysteresis suggest that the member states should examine their retraining policies, and the Commission should add retraining to the category of allowable aids to producers; indeed, any failure to do so, would encourage capital/labour substitution (Delors, 1994, p. 118). There is also a case for a co-ordinated rebasing of national tax systems to produce a sharper distinction between what is 'socially good' and 'socially bad' in industrial activity. The Commission is keen to cut taxes on employment and training and increase them on pollutants.
- There are also important failures on the capital side. Uncertainty about the future means that financial markets do not exist for all kinds of risk or for all time periods. One possible response is for a public body such as the European Investment Bank to use the Union's credit to guarantee loans in cases such as these.

- It will be impossible to avoid making some broad guesses about the sectors in which European producers stand the best chance of being competitive in the future. Only on this basis will public bodies be able to perform their roles in providing education, physical infrastructures and supports for research and development.

On the question of who should be the policy provider, Delors is interesting in presupposing that the nation state should remain at the forefront of these considerable challenges to public policy-making, but that the returns on national efforts will be nugatory in the absence of co-ordination within the EU framework. Although the programme as it stands assumes the participation of all states, a key issue will be how far it lends itself to being adopted by just some of the member governments. On the one hand, this would clearly be sub-optimal, given the emphasis the Delors report places on the inter-operability of networks. On the other, governments would, in any case, be the main deliverers of the programme and it is easy to identify particular clusters of states for whom it could be logical to go it alone or to go further than the rest under their own steam. For example, France, Germany and Benelux generate the bulk of the Union's GNP. They are geographically grouped. They all have regions where there are remarkably high levels of cross-border transactions; and, although the politics of European integration have become more problematic in France in particular, the ideas in the Delors report would probably be well within the permissive consensus of these countries for further inter-state co-operation. This, of course, brings us back to the question of 'Whither Britain?'

IV CONCLUSIONS

10   Conclusion

Paul Reynolds and David Coates

10.1   General features of British post-war industrial policy

How best to characterise the pattern of industrial policy adopted in the UK since the Second World War is itself a matter of some debate. To some commentators, the whole area – since the 1970s at least – has been characterised overwhelmingly by *discontinuity*: as permanence in industrial policy succumbed to the battle of competing ideologies (Walker and Sharp, 1991, p. 262; Hart, 1986, p. 157). To others, the ideological struggle over what the state should or should not do has only obscured underlying *continuities* and gradual re-adjustments over time (Grant and Wilks, 1983, p. 16); and where some have seen patterns of continuity and change, yet others have seen simply *inconsistency* and *incompetence* (Hart, 1992, p. 139). There is a shared understanding in much of the relevant literature that concern with industry grew in state circles as economic decline quickened in the 1970s and 1980s. There is agreement too that the centre of gravity of industrial policy in the 1970s differed from that which emerged from the middle 1980s; and there is some awareness that industrial policy towards civilian industry differed from that towards industries servicing military needs. But beyond this, there is no uniformity in the way in which the overall pattern of post-war policy is characterised and read.

For our part, we see a clear logic underlying this unevenness of policy and analysis, one rooted in an understanding of the nature and limits of the dominant paradigm informing state thinking on industry and its needs throughout the post-war period. At its core that paradigm was – and remains – an unambiguously *liberal* one: one built on a belief that industrial performance is best left in private hands, assisted

only at the margin by state activity of various kinds. Many commentators have observed the underlying liberalism of the UK political establishment (Marquand, 1988; Grant, 1990; Coates, 1994); and the more
sophisticated of them have pointed to its pervasive impact on the relationship of the British state to its local manufacturing economy. As
Wilks put it, in the industrial policy field, this ideological inclination
has translated itself into:

> an abdication of responsibility. The traditional response of the
> British liberal state has been to define industrial problems as, prima
> facie, the problems of industry, to be resolved by the market and
> with a presumption of government action.... Operationally, indus-
> trial policy is permeated by the norm of 'commercial freedom'. The
> market is seen as independent of the state rather than dependent on
> state regulation and support.... Thus a major operational value of
> British industrial policy is not maintenance of market principles (as
> in Germany) ... or the productivity of the enterprise (as in Japan) but
> rather a concern to sustain the autonomy of the firm. This concern
> might be regarded as the purest of market principles or, more cor-
> rectly, as the ultimate market ethic, since it really presupposes that
> national economic benefit (the good of all) is derived only from the
> individual's (in this case, the individual firm's) interpretation and
> unfettered pursuit of personal benefit.   (Wilks, 1983, p. 139)

Of course, liberalism has always been a porous as well as a dominant
political philosophy, one tolerant of both a narrow and a wide
specification of the role of state action in advancing individual freedom.
Liberalism in Britain has had, that is, both a conservative and a social
democratic face (on this, see Coates, 1990). In the sphere of industrial
policy, this internal liberal disagreement has crystallised around the
issue of how much state action was (and is) appropriate to produce
desired market outcomes. In each post-war decade in Britain one or
other face of the liberal tradition has been dominant: so that for
example 'in the 1960s, the guiding assumption, whether under
Labour/Conservative governments, was that the market economy could
no longer be left to its own devices', whereas, 'in stark contrast, the
guiding assumption of the 1980s was that the market economy *must* be
left to its own devices, and that Britain's economic deficiencies had
stemmed in large part from the state's creeping protection of individuals, firms and sectional interests' (Walker and Sharp, 1991, p. 262).

But for all their ferocity and significance, these disputes on the scale of state intervention have remained disagreements at the margin of policy in at least two vital senses:

- they have been disputes about the degree to which the edges of a market economy needed state regulation. They rarely extended into any basic questioning of the adequacy of markets as such; and
- they have been marginal to a remarkable and persistent consensus on what constituted the core of policy over time – a core built around limited help to civilian industry but consistent and extensive assistance to the agrarian and the military sector.

Industrial policy in Britain in the post-war period, that is, has been constructed not simply on the principles of liberalism (classic/social democratic as the fashion changed) but on the premises of an entrenched *liberal militarism*. Only on the Left of the Labour Party were both the liberal and the militarist elements of that consensus ever challenged – and then only late in the 1970s, when the erosion of economic strength was visibly undercutting the British state's ability to play a major and independent world role. Otherwise and until lately at least, post-war industrial policy has been forged by state élites committed to the maintenance of Britain's world role, as well as by one informed by an all-pervasive liberal common sense.

The *liberal* dimensions of the consensus have given industrial policy in the post-war UK certain unique distinguishing features. Policy to civilian industry has invariably been voluntarist, reactive and passive, limited in scale, and where consistent, primarily market-forming rather than market-shaping. Other than in relation to agriculture (which, as we saw in Chapter 5, has enjoyed a quite special set of policies with its own origins and history) industrial policy towards civilian industry in post-war Britain has been:

- *voluntarist*, relying on industrial co-operation, never directional – except in time of war – and if more ambitious than that (as with planning agreements in the 1970s) quickly abandoned;
- *reactive and passive*, coming in late in the day, normally to soften the effects of market processes (via aid to regions with declining industries, for example) rather than in any significant way strategic and anticipatory (the example of indicative planning which runs counter to that – in the 1960s – was itself quickly abandoned);

- *limited in scope* – certainly in the 1950s remarkably so (with aid to manufacturing industry on a much smaller scale than, say, aid to agriculture); and in the 1980s definitely so (with a generalised retreat of the state from public ownership, market regulation, and aid to industrial investment and research). The state was more active in the 1970s, attempting to find institutions and policies through which to play a larger and more interventionist role: but the 1970s were the exception; and
- *market-forming*: built around a consistent core of policies encouraging competition, sharing information, and aiding exports; normally *low on the political agenda*, subsumed under other priorities; and *largely self-defeating*, with government intervention often being too rushed and ill-thought out to be successful.

On the other hand, the *militarist* dimensions of the consensus has given industrial policy in post-war Britain a set of important characteristics often ignored (or treated as accidental) in the literature concerned with civilian industry–state relations.

- It has anchored policy-making on much of the growth sector of post-war industry in the *Ministry of Defence* and its predecessor ministries; thereby helping to explain the instability and political weakness of civilian industry departments in the British state.
- It has made *MoD procurement policy* a central instrument of state policy to industry in general – thereby giving military needs a disproportionate impact on the general pattern and effects of policy adopted.
- This explains why so high a percentage of *state-funded R&D* has been concentrated in just a few industries (aerospace and nuclear industries in particular) to the detriment of research aid to general civilian industry.
- It is also a clue to why the *aircraft industry* has been so central a concern to government industry departments down the years – bringing a litany of cases (from Concorde and Rolls-Royce right through to the European fighter aircraft) into the centre of the policy agenda.

In general and in consequence, the relationship between government and industry in Britain has been a paradoxical one: 'typified by industry's suspicions of *intervention* on the one hand' but infused with the 'curiously paradoxical recognition that government has a responsibility towards industry on the other' (Grant, 1980, p. 86). This paradox has been resolved at the level of the state largely by sticking to basic market-forming or market-supplementing policies. What has generally been missing on the continuity side of the industrial policy equation has been any extensive state involvement in the picking and creation of new industries – except in the 1970s, the future expansion in the economy's industrial base has largely been left to the market (and to the private corporate institutions dominant there). There is no sense in which, in relation to civilian industry at least, industrial policy has been developed to the point at which we can talk of the British state as an actively developmental or modernising one.

Rather, the cohabitation of liberal philosophy and militarist pretensions have combined in post-war Britain to weaken the institutions of civilian industrial policy-making. We can see this in:

● the *absence of any strong industrial civil service*, or tradition of state–industry movement by senior administrative or management figures in both sectors. This is to be contrasted with the extensive revolving door of appointments linking the MoD to the military-industrial complex in post-war Britain. As Wilks put it, 'a striking feature of government and industry in Britain is the relative isolation of … the three cultures of government, bureaucracy and enterprise. Isolation is evident in the form of different sets of ideas and assumptions, and also in the relatively low level of informal and institutional contact' (Wilks, 1983, p. 157).

● the *regular creation and destruction of civilian industry departments and institutions* – civilian industrial policy in Britain since 1964 is littered with institutions that have come and gone: the Department of Economic Affairs, MinTech and the Industrial Reorganisation Corporation from the 1960s; the National Enterprise Board and the Manpower Services Commission from the 1970s; the British Technology Group from the 1980s; even the NEDC was cut down at the start of the 1990s. It does look as though, for most of the post-war period, the rule was that 'the more closely an institution has become involved directly with selective intervention, the more vulnerable it has become to destabilizing change or even the threat of abolition' (Wilks, 1983, p. 135).

● the *persistent political weakness of the industry departments* remaining, and the recent erosion in the scale of the public part of the industrial sector itself. While Treasury dominance of economic policy remained intact, the DTI was the graveyard department for most of the Thatcher period, when its prime task (in company with the Departments of Energy and Transport) was to oversee the return of much of state-owned industry to the private sector.

This dominance of liberal militarism in the design of post-war British industrial policy has not, however, been without its challenges. On the contrary, the contradictions and limitations of the policies it has engendered regularly stimulated political debate on the adequacy of current industrial policy, and (less frequently) triggered a whole shift in the centre of gravity of policy itself. As earlier chapters have indicated, and as we shall discuss more fully later in this chapter, that shift began in the 1960s: first under the Conservatives (who created the machinery of indicative national planning and incomes control); and then under Labour (who used the machinery to the full, and created new agencies of industrial intervention – MinTech and the IRC). With a brief interlude, the trajectory carried on in the 1970s: being given a new set of powers and funds by the Conservatives (in the 1972 Industry Act) and briefly a very radical inflection under Labour (with planning agreements, further public ownership and the promise of industrial democracy). But a shift back to the centre (to a more voluntarist and passive industrial policy) then followed from 1976, held sway until 1983, and was itself then heavily curtailed by the privatisation and de-regulation initiatives of full-blooded Thatcherism.

Industrial policy in post-war Britain has thus oscillated around the issue of the role of the market – with state intervention peaking only in the early 1940s (under conditions of war) and in the first half of the 1970s (at the end of the post-war boom). As far as we can tell, this oscillation is the source of the policy inconsistency that was noted earlier, while the dominance of the commitment to predominantly market-based solutions explains how little policy inconsistency there has actually been.

10.2   Continuity and change in policy areas

This question of policy inconsistency can best be resolved by tracing patterns of policy over time, and as we do that here, we would refer you back to the discussion in Chapter 1 of key areas of policy concern. We listed them then as policies on the creation and exploitation of markets, on industrial ownership, on investment and industrial structure, on new and old industries, and on new technologies and labour skills. All those policy areas have been addressed by British Governments over time, as the intervening chapters of this book have documented; and we shall consider them here in a particular sequence, in order to prepare the ground for our later discussion of the rise and fall of particular policy 'packages'. We shall begin with policy on ownership, investment and regional aid; and then trace continuities and changes in policy on competition and small business, labour training and innovation.

(i) Ownership

Here we see a distinct pattern of change, with two periods of nationalisation being followed by one of privatisation.

- *1940s* – the pre-war nationalised industries/firms were supplemented by the public ownership of the basic utilities
- *1950s* – steel de-nationalisation was the only change in the public–private divide. Public sector industries were run at full capacity, with limited modernisation, and considerable autonomy from central government control.
- *1960s* – public sector industries were increasingly required to cover costs and earn a net return on capital employed. Existing nationalised industries (especially the railways and mining) were given help with restructuring; the size of the public sector was extended by the nationalisation of the fourteen largest steel firms, and by the IRC's purchase of equity.
- *1970s* – public ownership was extended to new industries and to individual firms.
- *1979 onwards* – the scale of the public sector was reduced by the privatisation of a series of publicly-owned manufacturing industries, and of parts of the state bureaucracy. Remaining parts of the public sector were subject to internal market criteria, competition from the private sector, and curbs on size and funding.

(ii) Investment aid to private companies

Here we see a steady increase in support peaking in the mid-1970s, followed by a significant reduction in state aid thereafter.

- *1940s* – beginnings of tax allowances on industrial investment (1945); and first moves in policy on foreign direct investment. The Attlee Government initially rejected a significant number of foreign firms seeking to invest in Britain because of a desire to develop indigenous suppliers of plant and equipment, but policy was quickly liberalised, and US companies and capital in particular were welcomed.

- *1950s* – tax allowances for investment in manufacturing plant and equipment were changed six times between 1952 and 1959 (depreciation allowances, initial investment allowances and new investment allowances all being used at various times to subsidise the purchase of new plant and equipment). Controls on the arrival of foreign capital were progressively loosened – with governments still prepared, on rare occasions, to block foreign entry into 'key or strategic companies' (in oil and the financial sector in particular), while allowing a growing US presence in the economy's leading export industry (motor vehicles).

- *1960s* – the scale of investment grants was raised significantly to industries deemed strategically significant; and there was active state support for strategic mergers. A serious attempt was made to create 'national champions' through exploiting economies of scale: and governments showed slightly greater concern about the scale of foreign investment or control in the UK manufacturing base (occasionally blocking attempts by foreign companies to buy into strategic industries, and seeking assurances on investment and export plans).

- *1970s* – investment grants were replaced by initial allowances again, but their introduction did not signal a reduction in selective state aid to industry. Just the reverse: the period 1972–79 was characterised in industrial policy by a complex series of selective assistance schemes, largely operated under the terms of the 1972 Act, by which large quantities of state aid flowed both to industries in trouble and to industries deemed strategically significant. A serious attempt was made after 1975 to forge an effective 'industrial strategy' based on the targeting of thirty-nine key sectors (each linked to government through a tripartite working party); and overall total state aid to industry declined in Labour's last two years of office.

- *1979 onwards* – an initial continuity on investment grants and public support for new industries gave way by 1985 to a sharp change of emphasis: a drop in funding to state and private industries (down to one-quarter of 1979 levels by 1987) and a general reduction in selective assistance. Only projects which promised 'exceptional national benefit' were funded, and only then on a very modest scale. High priority was given to the attraction of foreign inward investment.

(iii) Regional policy

As we saw in Chapter 8, the post-war period has seen the rise and fall of a particular kind of regional industrial policy. That policy had a number of distinctive features, It never took, except at the margin, the form of financing migration of labour to jobs: always jobs to labour. ...til the 1980s, regional policy always emphasised manufacturing ...uustry, gave priority to mobile plants – to attracting new firms into regions – and was highly centralised (at least, outside Scotland and Wales). Regional policy of this kind became by the 1960s what Morris and Stout called 'the deepest stratum of industrial policy' (Morris and Stout, 1987), moved into centre stage by the unemployment caused by the decline initially of basic industries (textiles, coal, shipbuilding) and later of cars and steel. Like investment aid, however, regional policy lost favour after 1976, as we can now document.

- *1940s* – the instruments of regional policy were created in the 1945 Development of Industry Act; industrial development certificates (IDCs), investment incentives and public provision of infrastructure were all used to attract firms to areas of high unemployment. There was a stringent use of certificates (needed before building industrial plant) to redirect employment to declining areas.
- *1950s* – regional funding of industry continued, with aid to individual firms and general provision of government factories. After being in abeyance 1951–7, the policy received a higher political profile from the late 1950s, with the Distribution of Industry Act (1958).
- *1960s* – regional policy was much strengthened by new Local Employment Acts providing grants for factory building (1960, 1963), and by the replacement of Development Areas by a greater number of smaller Development Districts (1963–6), new Special Development Areas (1966) with (from 1970) Intermediate Areas on their fringe. Overall a steady series of statutes and initiatives made the decade 'the most frenzied period of conscious regionalism' such

that 'by the late 1960s regional development in Britain received probably a higher priority and incorporated a greater range of measures than anywhere in Western Europe' (Barberis and May, 1993, p. 142).

- *1970s* – After briefly cutting investment grants, regional policy was confirmed in importance by the introduction of non-discretionary Regional Development Grants (RDGs) and by the introduction of a system of Regional Selective Assistance (RSA). The Labour Government extended the coverage of development areas, and set up the Scottish and Welsh Development Agencies. Policy changed after 1976, as the Government cut regional aid and narrowed the areas designated to receive it – out of a growing preference to put 'emphasis on selective, as against general, assistance to industry' (Grant, 1982, p. 59).

- *1979 onwards* – an initial continuity of regional aid, investment grants and public support for new industries gave way progressively to a sharp change of emphasis: the 1982 Industry Act scrapped IDCs; the 1983 White Paper, (*Regional Industrial Development*), moved policy away from RDGs and set cost limits on RSGs: and the 1988 White Paper, (*DTI – the Department for Enterprise*), scrapped RDGs altogether. In that process regional aid was significantly reduced: by a narrowing of the areas supported, and a progressive tightening of the criteria on RDGs and RSA. RDGs in their last phase (1984–8), were made available to service as well as manufacturing industry, tied more directly to job creation, and reduced to exclude replacement investment. In consequence, expenditure on RDGs and RSAs fell by two-thirds between 1979 and 1987. RSAs still played a key role in attracting inward investment.

(iv) Competition policy

Here the pattern of continuity and change has been very different. Competition policy has remained at the heart of industrial policy throughout the post-war period, with its impact only dulled between 1964 and 1970 (when economies of scale were given greater priority in the pursuit of international competitiveness). By the 1980s competition policy had become again *the* dominant element in British industrial policy.

- *1940s* – competition policy was strengthened by the creation of the Monopolies and Restrictive Practices Commission (1948).
- *1950s* – competition policy was extended through the splitting of the Monopolies and Restrictive Practices Commission into the Monopolies Commission and the Restrictive Practices Court (1956), and by the beginnings of moves against resale price maintenance (1958).
- *1960s* – competition policy was extended through the banning of resale price maintenance (1964), the public overseeing of mergers as well as monopolies (1965), the toughening of legislation on Restrictive Trade Practices (1968) and the attempt to enter the European Economic Community (from 1961).
- *1970s* – competition policy was extended through EEC membership (1973), and through Acts strengthening consumer rights (1973, 1974, 1977), encouraging Fair Trading (1973) and banning restrictive trade practices (1973, 1975, 1976). These left in place both a new Office of Fair Trading and the renamed Monopolies and Merger Commission (MMC). The decade also saw growing interest in the small firm sector (after the publication of the Bolton Report in 1971). A Small Firms Division was set up in the DTI and a series of policies initiated (tax breaks, extra finance and deregulation).
- *1979 onwards* – competition policy was extended through the Competition Act (1980) allowing the Director of Fair Trading to investigate (and refer to the MMC) any suspected anti-competitive practices, regardless of whether monopoly or merger was involved (these powers were also extended to cover nationalised industries). Privatisation was accompanied by both the encouragement of private competition (Mercury versus BT, for example) and the creation of consumer watchdog bodies for each industry. A myriad of initiatives was taken to strengthen the small business sector (loan guarantee schemes, business expansion schemes, enterprise allowances, one-stop shops); and the whole economy was exposed to greater European competition after the adoption of the single European market in 1992. Following a major review of industrial policy in 1988, after which the DTI was re-specified as the 'Department of Enterprise' and pulled back into largely an advisory role, 'competition policy' became the core of the government's industrial policy, and the deregulation of business became one of its central concerns.

(v) Education and training

Here the role of the British state has changed over time. but in differing
directions depending on which leg of this pair of policies is under view.
On education, the post-war British state was slow to intervene in the
determination of curricula and the direct shaping of vocational education, initiating reform under those headings only in the 1980s. But as
the Thatcherite state increased its powers over schooling, it withdrew
increasingly from the provision of training for people in work. State
initiatives on training for the employed came primarily in the 1960s;
and in the two decades that followed, governments trained primarily
the young unemployed, before turning even that responsibility over to
private employer-led provision in the 1990s.

- *1940s* – there was educational reform through the 1944 Act. Technical
  schools were established as one of three types of secondary school.
  The training of people at work was left to employers and unions.
  Some Government training centres were closed, and the numbers
  trained there annually reduced. Change came only in the 1960s.
- *1960s* – there was a big expansion of higher education (after the
  Robbins Report); and selective secondary education was replaced
  by comprehensives. Polytechnics were created (out of old technical
  colleges) to enhance vocational training within the higher education system. Statutory Training Boards were created on an industry-
  wide basis.
- *1970s* – central state direction of training was strengthened by the
  creation of the Manpower Services Commission. But training of the
  employed was still largely left to Industrial Training Boards and
  apprenticeship schemes, as the MSC increasingly concentrated on
  training programmes for the unemployed.
- *1979 onwards* – the autonomy of schools and local authorities in
  the design and management of the education system was eroded by
  the creation of the national curriculum, and by the exposure of
  schools to greater local parental pressure (league tables and the
  like). The MSC dominated the training of the unemployed: its
  schemes eroded the apprenticeship system; and Industrial Training
  Boards were allowed to collapse. In 1988 the MSC was shut, and
  the delivery of training was devolved to employer-dominated TECs.
  Both the MSC and the DES encouraged the spread of non-academic
  vocational training in schools and colleges of further education.

(vi) Policy on innovation

Government support for R&D has been a further major element in post-war industrial policy. That support has consistently been targeted at industries producing defence goods, and at closely related industries (particularly civil aviation and nuclear power). Agriculture too has received state aid in R&D. Half-hearted attempts were made in the 1960s to shift the focus on policy on to civilian as well as military research; and from the 1970s to encourage new industries based on the latest scientific and technology break-throughs. That policy was reset in 1988, to reinforce pre-competitive research on enabling technologies, and to cut the volume of public resources devoted to supporting both civilian and military R&D.

- *1940s* – the Second World War triggered direct state-funding of R&D, the creation of government R&D laboratories, and the use of military procurement to create new production capacities. These policies persisted after 1945, in the form of significant state support for R&D in the nuclear, aerospace, shipbuilding and electronics industries. The decade also saw some small amount of state aid to civilian R&D through the creation of the National Research Development Council (1948), and its supporting panoply of advisory councils.
- *1950s* – research expenditure was still heavily concentrated on military research and associated products: nuclear, advanced aircraft, military electronics and missile systems. 'In the 1950s more than half of total national R&D spending was devoted to defence'; and defence R&D as a percentage of total defence expenditure (at 14.7 per cent in 1958) was way higher even than that of the USA (10.10 per cent) and certainly than France (5.58 per cent) and Germany (1.47 per cent) (Edgerton, 1993a, p. 10). The aircraft industry was the main beneficiary: three-quarters of its output was military as late as the mid-1960s. Government civilian R&D expenditure in 1960/61 was £44 m. R&D expenditure by defence departments was £242 m (Grove, 1967, p. 268).
- *1960s* – the decade saw a whole new emphasis on civilian as well as military research. 'Indeed for the first time in its history the British state spent more on civil R&D than on military R&D' (Edgerton, 1993, p. 11). But by the end of the decade, spending on military-related R&D had risen again, notably on the Chevaline and

Tornado projects. By the end of the decade, too, responsibility for high-tech industries (atomic energy, machine tools, computers, electronics, telecommunications, as well as shipbuilding and engineering) had been temporarily brought together in the new Ministry of Technology.

- *1970s* – 'During the decade there was a steady increase in the proportion of R&D financed by government. It peaked in the early 1970s, at around one-half of total expenditure' (Walker, 1993, p. 173). By that point, government-funded R&D was heavily concentrated in aerospace and electronics: in aerospace, government funds consistently provided three-quarters of R&D resources for both military and civil aircraft; in electronics, half the total R&D budget was government-funded. Only in defence and agriculture did the state by 1978 spend more on research as a proportion of GDP than was the European norm: though within certain other categories it had unusually high contributions to make: to nuclear energy within the 'energy' category, to civil air transport within 'industry', and to building and water research within 'environment' (Pavitt, 1981, pp. 105–6). There was renewed emphasis on the importance of science and technology, and on the diffusion of new technologies – visible in measures such as the Product and Process Development Scheme (1977), the Microprocessor Application Project (1978) and the MicroElectronics Industry Support Programme (1978). But the sums involved were very small – £26 million a year for the first and about £110 million over several years for the other two together.

- *1979 onwards* – during the first half of the 1980s, expenditure on military and military-related R&D increased rapidly, but then tailed off slowly as funds were cut. Over the decade, the proportion of government R&D funding for defence projects going to private industry rose, from 54 per cent to 65 per cent. The bulk of that funding went to aerospace, electronics and mechanical engineering – (in particular GEC and Plessey, the UK's two key electronic firms, were still dependent for one-third (GEC) and 40 per cent (Plessey) of their turnover on military contracts as late as 1988 (Freeman, 1989, p. 209).

The initial continuity of policy on investment grants and public support for new industries gave way by 1985 to a sharp change of emphasis. Initially (1981) a new Minister (of Information Technology) was created to pull state resources away from old industries to new, and launched the Alvey programme, to stimulate

IT research through collaborative pre-competitive projects developed around certain general key technologies: intelligent knowledge-based systems (IKBS); the man/machine interface (MMI); software engineering; very large scale integration (VLSI); and computing architectures. The DTI also funded research into advanced manufacturing in electronics (AMIE) and advanced robotics (ARP). But by 1988 the DTI was reset as an 'enterprise department', concentrating the bulk of its R&D funding on pre-competitive research, especially collaborative research. It shifted the focus of its grants towards the funding of key enabling technologies (like microelectronics) likely to have benefits across industry as a whole; and towards non-project support, placing greater emphasis on technology diffusion (via advisory services, the encouragement of best practice, and improvement in the supply of skills). This change of policy was accompanied by a reduction in the level of state support for both military and civilian R&D.

10.3 Packages of policy

The rise and fall of particular areas of industrial policy on the agenda of successive British governments, and the different positions taken in each area, have been neither accidental nor unconnected. Rather, they have derived from the underlying *packaging of policy* characteristic of state–industry relationships in Britain in the post-war period as a whole. When policy is examined in the round, it is clear that two distinct 'packages' can be located – an old one and a new – the first social democratic, and the second neo-liberal, in origin and inspiration. The two faces of liberalism, to which we referred earlier, have shaped the content and interconnections of industrial policy in distinct and recognisable ways.

(i) The social democratic package

The 'old' industrial policy was underpinned by Keynesian assumptions about the effectiveness of a regulatory and interventionist role for the state in the national economy. Keynesianism gave a whole post-war generation of British politicians – both Labour and Conservative – the belief that they could, by managing the economy in a particular way, achieve certain national *economic* policy objectives (growth, low inflation, full employment, balance of payments surpluses) and certain *social* objectives too (welfare provision, social justice, and so on). Keynesianism also gave that generation of politicians the confidence to create state machinery to 'manage' the local industrial base as a coherent national economy.

So, at different stages between 1945 and 1979, regulatory machinery was established to manage trade, stimulate industrial development and co-ordinate the interplay of different sectors of the economy – industrial capital, finance and the unions, and even the manufacturing and service sectors of the economy. As we have seen, essential services, large-scale industrial resources (such as coal and steel), and provision for nascent new technology industries, all resided within the public sector between 1945 and 1979, kept there by a particular definition of the national and public interest, and sustained by a dominant, holistic concept of the national economy. Outside the public sector, private industry was supported by industrial subsidies and the manipulation of the taxation system to create a national environment of incentives for domestic (and later inward) investment. Subsidies, as with public ownership, serviced regional needs and policy objectives as part of the agenda for national growth and prosperity. Both public and private sectors were underpinned by a belief in the capacity of the state to influence markets, consumption, efficiency and modernisation in industry.

In this social democratic policy universe, governments regulated local industries partly to encourage their modernisation and partly to impose political and legal frameworks on that modernisation. In the event, such regulation, from health and safety to industrial relations, was invariably contested by business and on occasion by the unions (by the first as a constraint on the workings of the free market, by the latter as a constraint on the outcomes of free collective bargaining). The state judged itself ultimately by its ability to foster industrial development: initially through the provision of essential infrastructural services, later by actually 'picking winners', seeking to create and sustain 'national champions' in industries seen as strategically significant for long-term growth. In a social democratic understanding of the nature of modern capitalism, the task of government was to service the local economy, by correcting the imperfections of the market, managing industrial development, and providing a planning impetus for the growth of British-based firms. There was also a development logic at work within the social democratic package – a tendency for the state's role to extend and expand over time. In the language of the various state–market relationships explored in Chapter 1, the 'old' industrial policy shifted ideologically from market-shaping and managing towards strategies for market-creation and supplementation.

The 'old' social democratic industrial policy package disappeared in a formal political sense with the election of the Thatcher Government in 1979, but even before then it had attracted criticisms for its political failure and its conceptual limitations.

Politically, successive interventionist governments failed to balance the 'economic contradictions of democracy' as Brittan (1977) termed the failure of Keynesian economics to meet the different demands released by social democracy. Successive interventionist governments also failed to square the circle of industrial modernisation and Great Power status. As we have seen, the pursuit of an independent and major world role for the British state proved immensely costly and self-destructive over time: in high defence spending, the maintenance of a strong currency, and the failure to modernise the British state machine. At the same time, intervention to plan the national economy was undermined by the political pressures of the different interests affected by it – unions, business, investor interest groups and international economic actors. These political conflicts fettered rather than enabled successful intervention, since they blocked the construction of a coherent 'coalition for growth'. In Britain at least (and unlike either Germany or Japan) post-war governments failed to gain the confidence of either the local owning class (which held on to a belief in the market as the key to profit and wealth) or of the trade unions (which, even with Labour in power, did not trust government to protect the jobs and living standards of the groups they represented). The application of the 'old' industrial policy package stimulated de-industrialisation and winters of discontent whenever it was tried, for all that those advocating it sought only growth in investment and employment.

Their failure was not simply a policy one. It was also conceptual. The 'old' industrial policy was limited by the weakness of its grounding assumptions. These were too naïve about the market, too insensitive to the limits of the nation-state, too silent on the particularities of the local owning class. Keynesianism relied on the state as a 'handmaiden' to the market, mending rather than modernising or reorganising, and so being reactive rather than proactive. Keynesianism was also built on the premise that it made sense to treat national economies as whole, distinct and manageable units. Yet at critical points in the post-war story, it was clear that the national economy was not impermeable.

Global political and economic forces – transnational companies, international finance, the US government and the European Community – all imposed constraints upon British industrial development, and constrained political autonomy; and did so increasingly over time. The local owning class were themselves increasingly global players, with only limited degrees of commitment to the national industrial base. This was true of City institutions throughout the post-war period; and it was increasingly true of large, British-owned industrial concerns from the 1970s. When interventionist governments sought to 'modernise' the national economy by intervening in its central workings, they met an owning class imbued with a liberal distrust of state action, and increasingly linked to productive activity beyond the nation's shores. Blocked by the inadequacies of their underlying vision, and lacking adequate local social and industrial support, the social democratic project for industrial modernisation predictably stalled. It was effectively abandoned by the Labour government after 1976, and it was electorally routed from 1979.

(ii) The neo-liberal alternative

The failure of Keynesian political economy and statist industrial policy was met by a sustained 'New Right' critique which claimed to offer industrial policy which would be both ideologically and politically superior in its application to policy problems and address the new realities of the 1980s. Global penetration of UK markets, poor competitiveness, deindustrialisation, poor labour relations and the politicisation of the economy through state intervention, were all regarded as products of the 'old'; and the 'new' promised a mixture of change or accommodation in order to rejuvenate industrial performance.

A belief in the efficacy of market forces was central to this strategy. According to its adherents, only free-market signals in the private sector provided a discipline to economic activity, producing profits and efficient industrial organisation. Political power only fettered the market, distorting its signals and stifling and burdening economic activity. The task of industrial policy was therefore to create the conditions in which market forces could function to restructure the British economy and reconstitute its industrial competitiveness. The task of the state in that circumstance was overwhelmingly to exercise *restraint*: by committing itself to a series of monetary targets, to the removal of a series of impediments to the free play of market forces (especially in labour markets), and to a general rolling back of the state (to open up even greater market opportunities for private enterprise).

From these assumptions came Conservative strategies of popular capitalism, the enterprise culture and the property owning democracy. Privatisation pruned the public sector, moving as much as possible of what was in the public domain – industry, resources, people, administrative structures – into the private domain and under the discipline of market forces. Deregulation opened up competition in the finance and service sectors, and reduced state involvement in a range of industrial concerns. Employment legislation reduced union power, and opened the route to lower wages and greater labour productivity. Taxation was reduced for entrepreneurial and business interests, and realigned to reduce its progressive ethos and give incentives to competitiveness and performance. In the terms of the various state–market relationships explored in Chapter 1, the whole centre of gravity of thinking and action moved back to position 1: to the creation and defence of markets as the key to industrial growth and prolonged recovery. This represented a fundamental shift in the ideological underpinnings of industrial policy – and was recognised and presented as such, both by its advocates and its critics.

The 'new' industrial policy drew its capacity to redefine the terms of the policy debate so dramatically from three separate factors. First, though industrial policies underpinned by Keynesian economics had failed, much of the global and historical economic context which had conditioned that failure had been overshadowed by the immediacy of governmental mismanagement and the 'British' disease of poor industrial relations. This allowed for the easy stigmatisation of labour, and of intellectual and political interests who critically rejected the market. This stigmatisation was reinforced by the rightward shift of the political agenda, as both the Labour Party and some key trade unions interpreted the repeated Conservative electoral victories after 1979 as a product of popular support for market strategies and so abandoned their earlier commitments to common ownership, state regulation and planning.

Then, thirdly, the 'new' industrial policy claimed to answer the questions set by contemporary global economic change – questions set by foreign competitiveness, deindustrialisation and globalisation. It purported to answer the challenge posed by intensified foreign competition by the manner in which its mixture of labour regulation and industrial deregulation significantly lowered British labour costs. It sought to slow deindustrialisation in three ways:

(i)   by letting the existing manufacturing base shrink (the slack being taken up by an expansion in financial and other services);
(ii)   by encouraging small business enterprise; and
(iii) by attracting foreign direct investment from large transnational companies.

The new realities of a globalised economy were then to be confronted by a full immersion in them, with the Government's creation of a 'low-cost' economy challenging competitors on their own terms, and with deregulation allowing global speculators and investors to see Britain as once more a profitable and attractive location.

But, though ideologically influential, this neo-liberal package has quickly proved to be as economically ineffective as its predecessor. Market forces, if left unregulated, invariably prove to be cumulative rather than corrective, redeploying resources from weak economies to strong, rather than from strong to weak; and certainly in the context of a new international division of labour being forged by a fusion (in parts of the Third World) between transnational capital and developmental states, liberalism appears a remarkably weak base from which to seek industrial regeneration. In the global competition to attract foreign direct investment through low wages, Britain cannot match the desperation of the Asian peasantries; and the social costs of trying to do so are horrendous to contemplate. But the market alone will not re-skill the British labour force, or trigger the internal investment necessary to lift the local industrial base on to a high productivity, high-value added path. After more than fifteen years of neo-liberal industrial policies, the British economy still carries levels of unemployment and import penetration, and deficiencies in welfare provision and industrial investment, of a scale which can no longer be dismissed as the product of state interventionism. If the game was up for old-style, social democratic industrial policy by 1979, it is looking increasingly as though it is equally up for neo-liberalism in the mid-1990s. Industrial policy in Britain since 1945 has now moved through two distinguishable phases, without in any way achieving industrial renaissance. The question for the rest of the 1990s, and beyond, is whether a third and more successful package can yet be retrieved from the wreckage of the other two.

10.4   New directions for industrial policy?

One way of answering that question is to look briefly at the policy options currently being canvassed by leading political forces in the contemporary UK. 1994 was a particularly busy year in that particular respect, with the publication – in sequence – of the report of the Select Committee on Trade and Industry on the *Competitiveness of UK Manufacturing Industry*, the DTI's defensive response, the White Paper *Competitiveness: Helping Business to Win,* and the Labour Party's strategy for industrial success, *Winning for Britain.* The three reports offered overlapping sets of policy solutions – in that they shared common concerns to raise skill levels in the UK labour force, encourage innovation and the dissemination of best practice, and strengthen the viability of small and medium-sized enterprises. But the overlap was not total: they disagreed quite sharply on the kind of government action needed in each of those areas, and on the extent to which reform is needed beyond them: in City–industry relations, in labour market regulation and in the degree of direct government involvement. The centre of gravity of each package of proposals, as we might expect, sat at a different point on the spectrum of state–market relationships laid out in Chapter 1, with the willingness to intervene in market processes intensifying as we move from White Paper to Select Committee to Labour alternative.

Each package was built around its own big six policy proposals. For the Government there needed to be policy development:

- to strengthen vocational education and training, and increase the number of apprenticeships;
- to extend de-regulation (by cutting 40% of the rules constraining business) and encourage inward investment;
- to enhance innovation via a system of small grants, better university-business links, and exploratory talks with City working groups on the flow of finance;
- to help small business by the extension of the Business Links and Business angels schemes, and by government encouragement (though not legislation) to curb late payment of bills;
- to strengthen regional redevelopment through a new 'regional challenge' modelled on the City challenge, as a partnership of local funding and initiatives with government (and European) money; and

- concerted government action to ensure a stable monetary environment, with more privatisation, cost-effectiveness in the public sector, and tax regimes encouraging private wealth-creation.

All this, as Richard Caborn, the chairman of the Select Committee on Trade and Industry, said, was 'a million miles apart' from the thrust of the Select Committee's report. At the heart of their recommendations were:

- spending on training and education, financed by a levy on employers, with training controlled by the DTI rather than the Department of Education;
- support for deregulation, but opposition to regimes of growth built on low wages;
- greater public spending on R&D, particularly in key industries like aerospace;
- new rules on the City, to block hostile takeovers, restrain excessive dividend distribution and control over-generous pay to directors;
- better funding for small businesses through tax changes and loan guarantees;
- the establishment of national targets for growth in productivity, exports and share of world trade.

Labour's six were different again. They were:

- to increase investment funding by new rules on takeovers, the use of pension funds and the establishment of a Business Development Bank;
- to change the rules under which companies are run: to encourage longer-term investment by shareholders and greater involvement by workers;
- new tax credits to encourage greater R&D, especially in green technologies;
- a re-skilling of the labour force by a skills audit, and a strengthening of workers' rights to educational qualifications and industrial training;
- easing of the financial pressures on small businesses by taxation changes, a statutory right to interest on late payments, and a limited moratorium on corporate debts.
- the establishment of a network of regional development agencies and regional investment banks to renew and modernise the local economy.

The Select Committee wanted concerted action on financial institutions to end 'short termism'; the White Paper noted the problem, but suggested no action. The Select Committee wanted a levy on employers to finance training programmes; the White Paper shared their enthusiasm for training, but not for the levy. Both agreed on the benefits of deregulation and inward investment, but the White Paper stressed the benefits of low labour costs in ways the Select Committee did not. The Select Committee wanted more spending on R&D, and the setting of national targets; the White Paper did not. And between the proposals offered by Labour and those defended by the Conservatives were clear differences of governing philosophy. It is worth comparing the three reports's views on the proper role of government.

The Select Committee was suitably centrist and anodyne:

Government action is especially important in the following respects: provision of information and promotion of best practice; funding or part-funding activities where only part of the benefit is captured by the firms carrying them out (e.g. training and R&D); ensuring that the UK has the institutions essential for a successful manufacturing country; ensuring that the UK has high-quality infrastructure; using its hugh purchasing power to promote competitiveness; and exercising a strong co-ordinating role.   (HMSO, 1994, p. 126)

The White Paper agreed with most of that, but not with the last; and presented the overall case for government action in a far more limited and apologetic tone.

'Businesses – not governments – create wealth.... The Government's role is to create the conditions in which firms throughout the economy can improve competitiveness: by providing the stable macro-economic environment which enables business to plan ahead with confidence; making markets work more efficiently, and broadening the influence of market disciplines on resource allocation; pursuing tax policies which encourage enterprise and do not hinder economic efficiency; and improving value for money in those services which are best provided by the public sector. The Government must provide the legal framework.... Regulation may sometimes be needed to reproduce the effects of markets in natural monopolies or to reduce uncertainty, but over-regulation stifles innovation.... Where markets do not work well ... the Government has a positive and proactive role to play. It has a central role in areas critical to the process of wealth creation: ... good quality education ... the funding of research and development ... wider structural issues such as the supply of capital to small firms ... barriers to employment ... encourage employers to train their workforces .... law and order. Often the Government can help most by getting out of the way. (Cmnd. 2563, 1994, pp. 15–16)

Labour put it differently, and made much more of what the Select Committee called 'a strong co-ordinating role'.

It is not the job of government to run industry. It is, though, the role of government to promote within our economy and society those qualities that are essential if our industry is to be competitive. And nobody is in a better position than government to take an overview of the economy and whether the relationships between the different players in it are functioning effectively. Britain is handicapped in its efforts to develop a competitive economy by a government imprisoned by an ideology that is based on an outdated picture of industry.... We believe that Britain works best when we work together.... We believe that the market can encourage short-term priorities and may fail to promote long-term profitability.... We believe that an unjust society will product an inefficient economy.... Britain will always be handicapped in international competition while we alone [under Conservative leadership] are ruled by a government prevented by its ideology from ever admitting there could be a conflict between the short-term operation of the market and the long-term interest of the nation. (*Winning for Britain*, 1994, pp. 4–5)

10.5 A third way?

What we see in this set of proposals from the Labour Party is a hesitant move towards a third package, one already prefigured in the USA. For the simple answer to the question raised at the start of this section is that there is now a politically credible 'third way'. It is a third way built – if we recall the arguments about state–market relationships explored in Chapter 1 – around the Tyson/Zysman thesis for 'shaping markets': one in which policy is directed towards the achievement of competitive strength in key industrial sectors, through state intervention within a 'partnership' with corporate business. In this third package, the state's responsibility lies primarily with the provision of training, technology, R&D and capital modernisation, though at a broader level, the role of the state is that of selectively enhancing the prospects of indigenous capital. This to a small extent mirrors the impetus of the 'old' industrial policy to 'pick winners' and the state to manage domestic capitalism; but in this third package, the old social democratic preoccupation with direct state intervention and public ownership is replaced by the construction of a partnership between government and industry directed to the enhancement of corporate competitiveness in a number of key industries.

Behind this 'third way' is some sense of a need for the state to play a more *developmental* role in relation to its own industrial base, of the kind associated with successful Asian industrialisation (in places such as Japan and Taiwan) to which we referred when discussing typologies of state systems in Chapter 1. Neither in the USA nor in the British Labour Party is anyone seriously arguing for the very close state-industry linkages that are now seen to have been so vital to Japan's industrial take-off in the 1950s. Times, we are told, have changed, and no longer allow or require that. But nor can everything be left to the untrammelled workings of market forces. States must intervene, to shape the quality and availability of factors of production vital to industrial success; and must do so in an alliance with local corporate interests committed to industrial reconstruction and enhanced employment in their home economy.

The rhetoric behind this third way is politically important, because it offers a clearly alternative intellectual anchorage for policies that purport (and indeed seek) to be distinctive and different from neo-liberal (and earlier social democratic) policies. But the reality behind the rhetoric is what in the end will determine success or failure in programmatic terms (as distinct from merely short-term electoral ones); and here the novelty of what is on offer is less evident. One feature of the whole neo-liberal period in British industrial policy was the way in which market-based policies were juxtaposed to a crude stereotype of what life had been like in the heyday of social democracy: a time, we are repeatedly told, of lumbering, inefficient publicly-owned monolithic industries, over-planned and bureaucratically-hassled private wealth-creators, over-mighty trade unions and politically-motivated (and economically-illiterate) state intervention. Against that stereotype, of course, Labour's 'third way' looks new indeed. But the reality of policy (and of power relationships) in the old social democracy was very different from the stereotype painted of it by its political opponents; and in truth the new Labour package reads – ahead of time – much like the actual policy-mix adopted by post-war Labour governments in the second half of each of their previous periods of government. It certainly sits easily with policies advocated by a revitalised 'supply side' Keynesianism of the kind we often saw then: policies that include incentives for industrial development, and the prioritising of vocational education and training in skills development. Indeed, Labour is approaching office again in an intellectual climate increasingly shaped by Keynesian ideas, and by those of Will Hutton in particular. The Hutton 'package' proposes the radical restructuring of the institutional base of the political system as a precondition for effective economic and industrial policy, and looks for initiatives to lower capital costs, to strengthen shareholder commitment to long-term investment in companies, and to regulate the local financial sector (Hutton, 1995).

These echoes of the past make Labour's third way very attractive to a broad coalition of disillusioned Thatcherites and centre-left Labourites, and may yet be the electoral cocktail that the Party needs to return to power. But getting to power is one thing – using it is another; and here the similarity of the Blair promise with the Wilson practice still places large question marks over the long-term viability of this third package too. For the moment it has a freshness that rests on its capacity to distance itself from an exhausted neo-liberalism; but its credibility ultimately will turn on its capacity to tackle deep-seated weaknesses in the British industrial formation, and to do so in changing global conditions to which neither neo-liberalism nor old-style social democracy have yet managed to find an adequate answer. In opposition in 1994–5, the new Labour leadership placed the emphasis of their alternative route to industrial modernisation on its distance from the labour movement's traditional allies – the unions – preferring instead to court the support of the local business community and to set their face against increases in government expenditure and taxation. Yet such a business-led developmental model must then leave space – to its own left – for a more radical interpretation of the needs of local industrial reconstruction, and must remain open to the socialist critique that behind its rhetoric of modernisation very little of substance will actually change.

On that critical question of course – of whether there is substance behind the rhetoric – the jury must still be out; but there can be no doubt that substance will be required, since centre-left policy-makers in power in the next decade and beyond will face a particularly difficult set of both internal and external circumstances, circumstances which will not lend themselves to quick and easy solutions. Internally, centre-left governments in Britain stand to inherit a manufacturing sector whose contribution to GNP has shrunk from a third to a fifth since the last time Labour entered power, a manufacturing base whose total output is still only marginally higher than it was then, and one which still suffers from chronic under-investment and shortages of skilled labour. Externally, an incoming centre-left government will face a new international division of labour that has placed much industrial production in the Far East, will find itself the custodian of an economy within the EU that is outside the Community's industrial core, and will face an unprecedented level of global ownership in its industrial growth sectors. Weak internally, porous to external forces, and internationally on the slide, the British economy awaiting an incoming government after the next general election will be precariously placed indeed.

Elements within that economy are (and will still be) internationally strong (particularly aerospace, pharmaceuticals and financial services); but much of its manufacturing base is not of this quality. Certain of its regions are (and will still be) prosperous, and in employment terms still relatively secure (the South East particularly); but the North in general is not so well placed. Left without state intervention, the British economy in the 1980s has fractured industrially and regionally under the impact of global and regional market forces, and seems set to fracture more. But any moves that an incoming Labour government makes to correct that fracturing will need to confront and turn those market forces, and deal effectively with the interests that lie behind them. In opposition, Labour politicians seem convinced that they can do that by appealing to the interests of the local manufacturing class – to British private capital as it is presently constituted. But what if Labour is wrong, what if such a 'national bourgeoisie' has already been superseded by a more globally-orientated and externally-controlled industrial owning class? What then can Labour in power do to prevent a further export of capital, further unemployment and welfare erosion, further 'winters of discontent' and electoral rejection?

What it can do, of course, is explore the extent to which an even more radical set of industrial policies are available for implementation, a set of policies more in tune with the needs of Britain's contemporary industrial crisis. What it can do is consider the possibility of replacing its 'third way' by a more radical 'fourth'.

Fourth ways invariably settle at the radical end of the typology of state–market relationships mentioned in Chapter 1 (settle, that is, at the market-shaping/market-replacing end of the scale). In the early 1980s the socialist fourth way required British withdrawal from the European Community, and tight controls on private capital and trade; but arguably now, that anti-European moment has passed. These days a radical industrial policy needs a strong European dimension within it: to shape the pattern of trade policy pursued (by the EU as a whole) in relation to the other emerging trade blocs of the international capitalist world; to strengthen programmes of regional equalisation within the European Community; and to put real controls (at the European level) on transnational corporations. But a radical industrial policy needs a strengthened (and a democratised) British state as well: to set strategic targets for the development of British-based industries, to direct investment to those targets, and to subordinate industrial decision-making to democratic control (via public ownership, industrial democracy, and strengthened regional planning agencies).

Industrial planning and worker-power are not fashionable in Britain right now – and certainly are not in the circles surrounding the new Labour Party leadership – but it seems to us that they need to become so again (and quickly) if the political opportunity now opening up for a change of direction is not to be squandered in yet another attempt to modernise without reform, or to reindustrialise without adequately curtailing the power of those social forces responsible for deindustrialisation. The 1990s are closing with clear evidence that neo-liberal solutions to industrial decline do not work. It would be a tragedy if that lesson had to be learned all over again in the opening years of the next century, because an intervening period of more active but still modest industrial policy under a Labour government had failed to work as well.

Suggested Further Reading

For the general material discussed in **Chapter 1**, we recommend you read in particular W. Grant (ed.) *Industrial Policy* (Aldershot: Edward Elgar, 1995), and his earlier, *The Political Economy of Industrial Policy* (London: Butterworth, 1982); C. Johnson (ed.) *The Industrial Policy Debate* (Berkeley: University of Calefornia Press, 1984); P. Hall, *Governing the Economy* (Oxford: Oxford University Press, 1986); and the OECD annual review, *Industrial Policy in OECD countries* (Paris: OECD).

The material surveyed in **Chapter 2,** can be further extended by reading D. Coates, *The Question of UK Decline: the economy, state and society* (London: Harvester-Wheatsheaf, 1994); the second report of the House of Commons Select Committee on Trade and Industry, *Competitiveness of UK manufacturing Industry* (London: HMSO, 1994); and the forthcoming S. Lee, *The Political Economy of Manufacturing Industry in Britain* (London: Macmillan, 1996).

For **Chapter 3**, we recommend L. Budd and S. Whimster (eds) *Global Finance and Urban Living* (London: Routledge, 1992); A. Harrison (ed.) *From Hierarchy to Contract: Reshaping the Public Sector* (vol. 7, Policy Journals, Newbury); D. Liston and N. Reeves, *The Invisible Enemy* (London: Pitman, 1988); E. Noam, *Telecommunications in Europe* (Oxford: Oxford University Press, 1992); and R. Rhodes, 'The hollowing out of the state: the changing nature of the public service in Britain', *Political Quarterly*, vol. 65, pp. 138–51.

For **Chapter 4,** we recommend M. Armstrong, S. Cowan, and J. Vickers, *Regulatory Reform: Economic Analysis and British Experience* (Cambridge, Mass.: MIT Press, 1994); J. Roberts, D. Elliott and T. Houghton, *Privatising Electricity: The Politics of Power* (London: Belhaven Press, 1993); C. Robinson, *Energy Policy: Errors, Illusions and Market Realities* (London: Institute of Economic Affairs, 1993); and D. Toke, *Green Energy: A non-nuclear response to the greenhouse effect* (London: Green Print/Merlin, 1990).

For **Chapter 5**, we suggest A. Burrell, B. Hill and J Medland, *Agrifacts* (Hemel Hempstead: Harvester-Wheatsheaf, 1990); G. Cox, P. Lowe and M. Winter (eds) *Agriculture: People and Politics* (London: Allen & Unwin, 1986); R. W. Howarth, *Farming for Farmers?* 2nd edn (London: IEA, 1990); and M.

J. Smith, *The Politics of Agricultural Support in Britain* (Aldershot: Dartmouth, 1990).

For **Chapter 6,** we recommend P. Ainley and M. Corney, *Training for the Future: The Rise and Fall of the Manpower Services Commission* (London: Mansell, 1990); D. Finegold and D. Soskice, 'The Failure of Training in Britain: Analysis and Prescription', *Oxford Review of Economic Policy*, vol. 4, no 3 (Autumn 1988) pp. 21–53; N. Goldstein, 'The new training initiative: A great leap backward', *Capital and Class*, no 23 (Summer 1984) pp. 83–106; H. Rainbird, *Training Matters: Union Perspectives on Industrial Restructuring and Training* (Oxford: Blackwell, 1990); P. J. Senker, *Industrial Training in a Cold Climate* (Aldershot: Avebury, 1992); and J. Sheldrake and S. Vickerstaff, *The History of Industrial Training in Great Britain* (Aldershot: Avebury, 1987).

For **Chapter 7,** we recommend W. Grant, *Government and Industry: a comparative analysis* (Aldershot: Edward Elgar, 1989); P. Hennessey, *Whitehall* (London: Secker & Warburg, 1989); D. Judge, *Parliament and Industry* (Aldershot: Dartmouth, 1990); and K. Theakston, *The Civil Service since 1945* (Oxford: Blackwell, 1995).

For **Chapter 8,** we recommend N. Deakin and J. Edwards, *The Enterprise Culture and the Inner City* (London: Routledge, 1993); A. Eisenschitz and J. Gough, *The Politics of Local Economic Policy* (London: Macmillan, 1993); R. T. Harrison and M. Hart (eds) *Spatial Policy in a Divided Nation* (London: Jessica Kingsley, 1993); V. A. Hausner (ed.) *Critical Issues in Urban Economic Development*, 2 vols (Oxford: Clarendon, 1986 and 1987); B. Moore *et al.*, *Local Partnership and the Unemployment Crisis in Britain* (London: Unwin Hyman, 1989); and H. Morison, *The Regeneration of Local Economies* (Oxford: Clarendon, 1987).

For **Chapter 9,** we recommend J. Lodge (ed.) *The European Community and the Challenge of the Future* (London: Pinter, 1993); D. Audretsch, *The Market and the State* (London: Harvester, 1989); and C. Lord, *Absent at the Creation* (Aldershot: Dartmouth, 1995).

For **Chapter 10,** see P. Barberis and T. May, *Government, Industry and Political Economy* (Milton Keynes: Open University Press, 1993); D. Marquand, *The Unprincipled Society* (London: Jonathan Cape, 1988); and D. Coates and J. Hillard (eds) *UK Economic Decline: Key Texts* (London: Harvester-Wheatsheaf, 1995).

References

Abromeit, H. (1986) *British Steel* (Leamington Spa: Berg).

Addison, P. (1975) *The Road to 1945: British Politics and the Second World War* (London: Jonathan Cape).

Ainley, P. and M. Carrey (1990) *Training for the Future: The Rise and Fall of the Manpower Service Commission* (London: Conwell).

Anderson, P. (1987) 'The figures of Descent', *New Left Review*, 161, pp. 20–77.

Armstrong, M., S. Cowan and J.Vickers (1994) *Regulatory Reform: Economic Analysis and British Experience* (Cambridge, Mass: MIT Press).

Audretsch, D. (1989) *The Market and the State* (London: Harvester-Wheatsheaf).

Barberis, P. and T. May (1993) *Government, Industry and Political Economy* (London: Open University Press).

Barnett, C. (1986) *The Audit of War* (London: Macmillan).

Benn, T. (1987) *Out of the Wilderness: Diaries 1963–67* (London: Hutchinson).

—— (1989) *Against the Tide: Diaries 1973–76* (London: Hutchinson).

Bianchini, F. (1991) 'Alternative Cities', *Marxism Today*, vol. 35, pp. 36–8.

Blackstone, T. and W. Plowden (1988) *Inside the Think Tank* (London: Heinemann).

Blais, A. (ed.) (1986) *Industrial Policy* (University of Toronto Press).

Breitenbach, H., T. Burden and D. Coates (1990) *Features of a Viable Socialism* (London: Harvester-Wheatsheaf).

Brittan, S. (1977) *The Economic consequences of Democracy* (London: Temple Smith)

Broadbent, E. (1988) *The Military and Government: From Macmillan to Heseltine* (London: Macmillan).

Bromley, S. (1992) 'The Labour Party and Energy Policy', in M. Smith and J. Spear (eds) *The Changing Labour Party* (London: Routledge).

Brown, J. (1991) 'The State and Agriculture, 1914–72', in G. Jones and M. Kirby (eds) *Competitiveness and the State* (Manchester: Manchester University Press) ch. 10.

Bruce, R. (1986) 'The regulation of services: international perspective on the developing policy problems', in N. Garnham, (ed.) *Telecommunications: National Policies in an International Context*, London Centre for Information and Communications Policy Studies, Central London Polytechnic, pp. 15–46.

Bruce-Gardyne, J. and N. Lawson (1976) *The Power Game* (London: Macmillan).

Buck, N., I. Gordon and K. Young (1986) *The London Employment Problem* (Oxford: Clarendon Press).

Buckingham, L. and S. Whitebloom (1994) 'Tories preach capital heresy', *Guardian*, 12 March, p. 40.

Budd, L. and S. Whimster (eds) (1992) *Global Finance and Urban Living. A Study of Metropolitan Change* (London: Routledge).

Burnham, P. (1993) 'The impact of the Korean Rearmament Programme on the British Economy: the case of the Vehicle Industry', paper presented to the ECPR workshop: *The Political Economy of Postwar European Reconstruction*, University of Leyden, 2–7 April.

Burrell, A., B. Hill and J. Medland (1990) *Agrifacts* (London: Harvester-Wheatsheaf).

Burton, J. (1979) *The Job Support Machine: A Critique of the Subsidy Morass* (London: Centre for Policy Studies).

Cabinet Office (1988) *Improving Management in Government: The Next Steps* (London: HMSO).

Cairncross, A. (1985) *Years of Recovery: British Economic Policy 1945–51* (London: Methuen).

Calder, A. (1969) *The People's War* (London: Jonathan Cape).

Cameron, P. (1983) *Property Rights and Sovereign Rights: The Case of North Sea Oil* (London: Academic Press).

Canston, R. (1995) *Liberalising Telecommunications in Western Europe* (London: Financial Times Business Information).

Carson, W. (1981) *The Other Price of Britain's Oil* (Oxford: Martin Robertson).

Carver, M. (1992) *Tightrope Walking: British Defence Policy since 1945* (London: Hutchinson).

CBI (1991) *Competing with the World's Best. The Report of the C.B.I. Manufacturing Advisory Group* (London: CBI).

—— (1992) *Making it in Britain: Partnership for World Class Manufacturing. The Report of the C.B.I. National Manufacturing Council* (London: CBI).

—— (1993) *Manufacturing Facts 1993* (London: CBI National Manufacturing Council).

Cecchini, P. (1988) *The European Challenge: 1992* (Aldershot: Wildwood House).

Central Statistical Office (1992) *Standard Industrial Clasification of Economic Activities* (CSO Press and Publications).

Chalmers, M. (1985) *Paying for Defence: Military Spending and British Decline* (London: Pluto).

—— (1992) 'British economic decline: the contribution of military spending', *The Royal Bank of Scotland Review*, 173, pp. 35–46.

Chick, M. (ed.) (l990) *Governments, Industries and Markets: Aspects of Government-Industry relations in the UK, Japan, West Germany and the USA since 1945* (London: Edward Elgar).

Clarke, P. (l993) 'Industrial economic policy', in P. Hare and L. Simpson (eds) *British Economic Policy: a modern introduction* (London: Harvester-Wheatsheaf) pp. 141–64.

Coates, D. (1990) 'Traditions of thought and the rise of social science in the United Kingdom', in J. Anderson and M. Ricci (eds) *Social Science and Society: a reader* (London: Open University Press) pp. 237–95.

—— (1994) *The Question of UK Decline* (London: Harvester-Wheatsheaf).

Cockburn, C. (1987) *Two-track Training: sex inequalities and the YTS* (London: Macmillan).

Cohen, S. and J. Zysman (l987) *Manufacturing Matters: the myth of the Post-Industrial Economy* (New York: Basic Books).

Commission of the EC (1989) *Twenty-third General Report* (Bruxelles).

—— (199la) *Twentieth Report on Competition Policy* (Luxembourg).

——(199lb) 'Fair Competition in the Community Market: Community State Aid Policy', *European Economy*, no 48.

—— (1992) *Twenty-first Report on Competition Policy* (Luxembourg).

—— (1993) *Internal Market: Current Status*, 1 January 1993.

Connelly, P. (1992) *Dealing With Whitehall* (London: Century Business).

Conservative Party (1970) *A Better Tomorrow: The Conservative Programme for the Next Five Years* (London: Conservative Central Office).

Contemporary Record (1991) 'Witness Symposium: the Ministry of Technology 1964–70', *Contemporary Record*, vol. 5, pp. 128–48.

Corby, S. (1991) 'Civil service decentralisation: reality or rhetoric', *Personnel Management*, February, pp. 39–42.

Cowling, K. and R. Sugden (eds) (l990) *A New Economic Policy for Britain: essays on the development of industry* (Manchester: Manchester University Press).

Cox, G., P. Lowe and M. Winter (eds) (1986) *Agriculture: People and Politics* (London: Allen & Unwin).

Curzon Price, V. (l988) *Industrial Policies in the European Community* (London: St. Martin's Press).

Dasgupta, P. (1982) *The Control of Resources* (Oxford: Basil Blackwell).

Davis, E., S. Flanders and J. Star (1992) 'British industry in the 1980s', *Business Strategy Review* (Spring) pp. 45–69.

Dell, E. (1973) *Political Responsibility and Industry* (London: Allen & Unwin).

Delloitte, Haskins and Sells (1989) *Training in Britain: Employers' Activities*, IFF Research (London: HMSO).

Delors, J. (1994) *Pour Entrer Dans Le XXI Siècle, Le Livre Blanc de La Commission des Communautés Européennes* (Paris: Lafon/Ramsay).

Department of Trade and Industry (DTI) (1987) *Civil Research and Development. Government Response to the First Report of the House of Lords Select Committee on Science and Technology,* Cmnd. 185 (London: HMSO).

—— (1988) *DTI: the Department for Enterprise,* Cmnd.278 (London: HMSO).

—— (1991) *Innovation in Manufacturing Industry. Government Response to the First Report of the House of Lords Select Committee on Science and Technology* (London: HMSO).

Dietrich, M. (1992) 'The foundations of industrial policy', in K. Cowling and R. Sugden (eds) *Current Issues in Industrial Economic Strategy* (Manchester: Manchester University Press) pp. 16–32.

Dinan, D. (1994) *Ever Closer Union* (London: Macmillan).

Dockrill, M. (1988) *British Defence since 1945* (Oxford: Blackwell).

Edgerton, D. (1991a) *England and the Aeroplane* (London: Macmillan).

—— (1991b) 'Liberal Militarism and the British State', *New Left Review*, 185, pp. 18–169.

—— (1992) 'Whatever happened to the British Warfare State? The Ministry of Supply 1945–1951', in H. Mercer, N. Rollings and J. D. Tomlinson (eds) *Labour Governments and Private Industry* (Edinburgh: Edinburgh University Press) pp. 91–116.

—— (1993a) 'British Research and Development after 1945: a re-interpretation', *Science and Technology Policy,* vol. 6(2) (April) pp. 10–16.

—— (1993b), 'Research, Development and Competitiveness' in K. Hughes (ed.) *The Future of U.K. Competitiveness and the Role of Industrial Policy* (London: Policy Studies Institute) pp. 40–54.

—— (1996) 'The White Heat revisited: the British government and technology in the 1960s', *Twentieth Century British History* (forthcoming)

EEF (1992) *Industrial Strategy: Proposals for Recovery and Sustained Growth* (London: Engineering Employers Federation).

Exley, M. (1987) 'Organisation and managerial capacity', in A. Harrison and J. Gretton (eds) *Reshaping Central Government, Reshaping the Public Sector,* vol. 1, pp. 42–56 (Newbury: Policy Journals).

Foreman Peck, J. (1991) 'Trade and the Balance of Payments', in N. F. R. Crafts and N. Woodward (eds) *The British Economy since 1945* (Oxford: Oxford University Press) pp. 141–79.

Fothergill, S., S. Monk and M. Perry (1987) *Property and Industrial Development* (London: Hutchinson).

Freeman, C. (1989) 'R&D, technical change and investment in the UK', in F. Green (ed.) *The Restructuring of the UK economy* (London: Harvester) pp. 199–224.

Fry, G. (1981) *The Administrative 'Revolution' in Whitehall* (London: Croom Helm).

—— (1985) *The Changing Civil Service* (London: Allen & Unwin).

Garrett, G. (1992) 'The EC's Internal Market', *International Organization,* vol. 46, no. 1 (Spring).

Gentle, C. (1993) *The Financial Services Industry* (Aldershot: Avebury).

Geroski, P.A. (1991) 'European Industrial Policy and Industrial Policy in Europe', *Oxford Review of Economic Policy*, vol. 5, no. 2.

—— (1993) 'Antitrust Policy Towards Co-operative Research and Development Projects', *Oxford Review of Economic Policy*, vol. 9, no. 2.

Geroski, P. A. and A. Jacquémin (1989) 'Industrial Change, Barriers to Mobility and European Industrial Policy', in A. Jacquémin and A. Sapir (eds) *The European Internal Market* (Oxford: Oxford University Press).

Gillespie, A. and K. Robins (1991) 'Non-universal service? Political economy and communications geography', in J. Brotchie, M. Batty, P. Hall and P. Newton (eds) *Cities of the 21st Century. New Technology and Spatial Systems* (Harlow: Longman Cheshire) pp. 159–70.

Gilpin, Robert (1987) *The Political Economy of International Relations* (Princeton, NJ: Princeton University Press).

Goodman, D. and M. Redclift (1986) 'Capitalism, Petty Commodity Production and the Farm Enterprise', in G. Cox *et al.* (eds) *Agriculture: People and Politics* (London: Allen & Unwin).

Gosling, R. and S. Nutley (1990) *Bridging the Gap: Secondments between Government and Business,* (London: Royal Institute of Public Administration).

Grant, W. (1982) *The Political Economy of Industrial Policy* (London: Butterworth):

—— (1989) *Government and Industry: a comparative analysis of the US, Canada and the UK* (London: Edward Elgar).

—— (1990) 'Industrial Policy', in J. Simmie and R. King (eds) *The State in Action* (London: Pinter) pp. 25–42.

—— (1991) 'Government and manufacturing industry since 1900', in G. Jones and M. Kirby (eds) *Competitiveness and the State: Government and business in twentieth-century Britain* (Manchester: Manchester University Press) pp. 100–19

Grant. W. and S. Wilks (1983) 'British industrial policy: structural change, policy inertia', *Journal of Public Policy*, vol. 3(1), pp. 13–28.

Greenaway, David (1993) 'Trade and Foreign Direct Investment', *European Economy*, no. 52.

Grove, J. W. (1967) *Government and Industry in Britain* (London: Longman).

Gummett, P. (1980) *Scientists in Whitehall* (Manchester: Manchester University Press).

Hall, P. (1986a) 'The State and Economic Decline', in B. Elbaum and W. Lazonick (eds), *The Decline of the British Economy* (Oxford: Oxford University Press) pp. 266–302.

—— (1986b) *Governing the Economy: the politics of state intervention in Britain and France* (Cambridge: Polity Press).

Ham, A. (1981) *Treasury Rules: Recurrent Themes in British Economic Policy* (London: Quartet).

Hamilton, A. (1978) *North Sea Impact: Off-Shore Oil and the British Economy* (London: International Institute for Economic Research).

Harrison, A. (ed.) (1993a) *From Hierarchy to Contract, Reshaping the Public Sector*, vol. 7 (Newbury: Policy Journals).

—— (1993b) 'NHS health care services', in A. Harrison (ed.) *From Hierarchy to Contract, Reshaping the Public Sector*, vol. 7, pp. 87–106.

Hart, J. A. (1986) 'British Industrial Policy', in C. E. Barfield and W. A. Schambra (eds) *The Politics of Industrial Policy* (Washington DC: American Enterprise Institute) pp. 128–60.

—— (1992) *Rival Capitalists: international competitiveness in the United States, Japan and Western Europe* (Cornell University Press).

Hay, Donald (1993) 'The Assessment; Competition Policy', *Oxford Review of Economic Policy*, vol. 9, no. 2.

Hayward, K. (1983) *Government and British Civil Aerospace: A Case Study in Post-war Technology Policy* (Manchester: Manchester University Press).

Henderson, P. (1952) 'Development Councils: An Industrial Experiment', in G. Worswick and P. Ady (ed.) *The British Economy 1945–50* (Oxford: Clarendon Press).

Hennessy, P. (1989) *Whitehall* (London: Fontana Press).

Heseltine, M. (1987) *Where There's a Will* (London: Hutchinson).

—— (1989) *The Challenge of Europe: Can Britain win?* (London: Hutchinson).

Hill, B. (1989) *Farm Incomes, Wealth and Agricultural Policy* (London: Avebury).

HMSO (1993) *Realising our potential: A Strategy for Science, Engineering and Technology* (London: HMSO).

—— (1994) *Competitiveness: Helping Business to Win* (London: HMSO).

Hodgson, D. (1993) 'UK training policy and the role of the TECs', *International Journal of Manpower*, vol. 14 (8), pp. 3–16.

Hogwood, B. (1979) *Government and Shipbuilding* (Farnborough: Saxon House).

—— (1982) 'In Search of Accountability: the Territorial Dimension of Industrial Policy', *Public Administration Bulletin*, vol. 28, pp. 22–39.

—— (1988) 'The Rise and Fall and Rise of the Department of Trade and Industry', in C. Campbell and B. G. Peters (eds) *Organizing Governance: Governing Organizations* (Pittsburgh: University of Pittsburgh Press) pp. 209–30.

Holmes, M. (1982) *Political Pressure and Economic Policy: British Government 1970–1974* (London: Butterworth Scientific).

Hoskyns, Sir J. (1983) 'Whitehall and Westminster: An Outsider's View', *Parliamentary Affairs*, vol. 36, pp. 137–47.

—— (1984) 'Conservatism is Not Enough', *Political Quarterly*, vol. 55, pp. 3–16.

House of Commons (1994) *Competitiveness of U.K. Manufacturing Industry.* Second Report from the House of Commons Trade and Industry Committee Session 1993–94 41–I (London: HMSO).

House of Lords (1985) *Overseas Trade.* Report from the House of Lords Select Committee Session 1984–85 HL238–I (London: HMSO).

—— (1991) *Innovation in Manufacturing Industry,* Report of the House of Lords Select Committee of Science and Technology, HL18–I (London: HMSO).

Hughes, K. (ed.) (1993) *The Future of UK Competitiveness and the Role of Industrial Policy* (London: Policy Studies Institute).

Hutton, W. (1995) *The State We're In* (London: Jonathan Cape).

Jacquémin, A. (1984) *European Industry: public policy and corporate strategy* (Oxford: University Press).

Johnson, C. (1984) 'The idea of industrial policy', in C. Johnson (ed.) *The Industrial Policy Debate* (The University of California Press) pp. 3–26.

Johnson, P. (1985) *British Industry, an economic introduction* (Oxford: Basil Blackwell).

Jones, D. T. (1981) 'Catching up with our competitors: the role of industrial policy', in C. Carter (ed.) *Industrial Policy and Innovation* (London: Heinemann).

Judge, D. (1990) *Parliament and Industry* (Aldershot: Dartmouth).

Keegan, W. and R. Pennant-Rea (1979) *Who Runs the Economy?* (London: Temple Smith).

Keep, E. and K. Mayhew (1988) 'The assessment: education, training and business performance', *Oxford Review of Economic Policy*, vol. 4(3), pp. i–xv.

Keliher, L. (1990) 'Core Executive Decision Making in High Technology Issues: the case of the Alvey Report', *Public Administration*, vol. 68, pp. 61–82.

Kelly, I. (1994) 'A no-cost way to strengthen the DTI and empower local industry', *Centre for Industrial Policy Bulletin*, University of Leeds, no. 5, pp. 12–14.

Kirby, M. W. (1980) *The Decline of British Economic Power since 1870* (London: Allen & Unwin).

—— (1991) 'Supply side management', in N. F .R. Crafts and N. W. C. Woodward (eds) *The British Economy since 1945* (Oxford: Oxford University Press) pp. 236–60.

Lawson, N. (1989) 'The state of the market', in C. Johnson (ed.) *The Market on Trial* (Lloyds Bank Review) pp. 26–36.

—— (1992) *The View from No. 11: Memoirs of a Tory Radical* (London: Bantam).

Lee, D. (1979) 'Craft unions and the force of tradition – the case of apprenticeship', *British Journal of Industrial Relations*, vol. 17, (1), pp. 34–49.

—— (1989) 'The transformation of training and the transformation of work', in S. Wood (ed.) *The Transformation of Work* (London: Unwin Hyman) pp. 156–70.

Lesley Cook, P. and A. J. Surrey (1978) *Energy Policy: Strategies for Uncertainty* (Oxford: Martin Robertson).

Linklater, M. and D. Leigh (1986) *Not with Honour: The Inside Story of the Westland Scandal* (London: Sphere Books).

Liston, D. and N. Reeves (1988) *The Invisible Economy* (London: Pitman).

Llewellyn, D. T. (1990) 'Competition and structural change in the British financial system', in E. P. M. Gardener (ed.) *The Future of Financial Systems and Services* (London: Macmillan) pp. 15–35.

Lord, Christopher (1993a) *British Entry to the European Community under the Heath Government of 1970–4* (Aldershot: Dartmouth).

—— (1993b) 'The Maastricht Treaty: An Industrial Policy Sideshow?', *Bulletin*, no. 1 (Spring) (Centre for Industrial Policy and Performance, University of Leeds).

—— (1995) *Absent at the Creation. Why Britain did not join the Schuman Plan* (Aldershot: Dartmouth).

Marquand, D. (1988) *The Unprincipled Society* (London: Jonathan Cape).

Mather, G. (1992) 'Interview' quoted in M. Phillips, 'The tenders trap of Civil Service Plc', *Guardian*, 21 July, p. 21.

Ministry of Education (1963) *Half Our Futures*, Report of the Centre Advisory Council for Education (England), Chairman, John Newsom (London: HMSO).

Mitchell, D. (1982) 'Intervention, Control and Accountability: the National Enterprise Board', *Public Administration Bulletin*, vol. 38, pp. 40–65.

Moore, C. and J. J. Richardson (1989) *Local Partnership and the Unemployment Crisis in Britain* (London: Unwin Hyman).

Moran, M. (1991) *The Politics of the Financial Services Revolution* (London: Macmillan).

Morgan, K. and A. Sayer (1988) *Microcircuits of Capital* (Cambridge: Polity Press).

Morris, D. J. and D. K. Stout (1987) 'Industrial policy', in D. J. Morris (ed.) *The Economic System in the UK* (Oxford: Oxford University Press) pp. 851–94.

Mueller, A. (1985) 'A Civil Servant's View', in D. Englefield (ed.) *Today's Civil Service* (Harlow: Longman) pp. 100–8.

Muligan, G. J. (1991) *Communication and Control* (Cambridge: Polity Press).

Murphy, Sir L. (1981) 'Reflections on the National Enterprise Board', in *Allies or Adversaries? Perspectives on government and industry in Britain* (London: Royal Institute of Public Administration) pp. 17–28.

NAO (1987) Department of Trade and Industry: Assistance to Industry under section 8 of the Industrial Development Act 1982 (HC 329, 1986/87).

Newby, H. (1980) *Green and Pleasant Land* (Harmondsworth: Pelican).

Newton, S. and D. Porter (1988) *Modernisation Frustrated: the politics of industrial decline in Britain since 1900* (London: Unwin Hyman).

Noam, E. (1992) *Telecommunications in Europe* (Oxford: Oxford University Press).

OECD (1984) 'The contribution of services to employment', *Employment Outlook* (Sep.) pp. 39–54.

—— (1986) *Trends in the Information Economy* (Paris: OECD).

—— (1992) *Industrial Policy in OECD countries: annual review* (Paris: OECD).

Okimoto, D. (1989) *Between MITI and the market: Japanese industrial policy for high technology* (Stanford University Press).

Pavitt, K. (1981) 'Technology in British industry: a suitable case for improvement', in C. Carter (ed.), *Industrial Policy and Innovation* (London: Heinemann) pp. 88–115.

Perrings, P. (1987) *Economy and Environment* (Cambridge: Cambridge University Press).

Phillips, M. (1992) 'The tenders trap of Civil Service Plc', *Guardian*, 21 July, p. 21.

Piore, M. J. and C. Sabel (1984) *The Second Industrial Divide* (New York: Basic Books).

PEP (Political and Economic Planning) (1960) *Growth in the British Economy: A Study of Economic Problems and Policies in Contemporary Britain* (London: George Allen & Unwin).

Pollard, S. (1982) *The Wasting of the British Economy* (London: Croom Helm).

—— (1992) *The Development of the British Economy 1911–1990* (London: Edward Arnold).

Porter, Michael (1990) *The Competitive Advantage of Nations* (London: Macmillan).

Reed, A. (1973) *Britain's Aircraft Industry: What went Right? What went Wrong* (London: JM Dent).

Rhodes, R. A. W. (1994) 'The hollowing out of the state: the changing nature of the public service in Britain', *The Political Quarterly*, vol. 65, pp. 138–51.

Richards, S. (1987) 'The financial management initiatives', in A. Harrison and J. Gretton (eds) *Reshaping Central Government*, pp. 224–41.

Ridley, N. (1988) *The Local Right* (London: Centre for Policy Studies).

Roberts, J., D. Elliott and T. Houghton (1993) *Privatising Electricity: The Politics of Power* (London: Belhaven Press).

Robinson, C. (1993) *Energy Policy: Errors, Illusions and Market Realities* (London: Institute of Economic Affairs).

Rosenblatt, J., T. Mayer, B. Kaspar, D. Demekas, S. Gupta and L. Lipschitz (1988) *The Common Agricultural Policy of the European Community* (Washington DC: IMF).

Ross, George (1995) *Jacques Delors and European Integration* (Cambridge: Polity Press).

Rybczynski, T. (1984) 'The UK financial system in transition', *National Westminster Bank Review* (Nov.) pp. 26–43.

—— (1988) 'Financial systems and industrial restructuring', *National Westminster Bank Quarterly Review* (Nov.) pp. 26–43.

Sapir, A., P. Buigues and A. Jacquémin (1993) 'European Competition Policy in Manufacturing and Services', *Oxford Review of Economic Policy,* vol. 9, no. 2.

Sawyer, M. (1991) 'Industrial Policy', in M. Artis and D. Cobham (eds) *Labour's Economic Policies 1974–79* (Manchester: Manchester University Press).

—— (1992) 'On the theory of industrial policy', in K. Cowling and R. Sugden (eds) *Current Issues in Industrial Economic Strategy* (Manchester: Manchester University Press) pp. 3–15.

Scitovsky, Tibor (1958) *Economic Theory and West European Integration* (London: Unwin).

Scott, Andrew (1993) 'Financing of the Community: the Delors II Package', in Juliet Lodge (ed.) *The European Community and the Challenge of the Future* (London: Pinter).

Senker, P. J. (1992) *Industrial Training in a Cold Climate* (Aldershot: Avebury).

Sharp, Margaret (1993) 'The Community and new Technologies', in Juliet Lodge (ed.) *The European Community and the Challenge of the Future* (London: Pinter).

Sharp, M. and K. Pavitt (1993) 'Technology policy in the 1990s: old themes and new realities', *DRC Discussion Paper no 89*, Science Policy Research Unit, University of Sussex.

Sheldrake, J. and S. Vickerstaff (1987) *The history of industrial training in Great Britain* (Aldershot: Avebury).

Shepherd, J. (1987) 'Industrial Support Policies', *National Institute Economic Review* (Nov.) pp. 59–71.

Singh, A. (1977) 'UK Industry and the World Economy: A Case of De-industrialisation', *Cambridge Journal of Economics*, vol. 1, pp. 113–36.

Smith, D. (1980) *The Defence of the Realm in the 1980s* (London: Croom Helm).

Smith, J. (1993) Speech delivered to the Manufacturing Matters conference, Queen Elizabeth II Conference Centre, London, 20 October.

Smith, M. J. (1989) 'Changing Agendas and Policy Communities: Agricultural Issues in the 1930s and the 1980s', *Public Administration*, vol. 67, no. 2, pp. 149–65.

—— (1990) *The Politics of Agricultural Support in Britain* (Aldershot: Dartmouth).

—— (1992) 'CAP and Agricultural Policy', in D. Marsh and R. A. W. Rhodes (eds) *Implementing Thatcherite Policies* (Buckingham: Open University Press) ch. 9.

Swann, Dennis (ed.) (1992) *The Single European Act and Beyond* (London: Routledge).

Taylor, T. and K. Hayward (1989) *The U.K. Defence Industrial Base: Development and Future Policy Options* (London: Brassey's).

Thain, C. (1984) 'The Treasury and Britain's Decline', *Political Studies*, vol. 32, pp. 581–95.

Thatcher, M. (1993) *The Downing Street Years* (London: Harper Collins).

Theakston, K. and G. Fry (1994) 'The Conservative Party and the Civil Service', in A. Seldon (ed.) *The Conservative Party in the Twentieth Century* (Oxford: Oxford University Press).

Thompson, G. (ed.) (1989) *Industrial Policy: USA and UK Debates* (London: Routledge).

Townsend, A. R. (1987) 'Regional Policy', in W. F. Lever (ed.) *Industrial Change in the United Kingdom* (Harlow: Longman).

Treasury and Civil Service Committee (1988) *Civil Service Management Reform: The Next Steps, Vol II, Annexes minutes of evidence and appendices*, HC-494 (London: HMSO).

Tsoukalis, Loukas (1993) *The New European Economy: The Politics and Economics of Integration* (Oxford: Oxford University Press).

Tyson, L. and J. Zysman (eds) (1983) *American Industry in International Competition: government policies and corporate strategies* (Cornell University Press).

Tyson, S. (1987) 'Personnel Management', in A. Harrison and J. Gretton (eds) *Reshaping Central Government*, Policy Journal vol. 1 (Oxford: Transaction Books).

Wade, R. (1990) *Governing the Market* (Princeton University Press).

Walker, D. (1987) 'The First Wilson Governments, 1964–1970', in P. Hennessy and A. Seldon (eds) *Ruling Performance: British Governments from Attlee to Thatcher* (Oxford: Blackwell).

Walker, W. (1993) 'National innovation systems: Britain', in R. Nelson (ed.) *National Innovation Systems: a comparative analysis* (Oxford: Oxford University Press) pp. 262–338.

Walker, W. and Sharp, M. (1991) 'Thatcherism and Technical Advances: reform without progress?', *Political Quarterly*, vol. 62 (2/3), April/June, pp. 262–337.

Ward, S. V. (1990) 'Local Industrial Promotion and Development Policies 1899–1940', *Local Economy*, pp. 100–19.

Wells, J. (1989) 'Uneven development and deindustrialisation in the UK since 1979', in F. Green (ed.) *The Restructuring of the UK Economy* (London: Harvester) pp. 25–64.

Whitbread, C. and N. Hooper (1993) 'NHS ancillary services', in A. Harrison (ed.) *From Hierarchy to Contract, Reshaping the Public Sector*, vol. 7, pp. 69–86.

Whitebloom, S. (1994) 'Lukewarm response to PIA', *Guardian*, 22 February, p. 17.

Wiener, M. (1981) *English Culture and the Decline of the Industrial Spirit 1850–1980* (Harmondsworth: Penguin).

Wilks, S. (1983), 'Liberal State and Party Competition: Britain', in K. Dyson and S. Wilks (eds) *Industrial Crisis* (Oxford: Martin Robertson) pp. 128–60.

—— (1984) *Industrial Policy and the Motor Industry* (Manchester: Manchester University Press).

—— (1986) 'Has the State Abandoned British Industry?', *Parliamentary Affairs*, vol. 39, pp. 31–46.

—— (1989) 'The Department of Trade and Industry under Lord Young', *Public Money and Management*, vol. 9, pp. 43–46.

—— (1990) 'Institutional Insularity: government and the British Motor Industry since 1945', in M. Chick (ed.) *Governments, Industries and Markets* (Aldershot: Edward Elgar) pp. 157–79.

Williams, W. (1989) 'Central Government Capacity and the British Disease', *Parliamentary Affairs*, vol. 42, pp. 250–64.

Wilson Report (1980) *Committee to Review the Functioning of Financial Institutions*, Cmnd. 7937 (London: HMSO).

Wood, D. (1987) 'The Conservative Member of Parliament as Lobbyist for Constituency Economic Interests', *Political Studies*, vol. 35, pp. 393–409.

Young, Lord (1990) *The Enterprise Years* (London: Headline).

Young, S. and A. Lowe (1974) *Intervention in the Mixed Economy* (London: Croom Helm).

Index

283